Open Fire
Understanding Global Gun Cultures

Edited by

CHARLES FRUEHLING SPRINGWOOD

BERG

Oxford • New York

English edition
First published in 2007 by
Berg
Editorial offices:
First Floor, Angel Court, 81 St Clements Street, Oxford OX4 1AW, UK
175 Fifth Avenue, New York, NY 10010, USA

Berg is the imprint of Oxford International Publishers Ltd.

Library of Congress Cataloging-in-Publication Data
Open fire : understanding global gun cultures / edited by
Charles Fruehling Springwood. — English ed.
    p. cm.
Includes bibliographical references and index.
ISBN-13: 978-1-84520-416-7 (cloth)
ISBN-10: 1-84520-416-6 (cloth)
ISBN-13: 978-1-84520-417-4 (pbk.)
ISBN-10: 1-84520-417-4 (pbk.)
 1. Firearms—Social aspects—Cross-cultural studies.
 2. Firearms in popular culture—Cross-cultural studies.
 3. Firearms ownership. 4. Violence. 5. Gun control.
I. Springwood, Charles Fruehling.

    HV6016.O64 2007
    303.6—dc22   2006034258

British Library Cataloguing-in-Publication Data
A catalogue record for this book is available from the British Library.

ISBN-13 978 1 84520 416 7 (Cloth)
        978 1 84520 417 4 (Paper)

ISBN-10 1 84520 416 6 (Cloth)
        1 84520 417 4 (Paper)

Typeset by Avocet Typeset, Chilton, Aylesbury, Bucks
Printed in the United Kingdom by Biddles Ltd, King's Lynn.

www.bergpublishers.com

Open Fire

Contents

List of Tables and Figures   vii

Notes on Contributors   ix

Acknowledgments   xi

1   The Social Life of Guns: An Introduction   1
Charles Fruehling Springwood

Part I. Looking Down the Barrel of a Gun: Nation-States, Small Arms, and Local Victims

2   Gunscapes: Toward a Global Geography of the Firearm   15
Charles Fruehling Springwood

3   Gun Politics: Reflections on Brazil's Failed Gun Ban Referendum in the Rio de Janeiro Context   28
Donna Goldstein

4   Of Guns, Children, and the Maelstrom: Determining Purposive Action in Israeli-perpetrated Firearm Deaths of Palestinian Children and Minors   42
Frank M. Afflitto

5   Silent but Still Deadly: Guns and the Peace Process in Northern Ireland   56
Jeffrey A. Sluka

6   Warriors and Guns: The Anthropology of Cattle Rustling in Northeastern Africa   71
Nene Mburu

Part II. Locked and Loaded: Race, Sex, and Gender

7   Arming Desire: The Sexual Force of Guns in the United States   87
C. Richard King

8   Drawing a Virtual Gun   98
     Katherine Gregory

9   "Gun Rights Are Civil Rights": Racism and the Right to Keep
     and Bear Arms in the United States   111
     Christy Allen

10   "Man to Man": Power and Male Relationships in the Gunplay
     Film   125
     Robert Arjet

Part III. Playing, Dancing, and Thinking with Guns

11   Aiming for Manhood: The Transformation of Guns into Objects
     of American Masculinity   141
     Amy Ann Cox

12   "I Shot the Sheriff": Gun Talk in Jamaican Popular Music   153
     Carolyn Cooper

13   Playing at Hate: War Games, the Aryan World Congress, and the
     American Psyche   165
     Robert Rinehart

14   The Celebration of Violence: A Live-fire Demonstration Carried
     Out by Japan's Contemporary Military   178
     Eyal Ben-Ari and Sabine Frühstück

Notes   199

References   205

Index   225

List of Tables and Figures

Table

4.1 Corporal location of fatal woundings for "one-shot wonders" in exclusive designated areas (2000–2003)   48

Figures

1.1 Young males prepare for battle in the Democratic Republic of Congo, 2003   8

1.2 Members of a club in Belgium gathered for recreational gunplay with non-lethal Airsoft weapons   9

4.1 The view from Hindaza Hill towards Bethlehem's Manger Square and the spot where Johnny Thaljiya was killed   45

4.2 The view from the spot where Johnny Thaljiya was killed, in Bethlehem's Manger Square, through the narrow entrance leading out of the square, looking into the distance at Hindaza Hill   45

4.3 Satellite-generated map of the positions of perpetrators and victim in the Israeli gunfire-perpetrated death of Palestinian minor Johnny Thaljiya   46

4.4 Pie chart of corporal location of fatal woundings for "one-shot wonders" in exclusive designated areas (2000–3)   48

5.1 Loyalist paramilitary mural, Belfast, 2001   56

6.1 Turkana stool used as a pillow (when tending livestock), seat (during peace talks) and shield (during close combat)   77

6.2 Turkana wrist knife (a) with the safety scabbard on and (b) with the scabbard off   79

6.3 Map showing pattern of cattle rustling   81

Notes on Contributors

Frank M. Afflitto received his Ph.D. in 1998, from the Department of Criminology, Law and Society at the University of California at Irvine's School of Social Ecology. His first book details the social movement practices and justice perceptions of Guatemalans victimized by state violence.

Christy Allen received a Ph.D. in Sociology at the University of Essex. She teaches courses in American Studies, human rights, and criminology. Her dissertation "Living the Second Amendment" is an ethnography of gun rights activism in the United States, for which she joined pro-gun organizations and attended gun-rights activist training in several states across the US.

Robert Arjet researches violence in American culture as it relates to masculinity, gender, and extremist groups. He received his Ph.D. from Emory University's Institute of the Liberal Arts, and his dissertation on masculinity and firearms in American action films is entitled "Gunplay: Men, Guns, and the Action Films in the United States."

Eyal Ben-Ari, Professor of Sociology and Anthropology at the Hebrew University, is a widely published scholar whose research spans Japanese society, Israeli culture, early childhood education, military culture, and emotions. His recent books include *Body Projects in Japanese Childcare: Culture, Organization and Emotions in a Preschool* and *Mastering Soldiers: Conflict, Emotions and the Enemy in an Israeli Military Unit*.

Carolyn Cooper, Professor of English at the University of the West Indies, specializes in Caribbean literature. She authored *Noises in the Blood*, a collection of essays on Jamaican popular culture.

Amy Ann Cox, a doctoral student in US History at the University of California at Los Angeles, is interested in the history of firearms and gun-ownership, and gender. Her dissertation will explore the practical uses and cultural meanings of guns in early America.

Sabine Frühstück, Professor at the University of California, Santa Barbara, is a specialist in modern Japanese cultural studies. She has authored/edited many books and articles, including *Colonizing Sex: Sexology and Social Control in Modern Japan.*

Donna Goldstein, Associate Professor of Anthropology at the University of Colorado, is currently investigating HIV/AIDS pharmaceutical politics in Brazil, Argentina, and Mexico. She has written extensively on the intersection of race, gender, poverty and violence in Brazil, and authored *Laughter Out of Place: Race, Class, Violence, and Sexuality in a Rio Shantytown.*

Katherine Gregory, Assistant Professor of Communication at the University of Wisconsin-Parkside, is an ethnographer and filmmaker focusing on identity and resistance in marginalized social groups. Her recent book, *The Everyday Lives of Sex Workers in the Netherlands*, addresses the cultural practices and agency of transgendered and migrant sex workers.

C. Richard King, Associate Professor of comparative ethnic studies at Washington State University, has written extensively on the changing contours of race in post-Civil Rights America, the colonial legacies and postcolonial predicaments of American culture, and struggles over Indianness in public culture. His numerous books include *Team Spirits: The Native American Mascot Controversy* and *Postcolonial America.*

Nene Mburu, a retired military officer with experience in disarming pastoral communities in Kenya, has a BA in Politics (Nairobi) and an MA and Ph.D. in War Studies (Kings College London). Previously a lecturer in Cultural Studies in Her Majesty's Prison Education, he has authored *Bandits on the Border: The Last Frontier in the Search for Somali Unity* and numerous peer-reviewed articles on pastoral conflicts and disarmament.

Bob Rinehart, Assistant Professor at Washington State University, holds a Ph.D. from the University of Illinois in Kinesiology. The author of *Players All: Performances in Contemporary Sport*, his research interests include alternative sports and the use of qualitative methods within sport studies.

Jeffrey A. Sluka, Professor of Anthropology at Massey University, focuses on political anthropology and the analysis of violence and peace. Included among his many works is *Death Squad: The Anthropology of State Terror.*

Charles Fruehling Springwood, Associate Professor of Anthropology at Illinois Wesleyan University, specializes in the politics and symbolism of cultural knowledge, including representations of race. He co-edited *Team Spirits: The Native American Mascot Controversy* and co-authored *Beyond the Cheers: Race as Spectacle in College Sport.*

Acknowledgments

This project owes a great debt to the contributors to this book, who are responsible for whatever success it achieves. They responded with enthusiasm to my encouragement to think about and write about guns, some of them for the very first time. In particular, I am grateful to Frank Afflitto, for his efforts and sacrifices, and to C. Richard King, a loyal intellectual confidant who has talked guns with me for many years. Many other people have helped me along the way, and their assistance shall never be forgotten: Irv Epstein, Tom Lutze, Christina Isabelli, Rebecca Gearhart, Cade Cummins, Angie Glasker, Joshua Wagener, Patra Noona, Horacio Garcia-Servin, Alissa Hoffenberg, Jeff Sluka, Ilene Kalish, Students in my Anthropology 310 seminar, Myrdene Anderson, Dan Rose, Jean and Lyle Lockwood, Guy Tillim, and Tom Rosseel. I am grateful to the IWU Mellon Center for a generous support of an Artistic and Scholarly Development grant, and I wish to acknowledge the special assistance of the folks at IWU's Ames Library, including Tony Heaton, Kris Vogel, and Sue Stroyan. Leslie Coleman and Mallory Wendt kindly assisted in the preparation of the index. The folks at Berg were wonderful, especially Tristan Palmer, who proved to be a thoughtful and thought-provoking editor throughout. And finally, as always, with the writing and editing of this book, my debt to Jacob, Josua, and Cheryl Springwood—my beloved family—has deepened, my respect for them has grown, and my love for them has matured.

Charles Fruehling Springwood

CHAPTER 1

The Social Life of Guns: An Introduction

Charles Fruehling Springwood

On December 13, 2003, US forces finally captured Saddam Hussein near his hometown of Tikrit, in Iraq. Many still recall the television images of a disheveled Hussein being pulled out of an obscure underground bunker. He was alone when he was found, and he was clutching a pistol, which he never attempted to fire. In addition, the bunker contained two AK-47 assault rifles and some US$700,000, in cash. Hussein's handgun, in 2006, is in the possession of George W. Bush, the 43rd President of the United States, and it is kept in a small study adjoining the Oval Office at the White House. A small group of Army Rangers brought it all the way from Iraq in order to give it to their Commander-in-Chief. Reportedly, the President takes special pride in showing the gun to select visitors, and he clarifies that, contrary to certain media reports, the weapon contained no bullets when it was taken from Hussein (Gibbs 2003).

The *mise en scène* of George W. Bush brandishing the pistol of his captured arch-nemesis while strutting through musings of a war he authorized seems to demand some sort of analysis, almost surely of a psychoanalytic sort (see "Bush's Possession ..." 2004). Of course, the firearm has so frequently surfaced as a phallic metaphor, and the battlefield practice of annexing the weapon of one's vanquished foe as a symbolic castration souvenir started long before Bush amused himself with the deposed Iraqi leader's gun.

In this instance, the social and symbolic significance of the gun is primary. Guns matter, and although Hussein failed to utilize his firearm to wound, if not kill one or two of the many soldiers who converged on him, merely grasping it perhaps offered him some kind of comfort. And, in the hands of the President of the United States, it clearly means many other things. In fact, guns are frequently at the center of ostentatious stagings of political power and celebration. Hussein, indeed, made use of such symbolism himself, as he was frequently seen brandishing a rifle during public appearances. When George Bush Senior lost his reelection bid in 1991, Hussein reportedly shot his rifle into the air to celebrate. And within militant Islam the assault rifle is a requisite feature of video transmissions, and Osama Bin Laden is seldom pictured without a gun leaning against the wall behind him. In another instance, the firearm has been literally incorporated into the national flag of Mozambique, which—along with an open book and hoe—features at the center of its banner a Kalashnikov rifle.

Open Fire opens an interdisciplinary and transcultural dialogue about the social significance of guns, across time and space. It brings together the work of fourteen scholars, representing such disciplines as literature, history, peace studies, anthropology, and cultural studies, to constitute a collection engaging the material realities and the social meanings of firearms, in so far as they have impacted every cultural space in the world.

Gun scholarship has too often been framed by the Second Amendment controversies (see Kleck 1991; Kopel 1992, 1995; Funk 1999; Nisbet 2001), while other works focus on the social history or the manufacture of firearms (McNeill 1982; O'Connell 1989), particularly in the United States. Although many of these writings are of high quality, on balance, they seem unable to move beyond the intransigent pro-gun/gun control debate framework. Moreover, such work is too often founded by theoretical musings, legal lingo, or polemical opinion. What has been missing is a consideration of everyday experience with guns, especially the relationship of people to their guns. Moreover, previous work has failed to understand the ubiquity of guns across the globe or to appreciate the idiomatic meanings of guns in local spaces.

Additionally, in recent years, social scientists have taken their own disciplines to task for too often failing to engage the most ubiquitous features of social life. For example, ethnographies of local spaces frequently overlook their subjects' various involvement in such things as civil war, popular culture, or pollution. Cultural studies has made significant progress in opening itself up to a consideration of everyday practices. However, social scientists have yet persuasively to engage *guns*, arguably the most significant, highly charged register of material culture in the world today. A number of excellent studies have sought to foreground the importance of violence, even war, in terms of ethnic and state conflict. This important constellation of work (see Nordstrum and Robben 1995; Malkki 1995; Bourgois 1995; Simons 1999; Ferme 2001; Aijmer and Abbink 2000; Hinton 2002; Sluka 2000a; Anderson 2004) has challenged scholars not only to consider the everyday experiences of violence by people all over the world, but to understand its historical and sociocultural context.

None of the studies, however, turns on the prevalence or significance of the firearm. Indeed, the vast majority of them do not consider the weapons with which these regimes of terror are so often enacted. While numerous reseachers have worked with populations whose members variously desire, witness, own, sell, trade, fear, and indeed shoot guns, save for an occasional mention of the presence of such weapons in fieldwork settings, most studies attend rather to the larger-scale processes of conflict, including state and ethnic politics, displacement of peoples, diaspora, and refugee experiences.

Open Fire, in contrast, begins with an examination of the gun, as a crucial extension of cultural embodiment and as an "implement" qualitatively unlike any other. The following chapters, responding directly to these absences in the literature, are united by a sensivity to ways that guns are animated by myriad forms of (dis)empowerment, including race, displacement, gender, class, violence, and even play. The collection—while embracing examinations of guns as sociocultural signs motivated by powerful discursive frameworks—seeks especially to highlight the *materiality/thingness* of the firearm, as an element generating new economies, complex sets of social relations, embodiment, wealth, and poverty.

The guiding questions of the volume include: Why are guns so numerous, indeed ubiquitous, around the world? What does it mean to shoot a gun? To be shot by a gun? Who owns guns? Who doesn't? What does it mean to *own* a gun? In what ways is the firearm, as a manufactured "thing," both similar to and also very unlike other sorts of "things"? What are the cultural, psychological, and sensual dimensions of gun "play"? How do people think about guns in places where guns are largely non-existent? Why do guns move so easily between the symbolically slippery categories of "tools" and "toys"? How is gun activism—both pro and anti—important to broader understandings of power, identity, and community?

In Asne Seierstad's *The Bookseller of Kabul*, a recent chronicle of an Afghan household, one scene in particular motivates gun ethnography. Several Afghan fighters are watching a US soldier, Bob, talk into a wireless phone with the aid of a satellite dish he erected.

"Is he talking to America?" asks a long, thin man wearing a turban, tunic, and sandals. He looks like the leader ...The soldiers keep watching Bob ... they are interested only in the phone and how it works. They have hardly ever seen a telephone before. One of them exclaims in a sad voice, "Do you know what our problem is? *We know everything about our weapons, but we know nothing about how to use a telephone.*" (2004: 263–4)

Certainly, in tribal areas of Afghanistan, rifles animate local culture, as "traditional village weddings resound to the echo of .303 rifles made fifty years ago" (Poulton 2003: 414). Yet the ubiquity of guns is not merely remarkable in Afghanistan, but rather is a prevailing condition of contemporary life across the world, and perhaps nowhere more than in the United States.

This being so, what is needed are analyses that push beyond existing scholarship by refusing to ignore the power and the presence of the firearm, by struggling with the seductive transformation that a body, grasping and shooting a gun, undergoes, and finally, by listening to the unsettling, fearsome sound of gunfire, resounding in the ears of communities and victims. Whether or not the gun is an inherently bad thing, or a good thing, it is unquestionably a peculiar, resonant *thing*. In the United States alone there are approximately 200 million *privately* owned guns, and they are found in almost 40 per cent of American households. This doesn't include the many millions of guns owned by the government, police and military, nor illicit guns. And in Europe some 84 million guns are owned by private citizens. On balance, although it is virtually impossible to know how many guns exist in our world, I am confident in claiming that at least 700,000,000 guns ... nearly three-quarters of a billion guns exist in the world.[1]

Of Powder and Spark

Of course, there were not always so many guns around the world. The particular histories of guns have somewhat more identifiable starting-points than gun cultures. Although indispensable to how each of the scholars in the volume makes sense of firearms, history is significant more for the way in which it helps to unpack the continually emergent meanings and effects of guns rather than for a narrative account of the invention and development of early firearms. Nevertheless, it is critical to situate the "biography" of these portable weapons within time and space, and to discuss their origins. The terms "gun" and "firearm" are used interchangeably in popular parlance, and this is the usage that prevails throughout *Open Fire*. However, "gun" is used by arms experts in a more restricted sense, to indicate larger weapons with generally higher muzzle velocities, such as field guns or anti-tank guns. Properly speaking, then, the arms featured in this collection of essays are "firearms," weapons that fire moderately high-velocity projectiles using the energy produced by the ignition of a propellant, such as gunpowder, for example. Consequently, the chapters that follow examine the cultural meanings that accrue to firearms, and more particularly, small arms, which—because of their portable and often concealable nature—are conceptualized, circulated, and embodied in ways unlike larger guns and other weapons.

To begin simply, historians are in general agreement that the very first weapons that we should identify as guns were developed in China, in approximately 1290 AD (Goodrich and Chia-sheng 1946; McNeill 1982), at a time when when crossbows were already a widely used means of combat in East Asia. Crossbows, whose arrow-like projectiles were shot with a trigger mechanism, had been utilized since at least *circa* 220 BC (Cotterell 1981: 48–9). Gunpowder, a prerequisite for the invention of firearms, was invented, also in China, in 1000 AD (Ling 1947), where it was initially used as a general explosive element. By the middle 1300s, people in both East Asia and Europe were able to design hand-held machines that ignited gunpowder to propel projectiles through metal cylinders. By the middle 1300s, then, the gun—albeit primitive—was a modest transcontinental commodity. However, most weapons historians agree that technologically the firearm remained marginal in terms of military significance until, perhaps, the eighteenth century (McNeill 1982; O'Connell 1989).

Ultimately, guns and gun manufacture came to be viewed as much more significant to European nations than to the Chinese. Various historians have attempted to respond to Robert O'Connell's (1989: 108) assertion: "Why it was that the possibility of firearms largely bypassed the Chinese, while causing European rulers and artisans to invest entirely more energy in their development than pure efficiency would seem to have warranted, remains controversial." Kenneth Chase (2003) has speculated that the east and central Asian ecology of steppe- and desert-dwelling nomads was not ideal for warfare with firearms. William McNeill (1982: 83), preferring a more psychoanalytic reading, argued that "sexual symbolism presumably attached itself to guns from the beginning, and perhaps goes far to explain the European ... irrational investment in early firearms."

Since so much of the gun culture and violence discussed in this book is related to what is commonly referred to, variously, as a machine-gun or an assault rifle, it is important to address the history of these sorts of arms in particular. Semi-automatic guns, including many pistols, are those in which a single pull of the trigger will propel one bullet, often in rapid succession. A machine-gun, then, is a general term for a firearm designed to shoot *continually*, as long as the trigger is depressed. Hiram Maxim invented the first true machine-gun, a portable device with automatic firing capability, in 1883 (Ellis 1975). After the close of the Second World War and the beginning of the Cold War era, lighter, cheaper machine-guns emerged, most notably the AK-47 and the M-16 assault rifles. Mikhail Kalashnikov invented the former in the early 1940s, and Soviet factories began production of these gas-operated assault rifles in 1947. Widely used in many Eastern bloc nations during the 1950s, 1960s, and 1970s, these arms and a host of close variants, nicknamed Kalashnikov rifles after their originator, remain the most popular machine-guns in the world today. Indeed, they have "become the symbol of the small-arms trade," with somewhere between 35 and 70 million such rifles having been made since the end of the Second World War (Renner 1999).

I became interested in firearms, as a subject of scholarly inquiry, while conducting unrelated fieldwork in Japan, in 2003. I frequently encountered in Tokyo the most realistic, authentic "toy" pistols and rifles, known as "airsoft guns," I had ever seen. Sold in virtually every toy store, these guns—which actually discharge pellets—are widely popular, in a nation where handgun ownership among everyday citizens is virtually unknown and the police seldom carry weapons. As a cultural anthropologist, I began to reflect on the presence of guns, both the kind that shoot and those that do not, and their cultural importance in Japan as well as in my home country, the United States.

Lacking broad knowledge of the significance of firearms across the globe, and with no practical experience with guns and no familiarity with their manufacture and distribution, I invited several scholars to participate in writing *Open Fire*, to produce a book in which guns are paramount, rather than peripheral, to understanding people's worlds. In the interim, I have been consumed by researching guns, looking globally at the political and cultural economy of firearms (see

Chapter 2), and by talking with gun-owners and visiting gunshops, in the United States and in Mexico. Although I have not conducted any formal participant-observation research among gun-users, such as Abigail Kohn's project portrayed in her book *Shooters* (2004), I began to wonder whether or not I should learn to shoot, if not indeed own, a gun.

In order to converse with gun-owners and to understand firearms literature, I needed to become increasingly familiar with forms of knowledge that, previously, had been foreign to me. In addition to never having owned a gun and having fired one only once—a rifle owned by my wife's grandfather—I am also what might be conveniently termed a "gun-control liberal" opposed to the National Rifle Association (NRA), and my children do not own toy guns. Upon beginning firearms research, I was confused by the variety of numbers signifying the "caliber" of various weapons. Was a 9 mm bigger, if not better, than a .357 magnum? Weren't pistols and revolvers the same thing? And distinctions between a shell, a cartridge, and a bullet were surely significant, but I did not know what they were.

Nonetheless, as a child I had owned and played with toy guns, including cap guns, revolvers, squirt guns, and replica rifles. Such toys were important tools when playing cowboys and Indians, or alternatively, "modern warfare," with my neighborhood playmates. While I did not share the same level of excessive fascination with playguns as some of children, my enjoyment of them, I believe, was no less typical than that of other boys. However, I never owned a BB gun, and my parents did not encourage me to play with guns. I was not brought up in a household animated by "gun culture," in contrast to some of the other contributors to this volume. In fact, I was over forty years old before learning whether or not my father owned a gun or even kept one in any of the houses in which I was raised.

Though uninterested in conducting "autoethnography," ultimately I decided that, on balance, purchasing and shooting a gun would prove benefical in my efforts to study the symbolic interaction of guns and people. It seemed important to confront, if not overcome, my ambivalence about guns by having one of my own. If I my interests were centered on the "desire" various categories of gun-owners and users convey for their weapons, then it seemed incumbent upon me to resurrect, if at all possible while using a real gun, even a modest share of the pleasure I experienced as a nine-year-old, spraying my best friend Richie with imaginary bullets from my toy machine-gun.

Of course, Cheryl, my wife, refused to allow me to keep the weapon in our gun-free home, even after I promised to keep it unloaded and locked in a firearm safe, hidden in the basement. The gun is kept in a colleague's home, where I can retrieve it in order to shoot at the local range. Once committed to doing this, I felt as though I should enjoy the experience, if at all possible. That is, I wanted a nice gun, one that seemed attractive in my hand. I had heard of a Glock pistol, and the name resonated well to my ears, but I was disappointed that this was the make of gun that virtually all novice gun-buyers in the United States seek to purchase (Kohn 2001). Besides, I could not find one for less than US$500.00, so I settled on a Smith & Wesson 9 mm, for about US$330.00. When I opened the box, I did not know how to inspect the bullet chamber, which is common gun etiquette when picking up a pistol. My gun was accompanied by a used cartridge, which confused me. But I soon learned that this is provided by the Smith & Wesson employee who tested the weapon. To be honest, I think it is a handsome gun, and I enjoy holding it, but I have not yet learned to enjoy shooting it. In fact, when driving around town with the pistol in my trunk, I constantly worry that the police will surely stop me and ask me why I have a gun.

The feminist writer Cynthia Enloe penned an insightful poem in which she recalls the pleasures of gunplay in the American neighborhood of her youth:

> ... It was the early 1940s, when the evening radio brought
> wartime news and the Saturday matinee featured
> sharp-shooting western heroes.
> But as we shot at each other
> From behind suburban pines, maples, and azalea bushes,
> We seemed to have no need for
> Myths of White Hats, Civilization, or the Free World.
> We needed only rules, our rules.
> Kkhhgghh, kkhhgghh. You're dead.
> (2004: 310)

This reflection highlights how easily firearms become domesticated, sanitized of their potential to maim, and to meet any of a range of psychological and social needs. Semiotically, guns are slippery, sometimes "tools," sometimes "toys," usually both. Appositely enough, this polysemy of the firearm was illustrated last spring, when James Mattis, a US marine general, reflecting on combat in Afghanistan, told a reporter: "Actually it's quite fun to fight them, you know. It's a hell of a hoot ... It's fun to shoot some people." Enloe continues, clarifying that children do not even need a real object in order to conduct gunplay. "The weaponry wasn't important. You just took your right hand, bent your last three fingers in toward your palm. Then you pointed your first finger at your intended target and straightened your thumb vertically. You were armed" (2004: 311). A phenomenological treatise on guns and embodiment, if ever there was one.

In preparing this collection, I encountered two photographs, each of which struck me when viewed independently. But I came to realize that when juxtaposed, when viewed in tandem, they conspired to reveal the variety of contradictory layers of experience and meanings embodied by guns and those who use them. As such, I believe that they offer an invaluable way to frame the insights of *Open Fire*. The first photograph (Figure 1.1), taken by Guy Tillim, features a local defense militia, known as the Mai-Mai, in the Democratic Republic of Congo in early 2003. This particular group is led by a Mai-Mai general, Vita

Katembola, who was allied to a rebel faction known as the Rally for Congolese Democracy (Kisangani)—Movement for Liberation. That faction, then, was in turn allied with the Kinshasa government led by Joseph Kabila. The young men in the photo are training with wooden poles as guns for a two-week period before joining the RCD-KIS-ML army, after which they will fight Ugandan and Rwandan-backed forces. They are preparing, then, for deadly serious business.

In the second photograph (Figure 1.2), a number of Belgian men, members of the AirsoftBrugge club, are seen gathered for weekend wargames, during which they will use non-lethal weapons known as Airsoft guns. While the possibility of a sprained ankle exists, nobody will die nor even be maimed during this recreational outing. Allowing these two scenes to intersect forces one to begin unpacking a number of ironies and contradictions that speak to the uneven global contexts of social class, security, emobodiment, consumption, and gender.

In the chapters that follow, the reader will encounter analyses of the historical and daily reality of guns and their relationships with people, but not in a way that displaces interest in the larger social systems, institutions, state structures, and prevailing regimes of power. The particular things people do with guns, and the ways in which guns are made to be significant, we agree, generate insight into how the poltical economy of firearms is created. Firearm ethnography opens a

Figure 1.1 Young males prepare for battle in the Democratic Republic of Congo, 2003. Photo taken by Guy Tillim.

Figure 1.2 Members of a club in Belgium gathered for recreational gunplay with non-lethal Airsoft weapons.[2]

window into how the handlers of guns *produce*—through their usage—the range of possible meanings of guns (see Storey 1998: 226).

Open Fire is composed of three sections, which, in their own ways, advance the notion that firearms are powerful material objects with diverse meanings whose significance is shaped by both local contexts and global relations of power.

Part I, "Looking Down the Barrel of a Gun: Nation-States, Small Arms, and Local Victims," pays particular attention to the themes of the political economy of firearms and violence, issues of access and ownership, and the involvement of nation-states in both using and regulating guns. In its opening chapter, Springwood elaborates on several of the themes outlined in this introductory chapter. By describing how guns are deployed, both for war and for play, in a number of key regions across the globe, he seeks to trace the transnational routes of firearms and their meanings. Donna Goldstein then offers a detailed examination of the recent attempt to criminalize most forms of gun ownership in Brazil. Exposing the political maneuvering of various special interests to influence the outcome of a national referendum on the legality of firearms, she pays particular attention to the involvement of the US National Rifle Association in this struggle. Frank Afflitto's chapter applies novel techniques to investigate Israeli-perpetrated gunfire-induced fatalities of Palestinian children and minors during the Al Aqsa Intifada (September 2000–2005). His analysis features satellite mapping, used to examine spatial perspectives on the children's deaths through a single representative case study. Ultimately, Afflitto argues that gunfire-induced deaths of Palestinian children result from policy, and therefore are purposive in nature. In *Open Fire*'s fifth chapter, Jeffrey Sluka analyzes the precarious, ongoing peace process, with its series of negotiated paramilitary ceasefires, of Northern Ireland. Importantly, Sluka addresses the presence of arms carried by all parties to this famous conflict, including the British security forces as well as the loyalist and nationalist/republican paramilitary forces, as he suggests ways in which the gun might be extricated from Irish politics. Nene Mburu closes this section by offering another analysis of disarmament, but in a context very different than that in Northern Ireland. He attempts to understand the historical and symbolic significance of arms to pastoral peoples in eastern Africa in order to rectify misinformed efforts to disarm them. Importantly, in addition to local meanings and structures, Mburu argues that the prevalence of guns in the periphery of the state is partly due to international factors, particularly civil conflicts that began during the Cold War and the post-Cold War collapse of the state.

The chapters constituting Part II of *Open Fire*, "Locked and Loaded: Race, Sex, and Gender," interrogate the role of firearms in the construction of *difference*, especially in terms of race and gender. C. Richard King's reading of the contemporary entanglements of guns and sexuality in American popular culture opens this set of chapters. King argues that a series of overlapping themes, from phallocentrism to heteronormativity to misogyny, frame firearms in the popular imaginary. These gun stories and images serve, in the end, to reinforce prevailing social hierarchies and to naturalize patriarchy. Katherine Gregory's chapter highlights the discursive cyber-communities that have emerged in internet chat rooms on pro-gun websites. In addition to shaping identities in terms of pro-gun activism and nationalism, the conversations in these chat rooms may also raise important questions about the potential of the internet to transform politics. In fact, Gregory explores whether or not such cyber-discourse forges new, subversive forms of activism or merely obscures the relations of power that amplify gun ownership in America. Next, Christy Allen features the activism of three African American gun-rights proponents. Her study, while complicating prior understanding of pro-gun activists in the US as "angry White men," suggests that citizens of color may ally themselves with a largely white pro-gun lobby in ways that are surprising to both anti- and pro-gun activists. Amy Cox follows with a chapter tracing the history of the gun's ability to confer upon its owner a prevailing ethos of "manliness" to the eighteenth and early nineteeenth centuries. Originally, guns served merely as important tools for men to accomplish daily tasks, rather than more broadly to convey masculine prowess. But, as Allen explains, as manliness was reordered as a register of individual achievement, gun knowledge emerged as an indispensable tool wherein a man might prove himself a man. Finally, Robert Arjet examines the genre of gunplay films, which he views as popular allegories serving to amplify ideologies that link violence to masculinity. Through a careful analysis of the narratives of a number of such movies, he claims that the prevailing significance of guns is their role as objects through which men negotiate relationships *with other men* that are homosocial and framed by violence.

"Playing, Dancing, and Thinking with Guns," the final Part of the book, focuses its attention on the ludic dimension of the gun; but these chapters do more than suggest that firearms can be a common source of play. They reveal how guns, and more broadly weapons, are incorporated into performances of race, class, and nation. The first chapter is Carolyn Cooper's reading of Jamaican "guntalk," taken from her research on popular performances in Jamaican dancehalls, concerts, and film. She identifies the "lyrical gun" in Jamaican song as a not always violent but stylistic way of conveying a heroic "badness" originating in the rebellious energy of enslaved African people. In the following chapter, a chilling portrait of firearms and fascism, Robert Rinehart asks how, over the last 30–40 years, guns, masculinity, and youth programs have been linked as tools of socialization geared toward creating the so-called Aryan Homeland in the western United States. Eyal Ben-Ari and Sabine Frühstück, in *Open Fire*'s closing chapter, offer an ethnographic portrait of an annual public staging of the "firepower" of Japan's Self-Defense Forces. In addition to describing this live-fire performance by Japan's military—wherein violence functions as an object of spectacle, pleasure, and celebration—the authors add a theoretical perspective important to all the chapters in this book, which is an attempt to explain how violence is transformed from threatening and dangerous to natural, domesticated, and aesthetic.

The contributors to *Open Fire* do not suggest that global violence can in any way be reduced to the presence and flow of guns. Clearly, violence, even mass murder, existed before the invention of firearms. And incredible instances of genocide have occurred, even in recent decades, without exclusive reliance on guns, as was seen in the 1994 Rwandan massacre, for instance. And without a doubt, weapons far more powerful than firearms, from missile launchers to explosives to chemical agents, prevail in many conflicts around the world. Yet it is impossible to attempt an insightful analysis of patterns of armed violence, in global perspective, without accounting for the persistence and power of guns (Small Arms Survey 2001). Indeed, they "are the weapons of choice in contemporary conflicts—the weapons most often used in battle and in attacks on civilians" (Klare 1999). This volume, then, is preoccupied by the persistent ubiquity of guns, as material objects and as symbols of subversion and domination. Collectively, the ethnographic and theoretical engagements with firearms in the following chapters follow guns wherever they are, note with fascination those rare places where they are not, interrogate those who shoot, and listen to those who fear.

Part I

Looking Down the Barrel of a Gun

Nation-States, Small Arms, and Local Victims

CHAPTER 2

Gunscapes: Toward a Global Geography of the Firearm

Charles Fruehling Springwood

In recent decades, a tradition has emerged in many urban centers, both within and outside the United States, in which city governments invite citizens to bring their firearms to a central location in order to turn them over (Renner 1998: 145). More specifically, these events are staged as exchanges, and those turning over a gun—even one in disrepair—receive a sum of money, perhaps US$100.00, or a voucher to purchase groceries or other goods. Of course, the ostensible goal of these gun buybacks is to reduce the number of weapons in the community. Law enforcement officials usually supervise the exchanges, but usually no questions are asked regarding the legality or registration-status of the donated arms. Although one such program in Washington, DC, collected 2,306 guns over two days in 1999, some doubt the ultimate effectiveness of these programs, which — on balance—have little effect on crime. Nevertheless, many would acknowledge that the underlying purpose of these programs is largely symbolic.

In a turn highlighting the ease with which guns have always occupied the space between function and play, or more alliteratively, between tool and toy (Anderson 1987), *toy* gun buybacks have also become popular. Parallel to *real* gun buybacks, children may hand over their toys—rifles, revolvers, or sometimes even "rayguns"—in exchange for other, nonviolent playthings. And on at least one occasion, *Toys R Us* vouchers have been exchanged for real firearms (Worsnop 1994: 518). During the summer of 2005, I spoke to some parents in Mexico City who a year earlier had organized toy-gun exchanges in their local neighborhoods. A mother of four children, from the borough of Iztapalapa, remarked that, "Although this won't cause crime to drop, it discourages our kids from seeing guns as positive, pleasurable things." "Hopefully, it might also keep them from seeking out real guns," she added. Such programs reflect a concern about the psychological effects of gun violence on children, a desire to discourage children from becoming too complacent with guns, and a fear that they will ultimately be drawn to arms that really shoot.

As a case in point, in January of 2006 in Winter Springs, FL, a fifteen-year-old boy, Christopher Penley, was shot dead by a SWAT police officer at his high school because he carried a non-lethal but realistic-looking pellet gun to class. He allegedly pointed the pellet gun, nearly identical to a 9 mm pistol, at a police officer, who then shot him. Guns or imitation guns are not universally used by children as toys; but in numerous locations throughout the world, boys and often girls do amuse themselves with toy weapons. For example, a nine-year-old Druse boy, whose neighborhood in Lebanon was bombarded during the 1980s civil war, told the anthropologist Adel Assal (1992: 280–1):

> Whenever there was a lull we would call our friends to come to our house and play together ... Our favorite game was hide and attack. We made up machine guns and we had teams as armies so we throw bombs at them. We built barricades with chairs and pillows. We played the game "Souk Al Gharb."...We were defending Souk Al Gharb, and the kids from the neighborhood were the attackers.

The gunplay of these children is clearly framed by the tragic and daily violence of war; but even in places where not only is public violence rare, and lethal firearms are relatively absent, such as Japan, substantial numbers of children do enthusiastically play with guns.

In this chapter, I seek to situate guns within the intersecting structures and processes, and flows and assemblages, that produce the world around us. I seek, then, an analysis in which guns emerge as an important cultural object that promises to teach us about global connections between social relations, identities, economics, ideas, and power. Opening with a glimpse of these well-intentioned civic gun-buyback experiments allows me to begin with the assertion that in many places around the world, in surprisingly similar ways, guns are at once a contested object of community preoccupation, a commodity, and an object of both fear and desire. My intention, in the limited space of a single chapter, is not to forge an exhaustive social, political and economic model of firearm circulation; nor do I believe that a totalizing vision of the globalization of violence can turn exclusively on guns. Indeed, a grand theory of human relations and social connections is not only beyond the scope here; it is hardly a viable pursuit in the first instance. Instead, I argue that firearms cannot be left out of any attempt to theorize what it means to live in the contemporary world, and further, that firearms are a particularly useful starting-point in thinking about how to integrate the symbolic and the material, and to articulate embodiment and political knowledge.

A mature political-economic analysis of firearms will eventually address all of the following concerns: To begin with, it will trace the uneven flow of guns, across time and space, highlighting how this flow constructs difference, in terms of race, class, gender, etc. It will interrogate both the legal and illicit production and distribution of arms. The meanings of violence, and other possible meanings of guns, will be critical to any effort to describe an economy of desire and fear. And any global theory of firearms must engage the liminal and ludic dimensions of gunplay, considering how not only children but also grown-ups play with toy guns and real firearms. Such a study will explain how guns *embody*, and finally, framing all of these things, a useful global analysis of guns must contextualize how guns are gendered, asking why 'pistol practices' are so often masculine, if not *in nature* then *emergently*, in practice, when it is women, with their children, who are disproportionately the victims who flee gun violence.

In the balance of this chapter, I engage guns as a critical element in the historical and daily reality of people's lives, tracing the connections between these realities and the surrounding social systems, institutions, and prevailing regimes of power. The particular things people do with guns, and the ways in which guns are made to be significant, provide a vantage-point from which the underpinnings of the political economy of firearms are made more transparent.

Counting, Making and Buying Guns

In the introduction to this volume, I suggested that some 700,000,000 firearms probably inhabit the world. Western nations prevail as producers and exporters of firearms, and the top six players in the global market, the United States, Russia, France, the UK, Germany and the Netherlands[1] (four of whom are permanent members of the UN Security Council) account for about 85 per cent of worldwide arms transfers (Burrows 2002: 15). The majority of these exchanges are of small arms, identified by the United Nations as "all revolvers and self-loading pistols, rifles and carbines, assault rifles, sub-machine guns and light machine-guns, heavy machine-guns, hand-held under-barrel and mounted grenade launchers" and other anti-aircraft guns (Burrows 2002: 25). The majority of small arms, then, are guns, portable guns of various sorts and sizes that a single person can carry. They are extremely important cultural objects because, among other things, they are used by virtually all police and military forces and, in numerous countries, they are carried legally by common citizens. They exist in every land, commonly both legally *and* illegally.

In the United States, over 300 mostly privately owned companies are in the business of small arms production, and according to the UN Small Arms Survey 2002, in 1997 the total value of gun and ammunition production was US$2.059 billion (Small Arms Survey 2002: 27). Globally, more than a thousand manufacturers produce guns, including state-owned enterprises in China, Israel and Russia and many members of the Arab League of Nations. Absolute figures for the production and profit of firearms in global terms are difficult to configure, owing in particular to the lack of information from various manufacturers, especially those in China. Nevertheless, estimates based on both public and extrapolated sales and distribution numbers are available, and in 2000, the UN suggested that the worldwide production of military firearms and ammunition was at least US$3.3 billion and, for commercial firearms and ammunition, at least US$4.1 billion (2002: 15). The most popular kind of firearm in the world continues to be the AK-47 assault rifle, or "Kalashnikov" rifle—nicknamed after its Russian inventor. JSC Izhmash, a factory located in Izhevsk, Russia, has made and shipped somewhere between 35 and 70 million of these rifles since the early 1950s, which can be purchased for prices ranging from a few dollars to US$3,000 (Renner 1999; Small Arms Survey 2002). One of the largest exporters of guns, the United States, also imports more firearms than any other country, including 4.1 million pistols and revolvers in the late 1990s (Small Arms Survey 2002: 114).

Small arms are prolific in part because they are relatively cheap, and they are paramount in virtually all wars between nation-states, in guerilla warfare, and in international drug traffic conflict. As machines, they are not technologically complex, and they are durable, continuing to function long after they were made. Moreover, guns are portable, often easy to conceal and thus, easy to smuggle. They flow freely, openly exchanged at international arms fares in such places as England, and they flow invisibly, in such places at Mexico City's infamous black market, Tepito.

One place to buy high-powered sniper rifles or machine-guns—among other assorted warring weapons such as rocket launchers, bazookas, and even explosives—is at an arms exposition, or arms fair. These arms bazaars, which are sanctioned by the host government and sponsored by multinational weapons manufacturers, occur annually in many cities around the world, but are perhaps most common in England, the US, France, and Australia (Grech 1991; Mann 1993). These arms fairs are often "themed" in terms of the merchandise they are highlighting. For example, one high-scale fair in Virginia, USA, focused on displays of fighter planes, including the Stealth Bomber (Smith 1994), while others feature tanks or missiles. At the Defense Systems and Equipment International (DSEi) fair in London in September 2003, a large number of well-organized peace protesters gathered outside, an increasingly common occurrence at this kind of event. Inside the exhibition hall, in addition to heavy machine-guns, customers were able to shop for otherwise internationally banned shock and stun guns, which were being touted by TAR Ideal Concepts, an Israeli corporation, among others (Thomas 2005).

The Metropolitan Police served to protect the exhibitors inside from the peace protesters outside, and they actually invoked Section 44 of the Terrorism Act 2000 in order to search the protesters. Ironically, while no members of Al Qaeda were found among the protesters, it is likely that, at some point, some of the weapons available inside the building might have ended up in the hands of terrorist groups of a similar stamp (see Phythian 2001). Customers at these fairs include representatives of governments (of developing nations in particular), sometimes private citizens, and increasingly, multinational security firms. These latter include such companies as DynCorp, which has been hired by the United States government to perform various military functions in Iraq, and whose mercenaries were even deployed to patrol the streets—carrying semiautomatic assault rifles—in New Orleans in the aftermath of Hurricane Katrina in 2005.

For individuals not representing internationally approved governments or multinational companies, an easier way to locate and purchase guns is at a black market venue, which can often be found nestled in the back streets of an urban center or at an obscure location in the hinterland. I visited one such market, Mexico City's infamous Tepito, in the summer of 2005, but unaccompanied by a trusted informant, I was more than hesitant to inquire about arms. I did, however, see numerous *faux* weapons—paintball and pellet-ball guns—as well as an occasional revolver. The journalist John Ross visited Tepito, which also offers all manner of black-market goods beyond weapons, from clothes to videos to drugs, in order to interview a gun merchant. Ross describes Tepito as:

> ... shadowy and serpentine, its back alleys vanishing into sinister dead-ends. Here underground tunnels lead to thieves' dens, and clandestine warehouses are stuffed with stolen goods. You do not want to be caught out after dark in this "barrio bravo" when it crackles with gunfire. So far in 2003, 32 bullet-riddled corpses have turned up on these mean streets in battle for control over the flourishing drug trade ... Tepito is Mexico City's hottest drug "plaza," the city's pirate goods capital and ... a world class weapons bazaar. (2003: 18)

Ross's informant, Flaco, sells Glocks, Barretta 9 mm, and .357 Magnums, all for about US$300, but he also peddles *armas calientes* (hot guns), used in recent crimes, much more cheaply. Flaco will also make available to his customers Kalashnikov rifles (AK-47s), nicknamed Cuernos de Chivas, or "Goat Horns," in Mexico, M-16s, Uzis, and even grenade-launchers.

Guns sold in Tepito, like guns sold in most illicit open-air markets across the globe, are manufactured anywhere from Russia to England, from Israel to Brazil, or most likely from California to the eastern seaboard. Indeed, as is true with all guns in Mexico, probably 80 per cent of Tepito's firearms come directly from the United States (Ross 2003), much to the displeasure of many Mexican politicians. In fact, in 2001, Adolfo Aguilar Zinser, national security adviser to Mexican President, Vicente Fox, complained that the US "had not put this issue [guns flowing into Mexico] at the same priority level that they put the issue of drugs" (Weiner and Thompson 2001). Ross (2003: 18) explains: "... an enterprising dealer can legally buy one automatic weapon each day in El Paso, Texas, smuggle it across the river and pass it on for three times the U.S. price." Once in Mexico, the gun is liable to end up almost anywhere, from a stall in the Tepito market to the safe house of a drug lord to even the home of a police officer.

Although no nation of citizens buys and owns more firearms, per capita, than the United States—where no significant warfare has taken place for well over a century—it is impossible to exclude war from a political and economic analysis of guns. It is in the context of war, especially civil war and war in stateless societies such as Somalia, that those who have access to guns and who profit by controlling their circulation will prevail. It is not difficult to identity international sites where local violence is perpetrated, daily, by armies or paramilitaries of nation-states, or by rebel guerillas, or even by warring ethnic groups. While each of these violent struggles can only be fully understood with the nuanced context of their particular histories, they all tend to victimize relatively unarmed civilian communities, most often with military-style guns. In recent decades, the African continent has experienced more than its share of such conflict, in which well-worn gun routes have come to inscribe the continent in order to supply state militaries, paramilitaries, and rebels, from warlords to guerillas with guns (Wakabi 2004; Hoffman 2005). In spite of the presence of weapons much larger and more powerful than firearms, these hand-held devices continue to do the bulk of the killing in all forms of warfare (Klare 1999: 20).

One especially hot spot in Africa has been Sierra Leone (Hoffman 2005), where a tragic civil war has raged for years. Firearms, in particular Kalashnikov (AK-47) rifles, have proved very effective tools for the rebel warlords of the Revolutionary United Front (RUF), who have sold diamonds to raise gun money and to feed their soldiers. In contexts such as these, common throughout the world, guns are an important, albeit deadly form of capital. Of course, guns are patently useful in fighting battles against other armed groups. But groups that do not control the government, or groups that fear the loss of such control, may seek to stockpile assault rifles and other small arms in anticipation of future conflicts. Communities that, in the present, may enjoy the protection of a government, or of a local or international police force, may fear that their peace will be fleeting. As a result, they may stockpile firearms. In these landscapes of conflict, the local knowledge that a particular warlord, ethnic community, or police force is especially well-armed is meaningful. Having guns, lots of guns, with ammunition, is a persuasive form of symbolic capital, which conveys the obvious message that a group has the power to arm itself. Moreover, a well-armed group is perhaps communicating its ability to flout national or even international authority. Maybe most importantly, being armed may signify a range of emotional and psychological "comforts," from perceived protection to the "ownership" of conspicuous objects of power and resistance.

Boys' Play

For centuries, people have associated guns, and war, with men (Connell 2000). Evidence of the masculine nature of firearms is abundant, from media images of war to patterns of gun ownership. Even though women have often utilized arms to fight war, from the rifle-toting wives and mothers who took up arms in the Mexican revolution in 1991 (Poniatowska 1999) to the female soldiers in Zimbabwe (Lyons 2004), guns remain a masculine idiom. Any global examination of the circulation of guns and their meanings must address this, but not by merely accepting just-so theories about the intrinsic relationship between men and violence. Rather, masculinity needs to be conceptualized as diverse and multivalent, and rather than focusing on individual males, we must look at the way institutions and traditions of violence are masculinized. Men in so many different places turn to guns not only to protect themselves or to commit violence, but also to create an embodied sense of empowerment and pleasure, because masculinity itself is constituted within a global political economy. The meanings and vectors of masculinity cross borders much as people and objects do. Connell (2000) argues that: "The colonial empires from which the modern global economy developed were gendered institutions, which disrupted indigenous gender orders, and installed violent masculinities in the hegemonic position." Connell's viewpoint is instructive, especially, for understanding the range of meanings men convey when using and even playing with guns.

The gun is a cultural object with many meanings that work on its users and its victims in liminal ways. The practices of both toy and lethal gun buybacks, described in the opening of this chapter, illustrate the polysemy of the gun, especially in terms of its significance to forms of play as well as its importance as a tool for hunting, protection, and for committing violence. The dividing line between innocent play and horrific imaginaries can be razor-thin, as when a group of kids in New York City, ranging in age from 6 to 13, were observed using squirt guns to simulate a drive-by shooting in broad daylight (US House of Representatives 1989). In this chapter, I have endeavored to merge two sorts of insights about firearms in order to convey a nuanced model of their worldwide prevalence circulation. First, I have argued that guns are a commodity whose production, distribution, and consumption occurs through a myriad of circuits and contexts, from the sanctioned factories of state and private manufacturers to illicit international markets. Guns prevail in both regulated and unregulated spaces, and they emerge with dangerous impact wherever borders are contested within the global processes of deterritorialization and reterritorialization. Second, I also wish to pursue the notion that nuanced symbolic interaction between firearms, as cultural objects, and people is central to understanding the persistence and global flow of the gun.

Over the last two years, a fascinating situation has arisen in the southwestern United States, along the border between Mexico and the states of Arizona and New Mexico. A number of US citizens formed an organization known as the Minutemen in order to converge on the border to "assist" the federal border patrol by looking for Mexican migrants attempting to cross, undocumented, into the United States. The Minutemen are motivated by a preoccupation with the northward flow of what they term "illegal aliens," but their public relations campaign insists that they oppose all unauthorized immigration, regardless of which border is traversed, and that they only wish to assist the border patrol by spotting and informing authorities of attempted crossings. Nevertheless, perhaps the most conspicuous feature of these Minutemen, when they are performing their volunteer services, is that so many of them are armed. Minutemen volunteers frequently wear camouflage clothing and a holster revealing a protruding pistol (Ehrenreich 2005).

The identity of the Minutemen, shaped clearly by several convergent American mythologies of militia, firearms, freedom, and whiteness (Hosley 1999; Heston 1999), seems to turn on a desire to play the role of a deputized and conspicuously armed posse. Although the group adopted a no-confrontation policy, the original plan was to surprise "illegals," detaining and handing them over to the border patrol. One can only wonder, then, about the significance of the firearm to these, mostly white middle-aged men, who typically have driven across several US states in an RV (a Recreational Vehicle) to get to the border (Ehrenreich 2005). When seen in television interviews, often sporting high-powered binoculars and holstered guns, they seem excited by all the attention. They are enacting a drama embodying all the patriotic narratives that have given meaning to their racial identities and their investment in firearms. The Minutemen, at least those who choose to carry with them a favorite pistol or rifle, converge *expectantly* on a liminal territory, the US–Mexico border, themselves armed with a liminal object, at once a mechanical extension of their bodies, a toy, a weapon, and a symbol.

Packing Heat/Unpacking Power

The symbolic interaction that frames the relationship between guns and those who carry them turns on embodiment, or a redefinition of the boundary of the body in terms of the objects that surround it and the ideas it creates. The complex *relationship of embodiment* a gun has with its owner is a very useful starting-point for understanding the interpenetration of the cultural and the political, of the local and the global, and of the ideological and the material. Guns *too easily* merge with bodies, dissolving into one's self as unconsciouly as a cell-phone or purse. These not too sophisiticated machines form and conform to the body, transforming the psyches and boundaries of those whom they possess and of those at whom they are aimed. Importantly, and as a result, they also transform, and often *reinforce*, the psyches and boundaries of national and ethnic communities.

   Scholars in all the disciplines of the social sciences and the humanities have grown increasingly preoccupied with the body as a site of analysis (Bourdieu 1977; Turner 1984; Haraway 1985; Butler 1990), and, whether to build on his work or to argue against it, these writers have most often considered the writings of Michel Foucault. Foucault (1963, 1975) advanced an understanding of the body as a site critical to the interests of the state, and he persuaded researchers to appreciate the effects of power on the body. Foucault conceptualized the body in various ways, but rarely within a phenonomenological framework. While he used a theory of embodiment to critique the Western view of the body as unified entity with a bounded subjectivity, he avoided situating his analyses in terms of the viewpoint of the social actor. With little interest in the body as a lived phenomenon, in constrast to the phenomenologists, such as Marcel or Merleau-Ponty, Foucault instead sought the ways in which history inscribed power onto the "body." "The body of desire is not, for him, the phenomenal, lived body. It is not a corporeal, incarnate subjectivity. Desire, for Foucault, is neither expressed in the body, nor is the body the lived form of desire" (Lemert and Gillan 1982: 105).

In a similar fashion, I do not wish to locate desire—for guns especially—within the body, but, instead, as historically and socially constituted. Nonetheless, in the course of researching guns and learning to shoot one, I have become subsequently more persuaded by a phenomenological approach that allows me to think about the experience of the firearm from the viewpoint of the subject (Turner 1984: 54). Bruno Latour has highlighted the infamous refrain of the NRA and many pro-gun Americans, "Guns don't kill people; *people* kill people," in order to argue the ways in which humans and non-humans are "folded into each other." Latour explains that this phrase is a retort to the contrary claim that, "Guns kill people," which is "materialist: the gun acts by virtue of *material* components irreducible to the social qualities of the gunman" (1999: 176). That is, having a gun transforms the otherwise "good guy" into a potential killer. Latour (1999: 177) finds it somewhat amusing that the NRA touts "a *sociological* version more often associated with the Left: that the gun does nothing in itself or by virtue of its material components."

The essence of Latour's work has focused on developing semiotic–cognitive models of actor–action networks. Here, I wish to draw from his efforts to link mechanical objects with the human body, without necessarily purchasing the overall thrust of his arguments. He seems overly confident in the ability of his theories to predict the flows of power and social practice across time and space and to unite phenomena at the levels of the local and global. But his attempts to unite analyses of objects and subjects by highlighting the ways in which things leave traces, if not fully inscribed paradigms for action, on people, are insightful.

Clearly more "modernist machine" than "postmodern apparatus," guns offer the illusion of consolidation and unification of one's body. Their presence works to shape, for those who "carry," a system of embodied dispositions, possibilities, and potentialities, in the sense conveyed by Bourdieu's *habitus* (Bourdieu 1977). In agreement with Bernard Harcourt (2006: 146)—who has authored a study on what it *means* to "pack heat" among imprisoned male youths in Arizona—I am persuaded by Bourdieu's critique of an overly phenomenological approach, which "places too much confidence in the generative powers of the self and of the imagination." Bourdieu's *habitus* offers a more comprehensive way to unite an abiding interest in embodiment, of person, object, and space, with a concern for symbolic meanings and social relations.

In *The Logic of Practice*, Bourdieu (1977: 73) wrote that: "[t]he body believes in what it plays at ... it does not represent the past, it *enacts* the past, bringing it back to life." He continues, arguing that what the body learns is "not something that one has ... but something that one is" (p. 73). The gun, I think, becomes for many what one is rather than what one has. The gun becomes a medium for relating to people, things, and ideas. The gun becomes a tangible object of value inscribed with historical knowledge, knowledge of gendered social relations, violence, and power. Like many scholars who theorize embodiment, Bourdieu has attempted to situate analyses of the body and of practice within larger systems and structures of power and politics, and he has done so, more or less successfully, by conceptualizing the *habitus* as something that emerges within what he terms a social field, or a network of "objective" social positions—historically shaped—that maneuver for symbolic and economic capital.

Although it is potentially a beneficial starting-point from which to think about objects, such as firearms, in terms of how their relations with bodies and their contested global routes as commodities are mutually entangled, I have not assiduously applied Bourdieu's model of the "field" throughout this chapter. Indeed, ultimately an effective political-economic model of the circulation of guns, their meanings, their owners, and their victims, is beyond the scope of a single essay. What I seek to accomplish here, in the context of a broad configuration of theoretical tools, is to identify a number of articulated spaces where the meanings of guns converge and diverge and where guns matter.

I have been suggesting that the world is mapped with many diverse gunscapes, building on a series of metaphors coined by Arjun Appadurai (1996) to define novel cultural assemblages that direct global flows in ways that supersede national-state territories. A gunscape, then, is a dynamic yet delicate assemblage of firearm circuits, discourses, and practices that dominate a global region. In addition to the global economy of firearms, local and regional political relations shape these gun landscapes, which always interpenetrate and inform one another. Central Asia, from Afghanistan to Tajikistan, a violent spatial assemblage animated in particular by an abundance of Kalashnikov and British .303 rifles, would be an example of a gunscape (Poulton 2001). North America is another such gunscape, in which the effects of the firearm cultures of the United States extend northward and southward to impact on the prevalence and practice of guns in Canada and Mexico. The Minutemen, described above, are but one manifestation of the most gun-obsessed nation in the world. Their interest in reinforcing the border with Mexico centers on stopping the flow of humans, but pays no attention to the tremendous southward flow of illegal guns. And American guns flow northward too, as Canadian officials have complained repeatedly, but most recently in December 2005, when a gunfight among local teens at a shopping mall killed a fifteen-year-old girl. The Toronto mayor David Miller suggested that the tragedy was "a sign that the lack of gun laws in the U.S. is allowing guns to flood across the border that are literally being used to kill people in the streets of Toronto." Although realistically, one cannot completely blame the increase of gun violence in Canada on the United States, it is inherently more difficult for a nation to reduce access to firearms if its neighbors produce and circulate such weapons as ambitiously does the United States.

The gun cultures of the neighbors of the United States are not completely dictated by American society. In Mexico, a vigorous public debate continues over whether to liberalize gun laws, as a bill that would allow two firearms per household has come before congress (Araizaga 2005). Although in Mexico I have found nothing close to the mythological constellation of guns, patriotic citizenship, and nation that prevails in the United States, I have encountered a set of discourses and images in which guns are key symbols. In film, art, and museums, the rifle and the revolver emerge as positive icons of the Mexican Revolution of 1911. Indeed, on almost any given day, from village or city, rifles are highlighted as important peasant symbols in both indigenous and *mestizo* folk dances.

In Mexican popular culture, guns matter. Sometimes glorifed as essential tools in the more recent Zapatista rebellion, centered in Chiapas, at other times guns are viewed with ambivalence, as devices of terror brandished by local *narcotraficantes*, or drug lords. In recent decades, a genre of popular folk music— *narcocorridos*—has won the hearts of much of the Mexican population. In ways both similar and dissimilar to the guntalk defining the Jamaican dancehall (see Cooper, in Chapter 12 of the present work), these ballads glorify and at times castigate the figure of the gun-toting outlaw. Most commonly, the music highlights the lives of drug traffickers and their gunfights with authorities, but occasionally *narcocorridos* address government corruption, migration, and even the Zapatista rebellion in Chiapas (Wald 2001; Edberg 2004).

The balladeer Paulino Vargas's song, popularized by the leading *narcocorrido* recording group *Los Tigres del Norte*, conveys particularly well the desires and fears of an impoverished Mexican populace. *La Banda del Carro Rojo* ["The Red Car Gang"] tells a story about a car full of drug smugglers who crossed into Texas, on their way to Chicago, only to be pulled over by the San Antonio police:

> Surgió un M16, cuando iba rugiendo el aire,
> El farol de una patrulla se vio volar por el aire;
> Así empezó aquel combate donde fue aquella masacre.
> [An M16 blasted, as it roared in the air;
> The light of a patrol car could be seen flying through the air;
> That's how the battle began where the massacre happened]
> (Original lyrics and translation from Wald 2001: 34)

All members of the gang are killed in a shoot-out with the police, and the dying words of the leader are: "Lo siento, sherif, porque yo no sé cantar" ("I am sorry, Sheriff, because I don't know how to sing"). As the song closes, listeners are encouraged not to worry about the gang members, since—along with their leader—they will all certainly end up in hell.

While the line separating Mexico and the US is militarized by the weapons and tactics of the US border patrol, the druglords, and, less effectively, the volunteer Minutemen, the southernmost border region of Mexico is similiarly militarized, but for a different purpose and in a different manner. Certainly, a Mexican military presence punctuates the long border with Guatemala, in order to protect against arms and narcotics smuggling, in addition to illegal immigration. However, approximately one-third of the Mexican army is situated in the state of Chiapas, or in nearby Oaxaca and Yucatan, ever since the famed uprising of Lacandon Mayan peasants on New Year's Day in 1994. On that day, moments before the North American Free Trade Agreement would begin, an uncertain number of indigenous Mayans calling themselves the Zapatista Liberation Army attempted to occupy a few Chiapas towns, including San Cristobal de las Casas, the capital. The armed group's fighters carried machine-guns, while others carried rifles, pistols, or revolvers, and yet others brandished pretend rifles, carved from wood. The armed portion of the conflict, in which an estimated sixteen Mexican soldiers were killed and at least a hundred Zapatistas perished (Russell 1995), was short-lived, spanning eleven days; in the inter-vening years, the existence of large numbers of guns, in the hands of the Mexican military and police, local paramilitary gangs, and even the more well-armed segments of the Zapatista fighters, has come to characterize the region.

Yet, as armed rebellions go, this one has turned much less on guns than on clever public-relations campaigns, constant internet tranmissions, and large-scale public caravans of the masked Zapatistas, *without* their arms. Indeed, in 2005, the most public Zapatista figure, Subcommander Marcos, invited the renowned Italian soccer club FC Milan to a "home and away" match against his team of Mayan rebels. Such approaches have led some to label the Zapatista movement as a "postmodern guerilla movement" (Navarro 2005; Conant 2006). Nonetheless, the power and symbol of the firearm remain critical to at least some of the popular imagery of the Zapatistas. In fact, the wide availablity of photos, paintings, and even figurines of gun-toting Zapatista members offers a key sym-bolic bridge to the popular Mexican revolution, linked for ever with the (always armed) icons of Emiliano Zapata and Pancho Villa. In fact, Subcommander Marcos and his less well-known associates frequently sport a bandolier (a criss-crossed harness of bullets) with large, colorful shotgun cartridges, even though they carry machine-guns rather than shotguns (Conant 2006). And the command structure of the Zapatistas is almost never seen with heavy arms, conveying the message of "defiance of state authority" (Conant 2006: 46).

Responding to a proposal that the US Bureau of Alcohol, Tobacco, and Firearms be authorized to determine firearms safety standards, a bemused law professor Daniel Polsby reacted: "Firearms are supposed to be dangerous ... Their highest and best use is as weapons rather than as collectibles or hobby instruments ... their danger stems not from defects in their manufacture but rather from the way they're used" (Worsnop 1994: 12). It is difficult to find fault with this assessment, and in fact, this inherent feature of guns is what propels their encroachment on communities everywhere. The muderous potential of the firearm is undoubtedly a critical factor in the generating its inscription with a range of gendered desires and pleasures. The gun is a polyvalent object, a point illustrated perhaps all too concretely by a 1997 photograph featuring several Albanian men in the town of Memaliaj, surrounding a pool table. One of them, quite unfazed, is using his assault rifle as a pool cue (Renner 1998: 131).

I close by highlighting a snapshot from the fieldwork of Danny Hoffman (2005), who wrote about the 2001 disarmament of *kamajor* fighters (a pro-government militia) by United Nations forces in Bo, Sierra Leone. This portrait encapsulates the central message of the chapter, that firearms traverse local spaces only in so far as they have traveled global routes and have accrued layers of meanings generated both afar and near. Hoffman learned that both the Sierra Leone soldiers and the *kamajor* combatants commonly used popular images and narratives of commandos and guerillas to construct their identities. Popular *noms de guerre* included "Rambo," "Terminator," and "Delta Force." Others viewed themselves, variously, as Sampson (with dreadlocks) and as Joseph Cinque, the slave protagonist from the film *Amistad* (2005: 343). One of Hoffman's informants, a young fighter named Ibrahim, explained how he and others would stage ambushes along roadways. He boasted that the *kamajors* based their tactics on those used by the Viet Cong against the Americans: "Everyone knew that ... the Vietnamese were brave fighters and masters of the art of the ambush. His commander, [Ibrahim] claimed, had demonstrated this by screening films such as *First Blood* and *Rambo, Commando, Delta Force*, and *The Hard Way*" (2005: 345). Significantly, in addition to animating the practices of his militia with popular Hollywood narratives, Ibrahim also viewed the secret, local knowledge of *hale* to be just as important to military success. *Hale* are ethnic Mende medicines that, among other things, serve to bullet-proof the body.

In 2001, men such as Ibrahim converged on a soccer stadium in Bo in order to hand over their guns, typically assualt rifles such as Kalashnikovs, to representatives of the UN peacekeeping force. In exchange, they received about US$130 and, perhaps, some soap or a sleeping mat. What they failed to hand over, however, because it was impossible to relinquish, was their embodied knowledge of the firearm, especially of its accessibility and its power.

CHAPTER 3

Gun Politics: Reflections on Brazil's Failed Gun Ban Referendum in the Rio de Janeiro Context

Donna Goldstein

In this chapter, I wish to explore some of the global dimensions of the recent gun ban referendum in Brazil, taking Rio de Janeiro as a case study to think with. During research in the early 1990s in the shantytowns of Rio de Janeiro, I became aware of the local dimensions surrounding firearms, especially among male youths. The ethnography I wrote based on that research, *Laughter Out of Place: Race, Class, Violence and Sexuality in a Rio Shantytown* (2003), chronicles the violence of the 1990s in Rio through a close-up look at one *favela* (urban shantytown) I pseudonymously named Felicidade Eterna, located some 50 km from the city center of Rio de Janeiro.

In the final chapters of the book, I focused on the complex relationships between the residents living in the shantytowns, the drug gang members—most often boys and young men raised in these same communities—and the police forces, renowned for their use of lethal force against the poor and for their chronic corruption. During my last visit to Rio in 1998, residents in Felicidade Eterna expressed a solemn concern that the rules for appropriate revenge targets and the fragile peace at times established in their community between the police and the local gang had slipped away dangerously into a space of unpredictability. To these residents, the gangs of the 1980s were remembered as being more concerned about garnering the support of the communities they lived in, and seemed to live by fixed and somewhat stable rules of revenge that had a particular logic to them. In contrast, the gangs that had evolved in the 1990s seemed to exhibit characteristics distinct from their predecessors. Among other differences, they carried more powerful weapons and seemed to hesitate less often in using them. The clarity of the focus for a revenge killing seemed to slip from the perpetrator of the original crime to that person's family and friends, involving members of the community that would have otherwise considered themselves neutral toward the gangs. In the later chapters of *Laughter Out of Place*, I joined numerous other scholars of Brazilian violence in suggesting that the drug gangs had successfully created a kind of parallel state (Leeds 1996), one that provided some of the services—primarily access to housing and credit—and protection that communities required in the face of invasions from outside gangs.

But I did not fully foresee how deeply and destructively parallel these gangs would ultimately prove to be. In the new century, these organizations have grown more sophisticated and complex and have attempted to rival and even intimidate the Rio state government. For example, on September 30, 2002, stores, schools, banks, and offices in Rio were forced to close on the order of jailed gang leaders who were unhappy with their living conditions. Gang members also burned buses, paralyzing public transport. This day, which became known as "Black Monday," made it clear to *Cariocas* (residents of Rio de Janeiro) that beyond being able to impact the lives of the 1.5 million people living in the *favelas* of Rio, they were also able to exert a kind of parallel power upon the broader public, a power never directly experienced by the middle classes before. According to Zuenir Ventura, a newspaper columnist known for his essays that chronicle daily life in Rio de Janeiro: "On September 30 [2002] a border was crossed. Everything that the middle class has always observed from afar suddenly descended the mountain to take over the asphalt, and the result was fear, a generalized panic like I have never seen in this city" (Rohter 2002). One month later, gang leaders threatened to kill the governor, and, among other actions, successfully attacked police stations and patrol cars throughout the city.

At the same time, evidence of police abuse and impunity has grown proportionally, despite—and perhaps in reaction to—innovative experiments in public security instituted at the state and federal levels since 2000. In April 2005, at least 30 people were killed in drive-by shootings in the Baixada Fluminense, a region on the periphery of the city of Rio de Janeiro. The gunmen were believed to be military police officers angered by a recent campaign to crack down on police violence and corruption (Rohter 2005: A3). The Amnesty International Report (2001) titled "'People End Up Dying Here': Torture and Ill-treatment in Brazil," suggests that:

> torture or other cruel, inhuman or degrading treatment is widely and systematically used in many police stations and detention centres throughout the country's 26 states and in the Federal District. It occurs at the time of arrest, in police stations, in prisons, and in youth detention centres. It is used to extract confessions from suspects; to dominate, humiliate and control detainees; or, increasingly to extort money or serve the criminal interest of corrupt police officials. (Amnesty International 2001: 4)

Brazilians have become accustomed to ineffectual and corrupt police officials. In addition to the publication of periodic Amnesty International reports, they are witnesses to large-scale media spectacles of events that highlight police brutality. In 1993, a death squad of off-duty police killed seven homeless boys and wounded two others, spraying them with gunfire as they lay sleeping in front of the Candelária Church in the center of Rio de Janeiro. Also in 1993, twenty-one residents of the *favela* Vigário Geral in the North Zone of Rio were assassinated, also by off-duty police officers, prompting the founding of the Rio NGO Viva Rio, which emerged to promote gun bans.

During my residence in Felicidade Eterna in the early 1990s, guns were used casually and habitually to resolve a variety of conflicts between individuals, not only between the home gang and police, but also between members of the home gang and competing rival gangs. Throughout *Laughter Out of Place*, I describe the everyday struggle of Glória to keep all the children in her charge "off the street," out of trouble, and far from the influence of the criminal drug gangs. But Glória was not always successful in her quest, as I explain throughout the book. Her eldest child, Pedro Paulo, joined the gangs at a young age and died a violent death in a Red Command (imperialist drug-trafficking gang in Rio) shoot-out with police. Her young nephew, Lucas, also found himself attracted to the drug gangs, and echoing Pedro Paulo's explanation of why he needed to belong to a gang, explained that it was so that he would not have to "work like a slave at slave's wages, like his mother" (Goldstein 2003: 203). In Felicidade Eterna, the local gang controlled who could own a gun and who could not. Residents found it particularly frightening and destabilizing when a non-local gang gained control over the *favela*. In one instance that took place during my time in Brazil, a new non-local gang had invaded Felicidade Eterna, claiming it as its own territory. The reason for the invasion was that a resident connected to the local gang was known to have a gun and the new gang, known as ADA (*Amigos dos Amigos,* or 'Friends of Friends'), insisted that he give it up to them. This incident, described to me by residents in Felicidade Eterna in the early 1990s when the intensification of drug trafficking and firearms usage was at its height, was one of the many such episodes I related in *Laughter Out of Place* (2003: 192–3):

[The ADA] prohibited anyone who was not part of the gang from owning a gun and were especially wary of anyone with connections to Breno. Breno's brother-in-law, Franklin, a resident, owned a gun that the new gang insisted he give up. After numerous verbal threats, members of the gang resorted to force and one evening entered his home with the goal of confiscating his gun. His wife was at home alone. They had, by then, decided to kill Franklin if he resisted. His wife was severely beaten for being either unwilling or unable to tell them where the gun was hidden. While this was taking place, Franklin arrived at the entrance to the favela, and other residents alerted him to what was happening at his home.

Because at this time the local gang was nonexistent, Franklin had no recourse but to call for the help of the police. The police arrived, and a shoot-out with the ADA gang members ensued. The gang members escaped that evening, and Franklin and his wife had just enough time to gather a few possessions before fleeing their home. They knew they could not stay; it would only be a matter of time before the gang members returned to seek revenge, and the police offered no lasting protection. Franklin's only possibility for gaining access again to his house and his possessions was to carry out a successful reinvasion of the favela by allying himself with the gang's rivals, Cólegio das Árvores.

Franklin's predicament and the constant gunfire that emerged in the wake of his alliance provides a sober reminder of the nature of the rule of law as experienced by residents of Rio's *favelas*, where the police are ineffectual in providing protection to entire regions that are under gang control. While I sometimes experienced periods of relative calm while living in Felicidade Eterna, guns were nevertheless ever-present, particularly in their ability to define both the nature of leadership and the rule of law in this region beyond police control.

In the remainder of this chapter, I address local as well as global discourses surrounding the possibility of Brazilian gun control as it played out in the recent 2005 gun ban referendum—a referendum unique in the world for bringing one of the most radical proposals of gun ban legislation to the people for a vote. The referendum's inception began in December of 2003, when President Luiz Inácio Lula da Silva (President Lula) signed into law what later became known as the Disarmament Statute, a bill that legislated sweeping restrictions on the selling and carrying of firearms. The final provision of the bill called for an October 2005 national referendum, in which Brazilian citizens themselves would be asked to decide whether the proposed restrictions should be continued or revoked (Dias 2005: 40–8). If passed, the referendum would have dramatically changed the landscape of firearms and control: it would have required very strict legal procedures for the possession of firearms, increased the age limit for those who could own firearms, lengthened prison sentencing for those who carried firearms illegally, forced gun manufacturers to imprint bullets so that homicides could be traced to the original weapon, and made arms trafficking illegal in a manner parallel to the illegality of drug and animal trafficking.

The referendum ultimately failed, but the discourses that arose out of its consideration, produced within a matrix of local and global forces, reflect an important step in a longer process of democratization—a process so often criticized as problematic, if not dysfunctional, in the Brazilian context. Most notably, the rhetoric that developed for and against the referendum produced dramatic effects on the voting public. In polls taken at the very start of the campaign, approximately 70 per cent of Brazilians supported the gun ban. But surveys conducted just days before the referendum showed that the NO vote had gained significant momentum, estimating that at least 52 per cent would vote against the referendum at the polls (Phillips 2005: 3). When the gun ban referendum was finally put to a vote on Sunday, October 23rd, 2005, approximately 64 per cent of the public said "no" to the ban and only 36 per cent said "yes" (Resende 2005: A19). Read one way, the movement to ban weapons sales and to implement more stringent gun control in Brazil failed miserably, with the proposal failing to win a single state (Lobo 2005). Read another way, the very fact of the referendum's existence can be seen as an extremely positive development within the long-term process of redemocratization taking place in Brazil. In fact, the referendum marks the first time that any country, not just Brazil, has put a gun ban to a nationwide vote (Reel 2005: A13).

Regardless of how one interprets the outcome of the referendum, what happened between the beginning and end of the campaign that convinced Brazilians they would be better off without the proposed gun ban calls for analysis. This chapter seeks to provide that analysis by historicizing and contextualizing local debates surrounding the Brazilian referendum within global activist agendas emanating from left- and right-wing sources. There have been analysts that have speculated that the gun ban referendum and the "no" vote that was incurred could perhaps best be interpreted as a "no" vote to support for the Workers' Party and President Lula, in office at the time of the referendum. Just prior to the referendum it became known that the Workers' Party was involved in an influence-peddling scheme. This purported corruption of the party that had run on an anti-corruption platform shook the country and inspired disgust and disappointment even among traditionally loyal supporters. Many editorials in Brazil surmised that the cynicism provoked by this scandal might have caused voters to reject the gun ban referendum, a referendum wholly supported by President Lula. In contrast to these accounts, my own account of the referendum begins locally in the city of Rio de Janeiro, where a gun-weary population in many ways established the rhetorical terms of the debate. The discussion then moves outward to consider the effects of global interventions into the debate, considering the transnational trappings of a terrorist bombing in London alongside the imported rhetorics of global NGOs. Ultimately, my account returns to Brazil, where a unique configuration of discourses on gun control, violence, and poverty confirmed the referendum's failure.

The Political Economy of Guns in Rio De Janeiro

Although many organizations inside Brazil received funding and advice from global networks interested in seeing the gun ban referendum pass or fail, the discourses that emerged from the controversial referendum were already familiar to Brazilians, who experience almost 40,000 firearm deaths per year along with one of the highest rates of lethal police violence in the world. Much of the debate about the referendum emanated from organizations located within the city of Rio de Janeiro, one of the more vivid sites of crime, urban violence, and gun activity in Brazil. The Rio-based non-governmental organization Viva Rio[1] was central not only in coordinating the YES movement, but also in organizing an impressive group of scholars to investigate the basic political economy of guns in Rio de Janeiro. Their collection of scholarly papers provides much of the information found on this topic, and I cite their work throughout this section of this chapter. A common perception in Rio has been that criminals use military-style foreign-made small arms to commit crimes, while law-abiding citizens use registered Brazilian-made firearms for legitimate self-defense (Dreyfus, Lessing, and Purcena 2005). During the months prior to the referendum, this issue received increased attention as the Brazilian small arms industry exploited this perception when entering the political debates leading up to the final vote. Yet researchers at Viva Rio found that Brazil's own Small Arms and Light Weapons (SALW) industry is responsible for the production of a large percentage of the guns that are used by criminals and that contribute to the astronomic levels of armed violence in Brazil.

Currently, the Brazilian small arms industry is made up of a few companies, the two most prominent being Forjas Taurus SA and the Companhia Brasileira de Cartuchos, or CBC, which hold near-monopolies in handgun and small arms ammunition production. The other major company is IMBEL, a public company administered by the Ministry of Defense with strong ties to the Army, which primarily produces military arms and ammunition. Together, these companies have helped Brazil not only to consolidate its position as a medium-sized SALW producer and exporter, but also to become a dominant regional player in firearms production: the second largest producer of guns in the western hemisphere after the United States (Dreyfus, Lessing, and Purcena 2005: 50). Significantly, the production of permitted-use firearms in Brazil doubled between 1967 and 1995 from 400,0000 to 800,000, with handgun production key to that increase (Dreyfus, Lessing, and Purcena 2005: 67). The Brazilian production of SALW has thus grown steadily over the years, reaching a current market value of approximately US$100 million per year (Dreyfus, Lessing, and Purcena 2005: 68).[2] While the United States has been identified as the principal customer for Brazilian SALW since the late 1980s (Dreyfus, Lessing, and Purcena 2005: 75), Viva Rio researchers have pointed out that the surveying of the purchase and use of SALW firearms by Brazilian civilians themselves has been complicated by the lack of a federalized system:

> The purchase and use of firearms by civilians remained unregulated until 1980, when the Ministry of the Army enacted a regulation that established the number and type of weapons that civilians above 20 years of age would be able to purchase and also established the mandatory registration of those weapons (as a precondition for completing the purchase). However, small arms were registered with the Civilian Police of each state, with no national institution in charge of centralizing the data on firearms and their owners. (Dreyfus and Nascimento 2005: 96)

In 1997, the Brazilian federal government finally created a nationwide registry system called the National Arms Control System (SINARM), which instituted a federal system for the comprehensive registration of privately owned guns.

The increase in firepower in the city of Rio de Janeiro during the last three decades has been both quantitative (greater numbers of firearms) as well as qualitative (more weapons with greater firepower). The city provides a telling case study for understanding what happens to guns after they are purchased, particularly with respect to firearm movement between legal and illegal markets. According to the Viva Rio report titled, "The Value of the Illegal Firearms Market in the City of Rio de Janeiro" (Rivero 2005), out of the entire universe of arms seized by police during criminal activities in the state of Rio de Janeiro between 1951 and 2003, 81 per cent of the weapons were unlicensed; that is, just one-fifth of the weapons used in registered crimes were acquired legally. The report attributes the high number of illegal weapons in Rio de Janeiro to a lack of effective firearms controls in the state. As discussed in the report titled "The Value of Illegal Firearms in the City of Rio de Janeiro," the diversion of legal firearms to crime in the city of Rio began to increase dramatically from 1972 forward, coincidentally with the arrival of drug trafficking activities, especially marijuana trafficking, on a massive scale in Rio's *favelas* (Rivero 2005). Another important timeframe dates from 1981–2, when cocaine-trafficking became more common. This trend continued into the 1990s, and it was during this time that the diversion of firearms to criminal elements reached a peak. In short, increases in the drug trade coincide with increases in gun-related crimes and with the diversion of weapons from legal to illegal markets.

Yet the increase in firepower applies not only to drug traffickers, but also importantly to the police forces. In a series of recent interviews with the police, Rivero (2005) found that the police consistently talk about the desire to have firepower "equal to the traffickers" with the objective of exterminating them, a theme that many urban ethnographers of violence have noted (cf. Huggins 1991; Caldeira 2000). It follows that the desire for firearms manifested by police and drug gangs in Rio betrays a noteworthy class dimension. For instance, Lessing (2005), on the basis of interviews with middle-class citizens who participated in the Disarmament Statute of 2003 gun-buyback campaign, found that the vast majority of these citizens preferred to own firearms because of a perceived threat of property crime associated with the lower classes, together with the reality of ineffective law enforcement. In contrast, residents of Rio's *favelas*—whether directly involved as gang members or not—expressed the need for protection, status, and authority, as well as the socially mobile earning power associated with gun ownership.

The Man in London

On July 7, 2005, just two months prior to the vote on the referendum, London suffered a series of suicide bombing attacks in the subway and bus system during which four bombers and fifty-two civilians died. Two weeks later, on July 21, 2005, police found four additional explosive devices partly detonated in central London, near Shepherd's Bush station on the Hammersmith and City Underground Line, Warren Street station on the Victoria Line, and the Oval station on the Northern Line, and on a number 26 bus in the Hackney road, along with a mysterious package on some open ground at Little Wormwood Scrubs, in the West London suburb of North Kensington, that suggested a fifth explosive device (BBC News 2005a,b). The morning after this discovery, a 27-year-old Brazilian man by the name of João Alves Menezes, who in London preferred to be called Jean Charles de Menezes, left his apartment building and headed off to catch the bus that would take him to the Stockwell Underground station (BBC News 2005c). The son of a bricklayer from the city of Gonzaga in the state of Minas Gerais in Brazil, he had lived in London legally for three years working as an electrician. Mr Menezes now lived in an apartment block in Tulse Hill, South London, where he shared an apartment with two of his female cousins, Patricia da Silva Armani and Vivien Figueiredo (Past Peak Archives 2005; WRP 2005).

Plainclothes police had been staking out Mr Menezes's apartment building because they suspected that one of the bombers from the failed July 21 attacks, Hussain Osman, the prime suspect for the Shepherd's Bush attempt, might be living in the block, as they had found a gym membership card giving that address at the scene of the crime in Shepherd's Bush. When Mr Menezes emerged from the building at 9.30 a.m. on that fated day, he was therefore followed by police—who were still under the impression that he might be Hussain Osman—on to the bus that took him to the Stockwell Underground station and then into the station (which had apparently been the point of departure for three of the four would-be bombers the previous day) (BBC News 2005a,c). When Mr Menezes began to run down the escalator at the sound of an approaching Northern Line train, the police took this behavior to be an attempt to evade pursuit and rushed on to the train after him as it was about to depart, presumably in the belief that he might be their original Shepherd's Bush suspect about to engage in a second attempt to blow up a tube train (BBC News 2005e). Witnesses said the police then shot him five times in the head and neck, killing him instantly (Cowell 2005). The police report attributed the incident both to Mr Menezes's refusal to stop and to his wearing of a lengthy and potentially concealing jacket in summer weather, an anomaly that had apparently suggested to the police the possibility of a concealed bomb. But a Brazilian friend of Mr Menezes, also living in London, attributed his decision to flee to the fact that he had recently been chased by a London gang. One thing was ultimately clear to all parties, however: Mr Menezes was not a terrorist; he was merely a migrant worker from Brazil wearing a lengthy and potentially concealing jacket in warm weather (BBC News 2005d,e; Past Peak Archives 2005).

News of the circumstances surrounding Mr Menezes's death was bitterly received by Brazilians living in both London and Brazil. The Brazilian Artists website,[3] for instance, which is dedicated to Brazilian political issues as well as events related to Brazilians in London, posted a range of commentaries on his death, many of them suggesting strong parallels between the brutality of the police forces in Europe and Brazil, with the first fueled by racist anti-Arab sentiment and the latter by discrimination against shantytown residents. Although this tragic tale of the misreading of an innocent Brazilian migrant could have been a chance for Brazilians to reflect on a wretched gun-inflicted error made by one of the least violent police forces in the world, the mistaken shooting of João Menezes instead became a parable reminding Brazilians of the incompetence of their own police forces. This parable was quickly embraced by those opposed to the gun ban legislation and in favor of a NO vote on the referendum. Opponents successfully argued that because Brazilian police were incapable of protecting the civilian population from criminals, individuals should be allowed to own and carry firearms to protect themselves. There is a further hint of irony in the deployment of this rhetoric, given that President Cardoso had regularly invoked the British system of gun control when arguing for gun ban legislation in Brazil. In fact, it was after a diplomatic visit to England in 1997 that Cardoso became one of the earliest proponents of the Brazilian legislation leading to the 2005 referendum (Rohter 1999).

Global Players in the Brazil Referendum

Even though global players are credited as important actors in the outcome of the Brazilian referendum, it is difficult to measure the significance of their impact on the referendum. In what follows, I consider the effects of rhetoric produced by the US-based National Rifle Association on the one hand and transnational gun-ban NGOs on the other.

Brazilians on each side of the referendum claimed that the other side received outside, foreign, global support for their cause, both financial and strategic. On the left, for instance, ten Noble Prize winners lent their name and support to the YES cause. The International Action Network on Small Arms (IANSA), a UK-based global network of more than 600 non-governmental organizations favoring gun control, additionally expressed support for the Brazilian referendum, finding it to be a "historic opportunity to make people safer from gun violence" (IANSA 2005). On the right, the opposition to the gun ban gained powerful sponsors from outside Brazil, most importantly from the National Rifle Association (NRA) (Morton 2006). Already in 2003, when the Disarmament Statute neared a vote in Parliament, Charles Cunningham, an NRA lobbyist in Washington, traveled to São Paulo to meet with a pro-gun group. Cunningham's talks in Brazil were billed as offering "effective pro-gun strategies in an anti-gun culture."

Although many pro-gun activists stayed away from Cunningham's talks, fearing that their presence would be seen as a form of collusion with foreign interventionists, his appearance in the country was nevertheless seen as significant to the overall morale of the pro-gun groups (Morton 2006: 63). David Morton suggests that one of the NRA's simplest forms of influence on overseas groups may be to act as a "global pro-gun think tank" (2006: 65). While the NRA denied that they offered any direct funding to Brazilian groups, pointing out that their charter prohibits financial assistance, Morton argues that the NRA does indeed play a crucial role in international efforts, supplying strategies and rhetoric to pro-gun campaign efforts. Wendy Cukier (2005) of the Coalition for Gun Control agrees, noting that: "... the National Rifle Association has [put] pressure on the US Administration to block international efforts to combat the illicit trade in guns [and] American politicians have threatened to cut funding to the United Nations if it proceeds with these measures." While many gun-ban activists argue that these kinds of NRA campaigns are culturally inappropriate outside a US context and therefore inherently subject to failure, Morton holds that NRA campaign efforts abroad have been surprisingly successful. Highlighting the success of their efforts in Australia and Canada, he credits the NRA with the last-minute success of the Brazil campaign.

Yet representatives of Viva Rio noted that the Brazilian pro-gun lobby used both statistics and rhetoric that were indeed "culturally inappropriate" in the Brazilian context, using unintelligible campaign slogans that too closely resembled NRA television infomercials in the United States. For example, one TV spot in Brazil referred to the "right" to own a gun, while another argued for gun ownership because "it can take up to seven minutes for police to respond to your call" (Hearn 2005b). But the Brazilian Constitution does not guarantee gun ownership as a fundamental right (Hearn 2005b), and, as Viva Rio activists jokingly pointed out, every Brazilian knows it would take more than seven minutes for police to respond to a distress call. Still, there was something very effective about the pro-gun groups' depiction of gun ownership as a universal symbol of "freedom," suggesting that this seemingly US-constrained rhetoric appears to travel quite well and acquire new meanings in different contexts. In the end, it is perhaps unproductive to ask whether or not the pro-gun rhetoric was "culturally appropriate" in Brazil. While it is doubtful that any one advertisement or pamphlet tipped the referendum vote, the individual items of NRA-sponsored propaganda collectively worked to further the cause of pro-gun activists both abroad and at home.

Consider, for instance, a pamphlet distributed by the pro-gun lobby in Brazil, which featured an image of Hitler giving a Nazi salute. The choice of image was clearly meant to suggest a parallel between the dangers of disarmament and the dangers of Nazism. In fact, this image embodies a time-worn line of reasoning used by the NRA in the United States. The NRA-ILA website,[4] for instance, offers free downloads of an article entitled "Registration: The Nazi Paradigm." Written by pro-gun constitutional litigator[5] Stephen Halbrook, the article draws specific parallels with the 1938 Nazi policy to disarm the population and the genocide that followed. The argument is meant to associate the antics of gun-ban activists with Nazi policies, thus emphasizing the inherent genocidal risk threatening any population willing to disarm. Tellingly, the argument also succeeds in likening any government that supports disarmament to the Nazi regime.

But while this parallel might be understandable within the US context, given the country's involvement in the Second World War and the general population's level of knowledge about Hitler's genocidal policies, it is less clear how this rhetoric could have resonated within a Brazilian public that did not share this history. The law professor Bernard Harcourt's insights (2004) help to make sense of the NRA's coupling of Hitler's disarmament with contemporary gun control. He explores the NRA and Hitler-as-gun-control-proponent argument as one of the more fascinating internally fragmented aspects of the 'culture war' on gun control. He points out, for example, that while the pro-gun NRA and the pro-gun organization Jews for the Preservation of Firearms Ownership (JFPO) both deploy the Hitler-as-gun-control-proponent argument in their literature, the pro-gun white supremacist organization, National Alliance, reads the 1938 German gun registration laws as being a move toward gun liberalization. Harcourt's weighing of the evidence brings him (ironically) to side with the National Alliance interpretation of the 1938 edict; that is, that Hitler intended to liberalize gun control laws in Germany for "trustworthy" German citizens while disarming "unreliable" persons, namely opponents of National Socialism or Jews (2004: 26). By the end of his article, however, Harcourt finds it absurd even to "try to characterize this as either pro- or anti-gun control" (2004: 27), calling on scholars to examine the rhetoric behind the gun culture wars in a more serious manner. Harcourt's (2004) article caused me to ponder the possible interpretations of the use of the Hitler argument in the Brazilian context. If Morton is correct, this globally powerful pro-gun lobby was able to be successful even with the distribution of culturally inappropriate and questionable facts regarding Nazi gun laws.

The NRA-sponsored Hitler campaign was not the only ad campaign to misuse (non-US) globalized symbols of freedom. In one television commercial, an image of Nelson Mandela with a fist raised in a sign of solidarity was used to convince voters that the gun ban would strip them of their liberties by disarming them (Reel 2005: A13). Mandela's own lawyers, angered by the ad, wrote to Alberto Fraga, president of a key pro-gun group called Parliamentary Front for the Right to Legitimate Self Defense, and demanded that Mandela's image not be used in the campaign. They warned: "Mr. Mandela's fighting against apartheid … bears no relation to the issues described, i.e., the sale of guns" (Hearn 2005a). Although the organization responsible for the sponsorship of this particular ad remains unclear, the rhetorical exploitation of "freedom" to sell a pro-gun stance is highly reminiscent of the NRA campaign, suggesting, perhaps, that the NRA's influence goes far beyond what has traditionally been attributed to them.

Yet I have strong doubts that the vast majority of Brazilians would have been able to make sense of the discursive appropriation of either Hitler or Mandela. What they would have made good sense of, however, is the rhetoric put forth by the pro-gun lobby in Brazil, which was much more relevant to Brazilian practices and concerns. In short, the pro-gun lobby was able to convince the population of something widely known in the shantytowns of Rio de Janeiro and throughout Brazil: namely, that criminals have access to guns and will continue to have them, and that the police are unable to protect ordinary citizens. In the final weeks leading up to the referendum, the pro-gun lobby increasingly played on the public's insecurity and widespread skepticism about the police. In advertisements that seemed comparatively Brazilian in orientation, they projected the idea that voting for the gun-ban was a position supported by criminals. The ban would benefit them, the rhetoric went, since it would leave criminals as the only armed group besides the police.

In response to these campaigns, the gun-ban activists led by Viva Rio developed their own rhetorical strategies for combating criticisms of the referendum, exploiting local dynamics regarding the configuration of guns in Rio. Recognizing a gendered dimension to the gun culture debate in Brazil, they appealed to the large population of mothers and girlfriends who were conscious of an entire generation of youths being lost to death by gunfire. In the months prior to the referendum, Viva Rio helped organize a gun buy-back program that encouraged women to ask the men in their lives to give up their weapons. The "Mother's Day Campaign" of 2001, which ran the slogan, *"Arma Não! Ela Ou Eu"* ("Choose gun-free! It's your weapon or me"), reportedly collected one of the largest stashes of firearms ever in one day: approximately 100,000 guns occupying a 400-square-meter pile (Amnesty International 2003).

The Brazilian version of the gun-culture war thus seemed to incorporate class and gendered dimensions that prove complex even within the limited context of Rio de Janeiro. I was not in Brazil during the time of the referendum, so I was not able to track the debates as they took place among distinct class segments of the Rio context. But I have read numerous interviews provided by the news media with individuals living both in the shantytowns and on the "asphalted streets" of Rio, as the middle-class neighborhoods are known. These interviews reflect a wide range of opinions that are not easily codified by class position. Proponents and opponents of the referendum came from all classes, yet they arrived at their "yes" or "no" vote for very different reasons. For instance, residents of shantytowns who were opposed to gun control readily emphasized their fear of a future where only the police forces were armed, weary of the police's abusive behavior. In contrast, members of the middle class who were opposed to gun control readily expressed their fear of a future where only criminals were armed, weary of the police's incompetence. With or without global intervention, then, questions of violence and criminality are centrally important to Brazilian political debate. This is especially true in the city of Rio de Janeiro, where in the year 2000 more than 60 per cent of the population considered matters related to safety or security to be the main problem that both society and the State were confronting (Soares 2000: 1).

Conclusions

Since the late 1990s, Brazil has experimented with a series of bold policies that address issues of crime and violence in new and innovative ways, culminating in the gun ban referendum. In spite of the fact that the referendum of 2005 failed to win the majority of votes, this author remains optimistic about the future. Most critically, leftist civil society organizations and human rights activists are now surfacing who are willing to address issues of public security and policing, a subject that received comparatively little attention from the left in the 1980s.

The Brazilian anthropologist Luiz Eduardo Soares, who in recent years served as Public Security Secretary both at the Rio state level and at the federal level under President Lula, analyzes the ways in which the intellectual left was unable in past decades to address satisfactorily issues of crime, violence, and public security. Believing that crime is a symptom of social inequality and economic deprivation (Soares 2000: 15), leftwing activists of the 1980s and early 1990s chose to avoid crime and violence as political issues, focusing instead on socioeconomic reform. This leftist middle class, once vocal against police violence during the years of authoritarian rule (1964–83), was comparatively silent during the post-authoritarian period, when police violence was no longer directed against them, but instead directed at the lower classes. Their political involvement in the question of police violence shifted in the early 1980s, when state and police discourses moved from a "war against leftist subversives" toward a "war against crime" (cf. Huggins 2000). In short, the leftist middle class remained silent when police violence was no longer perceived as a middle-class issue. This silence was exacerbated by the lower classes, who also came to share an unwillingness to speak out against police violence. James Holston and Teresa Caldeira (1998) have written extensively about the disjunctive aspects of Brazilian citizenship within the process of redemocratization, suggesting that one of the most obvious aspects has been the widespread acceptance of routine police violence by the working classes themselves. After conducting a series of interviews among working-class residents living in the suburbs of São Paulo, Caldeira (2000) found that residents overwhelmingly held the opinion that criminals should be punished, even eliminated, regardless of the legality of the method. Caldeira later suggests that "increasingly and across the board, talk about and agitation for human rights seems to make less sense and be out of joint with the popular mood" (2002: 257).

In the last few years, there has been a further development regarding crime and violence in Rio de Janeiro that additionally calls for an analysis of the relationship between local and global dimensions of gun politics. In 2001, a UNESCO published paper (Geffray 2001) describes the drug-trafficking activities in the federal state of Rondônia, near the Bolivian border. The report found that stolen items from Brazil, such as cars, are being used to barter for Bolivian cocaine, which then makes its way back to Rio de Janeiro. A number of newspapers, both Brazilian and North American, have suggested that Brazilian drug traffickers have been supplying firearms to the Columbian leftist revolutionary organization FARC (*Fuerzas Armadas Revolucionarias de Colombia*, or "Revolutionary Armed Forces of Colombia"), also in exchange for cocaine. In April 2003, Rio newspapers, along with the governor of the state of Rio de Janeiro, began to speak of the "war on narcotraffic and violent crime" at home, invoking comparisons with the Iraq War and terrorism abroad in an attempt to justify the intensified police actions in the slums of Rio de Janeiro. Yet Paul Amar (2003) points out that this journalistic and governmental rhetoric stopped abruptly, shortly after it began. Suggesting that Rio's democratizing forces were ultimately able to sustain and support a democratic and progressive agenda,

Amar argues that in the last instance the city's leaders reinvigorated their efforts to resist "the hegemonic myths that have spurred counterproductive approaches to crime-fighting" (2003: 42). I would add another explanation to Amar's observation regarding localized skepticism towards these kinds of global narratives. I speculate that both left- and right-leaning political groups find something dangerous in invoking global comparisons within the Brazilian context, and still more in inviting foreign interventions into national political campaigns. The Brazilian appropriators of the Iraq War comparisons share with the NRA-influenced pro-gun activists a reluctance to embrace fully these globalized rhetorics, even if they will help their cause. While much of this reluctance can be explained by a unique form of Brazilian nationalism, groups across the political spectrum perceive the invitation of certain kinds of foreign intervention as dangerous to Brazilian sovereignty and disrespectful of the local.

In attempting to evaluate the role of both global and local discourses in the October 2005 gun ban referendum in Rio, I have ventured to explore some of the institutions that provide strategic and ideological support to these discourses. I am also reminded of the fabric of everyday life in the Rio shantytowns, where guns are central to young men in their quest for social mobility and in their quest for an identity that commands respect. I remember how Lucas, one of Glória's nephews who was only a pre-teen when I met him in the early 1990s, made a decision to join the Red Command, one of Rio's best-known drug-trafficking gangs. When he announced his decision, friends and members of his family replied that he had joined in order to have an early funeral; that is, in order to die young. Most significantly, Lucas was presented with a gun of his own when he joined the gang. Residents of Felicidade Eterna related to me multiple stories of how the new gun-owning Lucas readily made life threats to anyone he believed had wronged him in some way, whether major or minor. The reality and the dread of a gun in the hands of an angry young man was all too familiar to these residents, who are caught in the everyday crossfire between desperate gun-toting men and the violent police, who criminalize them. My sense, then, is that some day even the desire for protection will not trump the hatred of guns in these impoverished communities. Some analysts might interpret the failure of the gun ban referendum of 2005 as an indication that global conservative agendas, including the Hitler campaign of the US-based National Rifle Association and the US-influenced rhetoric surrounding the war on terror, were able to force their rhetoric and their logic on Brazilian referendum voters. I prefer to see the failure of the referendum to pass as an indicator of the widespread cross-class lack of faith in the institutions of police and government, particularly in their ability to enforce the laws that the referendum would have put into effect. The referendum, as an act in and of itself, proved that Brazil was capable of dreaming radical futures. Ultimately, however, the population needed broader guarantees of the functionality of the rule of law before it would place stringent limitations on access to firearms.

CHAPTER 4

Of Guns, Children, and the Maelstrom: Determining Purposive Action in Israeli-perpetrated Firearm Deaths of Palestinian Children and Minors[1]

Frank M. Afflitto

"*La rabia ... imperio, asesino de niños*"
Silvio Rodríguez, Cuban songwriter, "Días y Flores"[2]

Guns and their victims form intersecting, dialectical discursive frameworks of power, control, anxiety and resistance. The world was awakened to the gunfire-perpetrated victimization of Palestinian children by the Israeli military in October 2000, several weeks after the commencement of the period known as the Al Aqsa *Intifada*, or rebellion. This awakening occurred through internationally disseminated visual imagery of the death of twelve-year-old Muhammad Al Durra, in the Gaza Strip sector of the Illegally-Occupied Palestinian Territories (IOPT) when the boy, already wounded, was shot in the stomach with an explosive bullet by the Israeli Defense Forces (IDF) (Abdel-Nabi 2001), lay in the arms of his screaming, pleading father, and expired approximately one half-hour later (2001). The ambulance driver from the Palestine Red Crescent Society (an ICRC affiliate) who came to take the boy and his wounded father to the hospital was also shot by IDF troops upon arrival (2001), in clear violation of the rules of medical neutrality.

The theme of children in war is nothing new, and has been treated in depth in earlier social science and public health/medical literature. In addition, many international relief agencies and human rights monitoring organizations have, in recent years, focused mainly on children's roles in violent conflict (Anonymous 1999; Breen 2003; Singer 2001–2; United Nations, n.d., accessed 3/11/2005), in addition to disseminating the plight of refugee and displaced children within the, albeit fractured, family and community eco-system (Giacaman et al. 2002; Taylor 2004). A third main area of research and writing, perhaps the most flourishing by far, has been conducted with child victim-survivors of lethal conflict, and involves documentation of traumas and post-traumatic psycho-social conditions, in Palestine and elsewhere (Albina 2002; Anonymous 2002; Arafat 2003; Beauchemin 2004; Dickson-Gomez 2002; El-Sarraj 1996; Garbarino et al. 2002; Garbarino and Kostelny 1996; Gibson, K. 1989; Grassroots International 2000; Sait 2004; Save the Children 2004; Slovak 2002; Thabet et al. 2002; Wright, n.d.; Younes 2003; Zoroya 2002), along with calls for amelioration and reintegration into a more constructive, post-conflict society (see Máusse 1999). In recent years, though sparingly, researchers have begun to examine children as lethal casualties in armed conflicts, whether through being targeted (Geltman 1997; Kapp 2001; Marshall 2002; Schleunes 1996), as "collateral damage" (Mermet 1998) or through increased difficulties of childbirth and neonatal care and other healthcare resources (Christian/Base21 Media Activists 2003; Savitz et al. 1993).

The particularity of the firearm, and its specific use as a tool of assassination, in the construction of children and minors as lethal victims of armed conflict, is of interest herein. Firearm research has an extensive trajectory, particularly in the United States, where gun-perpetrated homicides reach into the thousands each year (Lott, Jr. 2003). US researchers have studied child and infant mortality in the areas of both intentional homicides (Eber et al. 2004; Fingerhut and Christoffel 2002; Fingerhut et al. 1992a,b; Murnan et al. 2004; Reich et al. 2002), and unintentional killings (Lott, Jr. 2003). The matter of intent in the perpetration of firearm-perpetrated killings is a primary focus of this chapter, as I seek to establish, through the use of a new methodology, the construct of intent in the gun-perpetrated deaths of Palestinian children and minors by the IDF and other state-sanctioned social actors.

Dead Children in the Popular Psyche

The war-induced deaths of children, and their subsequent perception as martyrs, is in no way specific to the Palestinian cause, nor to Islam, as many in the sociocultural West appear to think. Every September 13th, for example, Mexico celebrates its national holiday of the *Niños Héroes* (Child Heroes). This holiday commemorates what Mexicans consider to be a heroic battle and the subsequent massacre by US forces of a group of child military cadets at the Heroic Military Academy in Mexico City in 1847. The youths, from thirteen to eighteen years old, are clearly seen as anti-imperialist martyrs in the Mexican popular psyche. Perceived martyrdom of children, in predominantly Catholic countries like Mexico and El Salvador, brings to mind feelings of empathy, anger and resistance to the etiological factors that brought about such deaths for many in the populations in question. A popular saying in El Salvador during that nation's civil war was *"Sangre de mártires, semillas de libertad"* ("Blood of the martyrs, seeds of liberty"), and children and other members of the civilian population were certainly included in such social perceptions, along with political activists and those who were combatants in the revolutionary forces. A further case in point concerns the death of twelve-year-old Sandinista activist Luís

Alfonso Velásquez during that nation's anti-Somozan struggle. Luís was shot in the back and killed by a Somozan National Guardsman, and, at least during the Sandinista governments, a park commemorating his anti-Somozan social activism and perceived subsequent martyrdom was established in his name in the capital, Managua. Further examples abound, in Latin America, Sri Lanka and a host of other conflictive sites, for the interested reader to investigate.

The war-induced deaths of children in the internal conflicts in Sierra Leone and Uganda are current cases of international concern and sympathy. This is so particularly because, in both cases, the anti-government forces in each country did (Sierra Leone, Revolutionary United Front) and do (Uganda, Lord's Resistance Army) sequester and press-gang children into rebel military service. These cases are far from unique, and have garnered international sympathy because of the involuntary nature of children's participation in these armed conflicts and the subsequent abuses that were meted out to them, including forced labor conditions and sexual slavery (see Kapp 2001).

In turning to the issue of Palestinian children in the current period of unrest (late September, 2000 through to the time of writing in late 2005), over 645 under the age of eighteen years have died as a result of armed violence by Israeli state actors (soldiers, police and illegal settlers) (Amayreh 2005a; B'Tselem 2005a; Palestine Board of Health, cited in Cadigan 2004; Palestine Red Crescent Society 2005). These deaths, like those in El Salvador, Mexico and Nicaragua, are seen by the general populace as lamentable and painful. Beyond this, however, also in conjunction with the predominantly Catholic Latin American countries noted above, these deaths are additionally seen in the modal popular psyche as seeds sown in contribution to the struggle for justice against an oppressor. In the case of the unarmed, or rock-throwing/demonstrating, Palestinian child and his gunfire-induced death, Palestinians generally feel that only the most sordid social philosophy could put the blame for the deaths on the children themselves (see Hanley 2001). Thus the children are perceived as innocent victims of unjust, bellicose policies, and hence as martyrs in the Palestinian national cause.

The Case of Johnny Thaljiya, Age Seventeen Years

In Bethlehem, in the IOPT, in October 2001, seventeen-year-old non-activist and Eastern Orthodox Christian Johnny Thaljiya was gunned down by an IDF sniper in Manger Square as he coddled a four-year-old relative in one arm, and held a bag of rice for dinner in the other. This killing happened in front of his father, with whom he was chatting, on the way home from purchasing the rice.

IDF soldiers had re-taken an "Area B" which, under the Oslo Accords, was to be autonomously governed by the Palestinian Authority, with "security" provided by Israeli forces (http://en.wikipedia.org/wiki/Oslo_Accords, January 18, 2006, accessed January 19, 2006). While the re-taking of this area did not

Figure 4.1 The view from Hindaza Hill towards Bethlehem's Manger Square and the spot where Johnny Thaljiya was killed (Afflitto and ARIJ 2001–2).

Figure 4.2 The view from the spot where Johnny Thaljiya was killed, in Bethlehem's Manger Square, through the narrow entrance leading out of the square, looking into the distance at Hindaza Hill (Afflitto and ARIJ 2001–2).

include the majority of the Bethlehem conurbation, it did include Hindaza Hill, to the south, the highest point in the immediate area, from which the two shots, one to the heart, one to the abdomen, were fired, killing the young man instantly.

In a unique approach, developed by Afflitto (2001), and devised with the research staff and GPS Unit of the Applied Research Institute-Jerusalem, located in Bethlehem, IOPT, GPS data were collected from the site where the minor was killed, and from the site where Israeli soldiers had previously been camped during the re-taking of Area B, both events having occurred prior to funded fieldwork in December, 2001 and January, 2002. The GPS methodology was developed for, amongst other reasons, determining the approximate distance between the child victims of Israeli gunfire, and the Israeli snipers themselves (Afflitto 2001; Afflitto and ARIJ 2001–2). Distance was deemed to be an important variable in the empirical analysis of purposiveness, or intent, in the gunfire-perpetrated killing of children and minors in the IOPT (Afflitto 2001). Figure 4.3, a visual image of the area, illustrates the location of victim and perpetrators in the killing of Johnny Thaljiya, as well as documenting the estimated distance of 968 meters between the two.

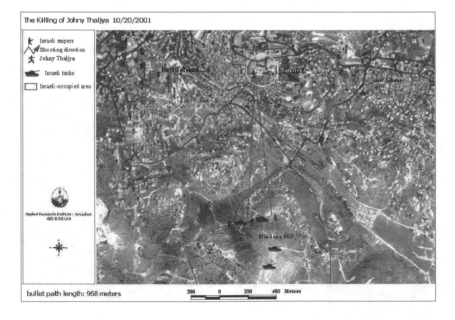

Figure 4.3 Satellite-generated map of the positions of perpetrators and victim in the Israeli gunfire-perpetrated death of Palestinian minor Johnny Thaljiya (Afflitto and ARIJ 2001–2).

Numerical Breakdown of Palestinian Child Deaths in the Al Aqsa Intifada (2000–5)

The Israeli gunfire-perpetrated death of seventeen-year-old Palestinian minor Johnny Thaljiya is far from unique. Children from both nationalities in the more than five-year-old conflict have died. Although Palestinian children have died in greater numbers, the percentage of child fatalities from the total pool of fatalities for both Palestinians and Israelis is about the same, oscillating between 20 and 25 per cent of those totals. The main difference between the modes of death of children in these two groups has been the means of violence perpetration. While a substantial proportion of Palestinian children and minors have been killed by Israeli-perpetrated gunfire,[3] the vast majority of Israeli children and minors have been killed by Palestinian-perpetrated body-bombings. This difference is significant, and its substantiation served as a precursor to the development of the present line of research for two primary reasons.

The first of these involves the selectivity of targets in the deaths of the Palestinian children. To date, Palestinians have not specifically committed body bombings focused on places where children and minors are exclusively concentrated, except for, perhaps, the Tel Aviv Dolphinarium dancehall body-bombing, which was perpetrated on June 1, 2001. In contrast, sniper fire at Palestinian children necessitates choice of individual targets, and choice of an individual corporal target location before the pulling of the trigger, when a tank-mounted or individual-wielded firearm is used. But this is not necessarily true of firearms mounted on helicopter gunships, and so I make that distinction here.

The second facet of relevance to the initiation of this research is the argument that choice is somehow a mask for intent, or at least that the two are somehow interrelated. It should be apparent that, upon choosing a child target, and upon making a decision to select a certain part of the intended victim's body, and to subsequently pull the trigger, this array of choices, once followed through, necessarily represents a process of the imposition of intent by the shooter him- or herself, in terms of a range of possibilities, from shooting off-target to frighten, to light wounding, to grave wounding such as blinding, or brain death, and on to physical death itself. Add to this the repertoire of available ammunition utilized with regularity by Israeli forces, including the internationally condemned "dum-dum," or explosive, bullets, mushrooming bullets, and the Israeli-misnomered "rubber bullets,"[4] along with tank-fired flechettes, and it becomes a rational deduction that a clear intention to kill children and minors exists among the IDF and other Israeli state forces.

Corporal location of lethal gunshot wounds provides a preoccupying portrait of Palestinian child deaths for anyone concerned with the rights and safety of children. Of a total sample of gunfire-perpetrated child deaths from September, 2000 through to December, 2003, where available data provide corporal location of the fatal wound, 109, or 65 per cent of a total of upper-body "one-shot wonders" were killed by exclusive headshots, four, or 2 per cent by exclusive neckshots, and

56 or 33 per cent were killed by exclusive heart–chest shots.[5] An additional 90 children and minors, or 21 per cent of a total of 427 dead in three and one-quarter years, were killed by gunshots on two or more corporal locations, many including one or more of the three vulnerable areas already mentioned, such as head–chest and neck–chest combinations.[6]

Table 4.1 Corporal location of fatal woundings for "one-shot wonders" in exclusive designated areas (2000–3)

Year	2000	2001	2002	2003	Total
Head	35	21	29	24	109
Neck	0	0	1	3	4
Chest–heart	18	10	17	11	56
Total	53	31	47	38	169

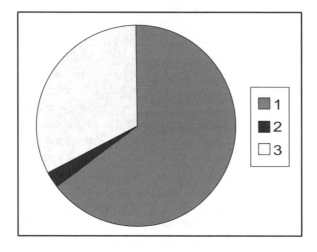

Figure 4.4 Pie chart of corporal location of fatal woundings for "one-shot wonders" in exclusive designated areas (2000–3): 1, head; 2, neck; 3, chest–heart.

Eighty-three Palestinian child/minor deaths occurred in the last three months of 2000, 76 of the same in 2001 (with more than half of those—forty—occurring from September 12 through December, in the post-9/11 era), leading to an astounding 172 deaths in 2002, during Israeli incursions into what had once been Palestinian Authority-controlled areas, and 96 in 2003. In total, in the first three and one-quarter years of Intifada, 427 Palestinian children and minors were killed by Israeli security forces and illegal settlers, with 169, or 40 per cent, being killed by "one-shot wonders" in the head, neck or heart–chest.

Of Gunshots, Headshots, Neckshots, and Heartshots

The headshot is the most frequent, and certainly the most problematic, of the "one-shot wonders." Constituting the smallest reasonably-lethal target on the body, except for perhaps the neck, which, with such infrequency of targeting is not so telling in data tallying, although it has been one of the main corporal areas cited (Palestinian Center for Human Rights, Gaza 2005) and has thus been used, one must ponder how the frequency of headshots, adhering to a null hypothesis, could be random. Out of approximately 39 months, 109 fatal headshots would represent an average of 2.8 per month in the timeframe under study, along with 1.44 fatal heart–chest shots per month. All together, in the time period under study, Palestinian children and minors have been fatally wounded in "one-shot wonder" upper-body shots in two of the designated areas under consideration at roughly a rate of 4.24 per month, or about one per week.

The headshot and subsequent destruction and/or removal of brain matter brings a definitive end to life, serves to mutilate the victim, at times beyond recognition, breeds fear into the wider community, who must clean up the mess left by these headshots, and is highly symbolic. A case in point is that of the gunfire deaths by high-powered explosive bullets at close range of six Jesuit priest-professors at the University of Central America "José Simeón Cañas" campus in San Salvador. This occurred in the early morning hours of November 16, 1989, and was perpetrated by the US-trained Atlacatl Batallion of the former Salvadoran military. In addition to being shot in the head at close range by these high-powered weapons, the professors' corpses were dragged, and at least three of them, those who had published internationally the most, had their brains largely removed from their cranial cavities. The symbolic message to the intellectual and national community was that their academic conceptualizations were dangerous, subversive and not to be tolerated. Because of this, the brains were destroyed and removed so that they could no longer subvert the military-oligarchical status quo. Though death itself would have served the same purpose as the destruction and removal of the brains themselves, only the destruction and removal could have embodied such a message of intolerance to thought.

A similar discourse can be deciphered in the headshot-induced brain attacks on Palestinian children and youth. The death is unquestionable and definitive, whether it is via the thousands of cases of brain-dead vegetative states, or physical death in its entirety. Both vegetative and physical deaths are deaths of the intellectual capacities, as it were, and hence, death itself.

Under some further exacerbatingly preoccupying circumstances, some youth and prepubescent children have been sniped in what appears to be a form of intergenerational vengeance. On July 7, 2001, for example, eleven-year-old Khalil Al-Mughrabi had his brains blown out in the midst of his friends while resting after a soccer game, in the Gaza Strip, from a long-distance shot emanating from an IDF post. His crime ...? An adult family member, Laila Al Mughrabi, had, in the 1970s, hijacked a bus and shot up the coastal road indiscriminately, killing Israeli civilians (Anonymous, personal interview, 2002). In the West Bank sector's Dheisheh Refugee Camp, outside Bethlehem, later in 2001, fifteen-year-old Kifah Abed was shot in the heart and killed, while throwing stones at Israeli soldiers. His crime? Kifah was known as one of the best stone-throwers amongst the youth in Dheisheh, and was frequently involved in such activities. Additionally, and perhaps more importantly for this discussion, he was a child friend of the "living martyr" Muhammad Abu Aker, also from Dheisheh, who, in the first Intifada (1987–93) was shot with a "dum-dum" round in the abdomen, and lived, after successful surgery in Boston, for a couple of years, without intestines and with the limited ability of drinking soup broth and mint–sage tea until physical death eventually overcame him. Materials handed out at the "*taabeen*," or fortieth-day memorial service, for Kifah featured photos of him throwing stones with dedication, as well as on the lap of the "living martyr" Abu Aker, before Abu Aker's death, while Kifah was just a toddler.

Lethal Israeli Gunfire as Social Discourse

In the first Intifada, Israeli sniper fire was used more for the purposes of maiming, as opposed to killing. During fieldwork in Jenin in 1989, for example, I witnessed dozens of youths who had been shot in the bicep with "dum-dum" rounds as they threw rocks at Israeli troops, leaving their right arms useless for the remainder of their lives. Lethal headshots were a rarity, in comparison to their frequency of employment during the Al Aqsa Intifada (September 2000–present).

A number of individual authors and institutional reports have concluded that Palestinian children, in the current period, have been "direct targets of Israeli military violence" (Jabr 2004; McGreal 2004; Palestinian Centre for Human Rights Monitoring Group, cited in McGreal 2004; Physicians for Human Rights–USA, cited in Amayreh 2004). The Israeli author Gideon Levy (2004) asserts that the killing of Palestinian children is a "routine matter" for the Israeli security forces, as these forces are wont to kill Palestinians, including children, with "striking ease" (Amayreh 2004). The Israeli army teaches its personnel that the killing of Palestinians should be taken "lightly" (B'Tselem, as cited in Amayreh 2005b) as each is a "potential suicide bomber" (Director of Human Rights Watch, as cited in Cadigan 2004).

The case of the shooting death of thirteen-year-old schoolgirl Iman Al-Hamas by an IDF officer in 2004 is also an example worth additional consideration, and highly representative of child mortality trends induced by Israeli firearm employment. Ms. Al-Hamas was killed on her way home from school, near a Rafah border fence, by "Captain R", who was "cleared of wrongdoing" by an internal IDF investigation "and returned to his post" in the southern Gaza Strip (Amayreh 2005a; see also El-Haddad 2005). Palestinian medical professionals counted more than 15 separate bullet rounds in her body (Al Mezan Center for Human Rights 2004), as Captain R, in front of IDF witnesses who later testified against him, approached the girl after wounding her, and emptied his clip into her, "verifying" (Newsbrief, source unknown, 2004), or "confirming" the "kill" (El-Haddad 2005; Levy 2004). The fact that Captain R was cleared by the internal Israeli military judicial system and returned to his post is a more clear and stark message than is the assassination itself. In fact, as of recently, less than two dozen cases had been rendered indictable by the Israeli military or civilan justice systems, and only two convictions had been handed out, for the killing of any Palestinian civilians, in five years of conflict (Amayreh 2005b). Perhaps, as the Israeli Knesset member Yehiel Hazan publicly stated, Arabs really are "worms" (*Al Jazeera*, 12/13/04, as taken from Agence France Presse) and therefore, undeserving of the application of international justice standards.

The explicit, purposive killing of Ms. Al-Hamas calls into question the lethal use of firearms in the demarcation of boundaries, spatially and between people, and as part of the potential pool of sociocultural capital in subsequent generations. A spatial perspective on lethality in conflict is supported via ethnographic research conducted in Northern Ireland by Jeffrey Sluka (1989), who posits a strong relationship between spatial configuration and sectarian murders, particularly in and around the Catholic ghettos of Belfast. In the same land, Allen Feldman (1991) links geography and symbolism as he explains the reconstituting effects of, and intentions behind, sectarian violence, particularly that which is sanctioned by the state. Feldman (1991) cites observations by the geographers Boal and Murray, who have stated that "violence becomes a deliberate tool of social engineering" in the context of sectarian conflict, and that the areas (re)created and (re)constituted through involuntary or voluntary population movement post-violence are demarcated as "ensuring social homogeneity" (1977: 364, cited in Feldman 1991).

"Topographic detail," for Feldman (1991), is imbued with "precise historical meanings" and a "destabilization of topos instigates the concentration of its value form in symbolic performances directed at the rendering of persons and place" (1991: 28). Such symbolic performances include, for example, in often dialectical relationship, stone-throwing at occupying forces, and the head-shooting of children near border fences, schools, and on the rooftops of their own homes, as well as the body-bombings at Israeli military roadblocks and in Israeli population centers. The violence becomes a means to "set and/or extend" "territorial boundaries" (1991: 28) and, I argue, sociocultural futures.

The lethal gunfire violence against Palestinian children is a means to engender a "destablization of the topos" both geographically and socioculturally. When pressed to give an explanation for the killing of their son, the parents of Johnny Thaljiya stated that it was "just killing" (Personal interview, 2002). That, in fact, the killing in and of itself was the intent of the IDF soldiers, not as punishment for any crime other than for that of being a Palestinian youth armed with a nephew and rice, and for being the spatial and intellectual future of the state of

Palestine. The killing of Palestinian children in the patterns, and by the means, observed, is a form of long-term diminishing of potentially available sociocultural capital, and a programmed, preventive intended preemption of both Palestinian statehood and resistance to the illegal military occupation of Palestine imposed by Israel. The child death not only signifies that "this land is mine," but, in the killing of a generation, the restructuring of a generation via lethal firearm employment, the ghettoization of those children and their repertoire of self-actualizing possibilities, that the future, to the Israeli state, is also "mine."

This pattern of child-killing via firearms occurs in the context of other violence-induced (re)arrangements of topos. In conjunction with the Israeli gunfire-perpetrated deaths, and wounding, of Palestinian children and minors come the deaths and wounding of unarmed adults (approximately 1,300), the confiscation of land, the erection of a separation barrier that invades illegally-occupied land inside the internationally-recognized 'green line', the destruction of massive amounts of farms, farmlands, and olive trees, the closing of schools and educational possibilities, and the demolition of hundreds of Palestinian homes.

From the Horse's Mouth

B'Tselem (as cited in Amayreh 2005a) states that Israeli military and judicial explanations of the numerous fatal shootings of Palestinian children are "organized lies." Israeli firing instructions during the current Intifada are quite different from those employed in the first Intifada (Ron 2000), and clearly indicate to soldiers that they should "fire at anything moving" (Amayreh 2005a) as in the frequently employed "free-fire zones" used by US troops during the war in Vietnam.

Israeli media interviews in recent years have referenced Israeli soldiers making unambiguous statements, such as having orders to shoot anyone who "looked twelve and over" (Haas 2000). An Israeli soldier, on December 15, 2001, stated on Israeli national television, several months after the occurrences of September 11th, that "now we can shoot them in the head, and no one cares" (Keller and Zilversmidt 2001).

Israeli "Open Fire Regulations" employed before the Al Aqsa Intifada allowed Israeli security forces to initiate the use of gunfire, including lethal gunfire, in three instances only:

1. When the lives of security force personnel were threatened.
2. In order to quell violent disturbances, after other means had been exhausted.
3. In order to apprehend suspects, by shooting them in the legs (B'Tselem 2005b).

In the current Intifada, the interpretation of these regulations has been expanded, to include "stone throwing" as a "life-threatening situation", as well as by allowing the firing of live rounds for the purposes of enforcement of the numerous curfews that have been imposed, and the delineation of Palestinian "no-go" areas, which are nothing more than "free-fire zones." All in all, such interpretations and nuanced changes have been responsible for the "routine use of lethal gunfire in non life-threatening situations" (B'Tselem 2005b).

Since "Israel defined the violence that has taken place during the Al-Aqsa Intifada as an armed conflict, or ... war ... [t]he change in definition ostensibly justified the making of significant changes in the Open-Fire Regulations" (B'Tselem 2005b).

Distance as a Predominating Variable in Determining Purposiveness

The question of distance between perpetrator and victim in the use of Israeli firearms against children and minors in the IOPT during the Al Aqsa Intifada speaks clearly to the construct of intent, or purposiveness, in these deaths. This is so particularly when viewing the high frequency of these deaths in the spatial-corporal locations of fatal wounding. If, in fact, Israeli soldiers are currently justified, by the new Open Fire Regulations, in shooting those "twelve and older" when they feel their lives to be threatened by activities such as stone-throwing, how can deaths such as those of Khalil Al-Mughrabi and Johnny Thaljiya and a host of others be fitted into such a paradigm?

In the one case that it was possible to elaborate before the Israeli incursions into Palestinian areas A and B in early 2002 necessitated the cessation of field-work, despite the receipt of funding to continue the project on the basis of the successful presentation of this first case, it is clear that the minor Johnny Thaljiya posed absolutely no threat to the lives of the Israeli soldiers 968 meters away on Hindaza Hill. Whatever the reasons those soldiers, or that soldier, might give for having pulled a trigger after taking careful, long-distance aim at an unarmed youth, the fact that they felt their lives to be immediately threatened cannot be one of them. It seems that the immediate threat in these killings is not to the individual lives of individual Israeli soldiers, but rather, the threat is to the status quo of military occupation and domination itself, and the threat to the future of the land that the illegal settlers and Palestinians both call their own.

Conclusion

Even ignoring the 10,000–20,000 (Hanley 2001; Amayreh 2004) injured, largely by gunfire and other ammunition utilized, such as tank shells, bombs from planes and missiles from helicopters; even ignoring the maiming, brain death and crippling effected by Israeli munitions on Palestinians who were either unarmed or armed only with stones at a questionably effective distance, the lethal Israeli violence employed via the use of firearms should be seen as disturbing and preoccupying to those concerned with the welfare of children. These killings, especially when calculating in distance as a variable, indicate a level of lethal intent and purposiveness on the part of the Israeli security forces, and to a less frequent extent, illegal settlers, in the (re)shaping of Palestinian youth.

The killing of the most vulnerable is always far-reaching symbolically in any social conflict. Guatemalan counterinsurgency soldiers in that country's armed internal conflict often thrived on tying parents, grandparents and other adult relatives to chairs or trees while they raped the family's/community's young women, and then killed them, in front of their eyes. The act causes intense and incomparable anguish, and the message sent to the bound witness is one of the omnipotence of the perpetrator counterpoised with the impotence of those who remain alive to tell the tale. "Because Palestinian homes, normally places of shelter, are major targets of Israeli army raids, children come to feel they are without protection" writes one author (Marshall 1993).

As in all state-sanctioned terrorism, wanton killing not only breeds pain and impotence, but resistance to the forces that perpetrate such acts (Afflitto 2000; Poniatowska 1971/1991). CNN reports that the killing of twelve-year-old Muhammad Al Durra "has made a deep impression on young Palestinians" (CNN 10/9/00). What this says for the future of Palestinian and Israeli relations, as a generation of victimized, angry youth, those who are left, come to adulthood, is going to be, at least in part, a product of the profound losses suffered. These losses include such phenomena as years of lives lost (YLL) (Arnold et al. 2002), which have radically re-shaped the social demographics of Palestinian futures, the excess mortality (Roberts et al. 2004) perpetrated by Israeli men and women with names, faces and guns on children, and the ensuing radical disruption of family, home, society and childhood itself. "Kill a child, kill a [future] family" is the way in which one Palestinian worker for a non-governmental organization characterized the child killings.

A major indicator of "the deliberate targeting of [Palestinian] children is the fact that 20% of the total number of Intifada victims were children going about their normal daily activities such as going to school, playing, shopping or simply being in their homes"[1] (see Cook, date unknown, as cited by Defence for Children International – Palestine Section 2004). The theory of crime victimization originally proposed by Cohen and Felson in 1979 (see website below) may be of analytical assistance in viewing the Israeli-perpetrated gunfire deaths of Palestinian children and minors in the Al Aqsa Intifada. According to the two criminologists, when the three factors of "motivated offenders, suitable targets, and the absence of capable guardians" (http://home.comcast.net/~ddemelo/crime/routine.html) unite, "predatory" criminal victimization becomes possible. Palestinian children are killed in large part while going about their routine activities. Those routine activities themselves have been shaped by stifling curfews and angry reactions to military occupation, degradation and depredation. At least some Israeli soldiers are actors motivated to kill those children. Those children, institutionally speaking, have become "suitable targets," as they are often over eleven years old, and "threaten the lives" of well-armored Israeli soldiers by throwing stones, generally from impotent and ineffective distances. Evidence does exist, indicating that Israeli soldiers do, in fact, intend to kill Palestinian children and minors through the purposive, lethal use of firearms. Whether or not to agree with this Israeli approach is the individual choice of the reader.

CHAPTER 5

Silent but Still Deadly: Guns and the Peace Process in Northern Ireland

Jeffrey A. Sluka

The gun of the IRA has been taken out of Irish politics. The weapons of the IRA are gone in a manner which has been witnessed and verified.
(Irish Prime Minister Bertie Ahern, September 26, 2005)

The gun has not gone out of Irish politics.
(DUP leader, Reverend Ian Paisley, September 26, 2005)

There is a political reality we do not have a name for. In Angola, I have heard people call it a time of "not-war-not-peace." Essentially, it is a time when military actions occur that in and of themselves would be called "war" or "low-intensity warfare," but are not so labeled because they are hidden by a peace process no one wants to admit is failing.
(Nordstrom 2004:166–7)

Figure 5.1 Loyalist paramilitary mural, Belfast, 2001. From Rolston 2003: 40.

Introduction: "Not-War-Not-Peace" in Northern Ireland

At the time of writing the paramilitary "ceasefires" in Northern Ireland were continuing to hold in an ongoing but fragile peace process that, beginning in 1993, had been going on for over twelve years. But while the guns have been *relatively* silent for over a decade, and hundreds of lives that would have otherwise been snuffed out in the endemic ethno-nationalist conflict have undoubtedly been saved, political violence has continued, though at a reduced rate. The peace process has been purposely delayed and repeatedly nearly scuppered by Protestant-unionist intransigence and their refusal to participate with the elected representatives of the Catholic-nationalist community in the power-sharing governmental institutions established as the key element of the peace process. In flagrant violation of the provisions of the peace agreement regarding the decommissioning of weapons, they demanded not only *unilateral* Irish Republican Army (IRA) disarmament but that it be done in a public ritual act of symbolic humiliation. Ian Paisley's Democratic Unionist Party (DUP) insisted on a complete photographic record of IRA disarmament, and Paisley said that the IRA needed to be humiliated—that they had sinned in public and needed to "wear sackcloth and ashes" and "repent in public." For well over a decade Protestant politicians in Northern Ireland, the British government, and a complicit media inaccurately presented the refusal of the IRA to conform to this *diktat*, external to the peace process agreement though it was, as the major obstacle to progress. This was in spite of the fact that the IRA were, in fact, meeting all their obligations concerning disarmament under the Good Friday Agreement on which the peace process is based, as verified by the disarmament commission.

In order to break the stalemate and compel Protestant politicians to accept and enact their obligation under the peace agreement to participate with Catholics in a democratic "power-sharing" local government for Northern Ireland, in the summer of 2005 the Provisional Irish Republican Army, after more than a quarter-century of guerilla warfare aimed at achieving a united Ireland, unilaterally declared that their "armed struggle" was over, and the organization disarmed and disbanded. While the rest of the world celebrated this historic occurrence and optimistic commentators suggested that it signified that the gun had finally "gone from Irish politics," Ulster Protestant politicians responded negatively, and still refuse to share political power or sit in elected bodies with the Sinn Fein politicians who represent the majority of the Catholic community.

This chapter describes and analyzes this situation. It outlines the arms context in Northern Ireland, including those held by all parties to the conflict—the British security forces (army and police) and both the loyalist and nationalist/republican paramilitaries—and the role of disarmament in the peace process. I argue that the unionist demand for unilateral IRA disarmament was the single major impediment to progress, and was an intentional political "red herring" employed by significant pro-unionist elements in the British government and by unionist politicians in Northern Ireland opposed to the power-sharing on which the peace process is based. These anti-peace process elements work to a secret agenda either to scupper the peace process completely or to subvert it into a covert counterinsurgency strategy aimed at—not peace, justice and reconciliation, but rather—the defeat of the IRA, the prevention of any form of power-sharing or democratic government with the Catholic population, and the political *status quo* of Protestant domination and the maintenance of the union between Northern Ireland and Great Britain.

Today, there are many ongoing peace processes, including those in South Africa, the Philippines, Mexico, Indonesia, Burma, Kashmir, India, Northern Ireland, Palestine, El Salvador, Guatemala, Colombia, Angola, Mozambique, Sudan, the Democratic Republic of Congo, and a number of other places around the world. Carolyn Nordstrom (2004) argues that many of these contexts represent a kind of surreal, liminal political space that is neither war nor peace. There is still violence, and many of the conditions that obtained during the war years still continue, largely unchanged or only slightly modified. The soldiers and paramilitaries are still there, they are still armed, and they still operate, organize, recruit, train, and acquire new weapons. The informal and illegal networks (such as the black market or the underground economy) developed during the war still operate. The political issues that underlay the conflict remain largely unresolved, but an illusion of "peace" is maintained; it is not real peace, but it is more peaceful, so to speak, than it was during the war. Nordstrom argues that peace, like war, becomes institutionalized and bureaucratized. "This scenario helps to explain why countries undergo round after round of political violence; why war keeps 'breaking out' time and again. In a very real sense, it is the same war, a war that never ended except on paper" (2004: 170).

In what follows I review the role the gun played during the war years in Northern Ireland from 1969 to 1994 and the role it has played since the peace process replaced the war process, analyze this as an example of "not-war-not-peace"—a semi-permanent (or permanent?) state of "peace process" that is somewhere between war and peace but not peace itself—and look at the prognosis for whether the gun has gone out of Northern Irish politics or not.

The War in Northern Ireland, 1969–94

Between the outbreak of the war in Northern Ireland in 1969 and the paramilitary ceasefires declared in 1994, there were approximately 50,000 "terrorist incidents," including some 35,000 shootings and 16,000 bomb and incendiary attacks; the security forces captured over 11,000 weapons and 150 tons of explosives, over 14,000 people were charged with "terrorist offenses," and 3,168 people were killed and 35,000 injured as a direct result of political violence (Weitzer 1990). The fatalities break down into the following categories (O'Duffy 1995: 772):

Security Forces	1,045	(33.0 per cent)
Republican Militants	314	(9.9 per cent)
Loyalist Militants	89	(2.8 per cent)
Catholic Civilians	1,067	(33.7 per cent)
Protestant Civilians	571	(18.0 per cent)
Political Activists	45	(1.4 per cent)
Unclassified	37	(1.2 per cent)

It should also be noted that, of the 571 Protestant civilians killed, 114 (20 per cent) were killed by loyalists, usually under the mistaken impression that they were Catholics.

These casualty figures demonstrate that the two largest categories of fatalities were Catholic civilians killed by members of the security forces and loyalist paramilitaries, and members of the security forces killed by republican guerrillas. The largest category of deaths was innocent Catholic civilians. The breakdown of those responsible for the 1,067 Catholic civilians killed is:

Killed by Republicans	192	(18.0 per cent)
Killed by Loyalists	662	(62.0 per cent)
Killed by Security Forces	144	(13.5 per cent)
Unclassified	69	(6.5 per cent)

Statistically, those most at risk of death in the conflict were innocent Catholic civilians, over 800 of whom were killed by the security forces and loyalist death squads.

This supports the assertion of Catholics, generally ignored by the media because of effective British propaganda, that there were two campaigns of violence in Northern Ireland, essentially the republican war against the British state and security forces, and the security forces' and loyalist paramilitaries' counterinsurgency war, not just against militant Irish nationalists (republicans) but against the Catholic civilian population as a whole. This is further demonstrated by the following statistics (Weitzer 1990):

Civilian Deaths from Political Violence, 1969–88
Civilian deaths as a percentage of deaths by this agency:

- Security Forces: 54.6 per cent
- Nationalist Paramilitaries: 37.3 per cent
- Loyalist Paramilitaries: 90.1 per cent

Over half of those killed by the security forces were civilians; less than one-third of those killed by the IRA and other republican guerillas were civilians; and nine out of ten of those killed by loyalist paramilitaries and their death squads were innocent civilians killed in sectarian attacks—that is, by death squads who selected their victims solely on the basis of their (Catholic) religion (Sluka 2000).

Furthermore, in 1988 the loyalist paramilitaries were rearmed, under the direction or with the connivance of British intelligence, with weapons smuggled from South Africa by British agent Brian Nelson (Sluka 2000). This resulted in a major increase in sectarian killings in the first half of the 1990s—that is, in the years just prior to the development of the peace process—with loyalists for the first time claiming more victims than the republican campaign by the IRA and Irish National Liberation Army (INLA) and emerging as the single major source of political violence in Northern Ireland. In the six years before the arrival of these weapons, from 1982 to 1987, loyalist paramilitaries killed seventy-one people, forty-nine of whom were innocent Catholic civilians killed in sectarian attacks. In the six years following, from 1988 to 1994, they killed 229 people, of whom 207 were killed in sectarian killings, i.e. a threefold increase on the previous five years (Relatives for Justice 1995: 3).

"Terrorism" usually refers to violence against civilians for political ends, whereas "war" refers to armed conflict against political and military targets. If those definitions are applied to the conflict in Northern Ireland, these statistics show the republican guerillas, the only parties to the conflict officially defined as "terrorists," were, in fact, the least likely to kill innocent civilians and more discriminate in their violence than both the British security forces and the loyalist paramilitaries. And if we further sharpen the definition of terrorism to mean only the *intentional* rather than the "incidental" killing of civilians, then the label "terrorism" applies exclusively to the violence perpetrated by the loyalist paramilitaries. Nonetheless, only the republican guerillas in Northern Ireland are generally referred to as "terrorists" by the authorities and media.

The Peace Process in Northern Ireland, 1993–2005

Chronology

The following timeline presents the main points in the chronology of the peace process:

1993   "Irish Peace Initiative" by the Catholic parties Sinn Fein and the Social Democratic and Labor Party (SDLP) launches peace process, involving British and Irish Governments, who issue Downing Street Declaration in support.

1994   IRA ceasefire declared in August, followed by loyalist ceasefire in October.

1996   *February*; IRA ends ceasefire as a result of negative response by Tory (John Major) government to peace initiative.

1997   *May*; Labor Government (Tony Blair) elected. *July*; IRA resumes ceasefire.

1998   Good Friday Peace Accord ("The Agreement"); 94 per cent support in Ireland, but in Northern Ireland 71 per cent in favor (Catholics 97 per cent, *Protestants 52 per cent*). *That is, overwhelming support by Catholics, but only grudging support by Protestants*. INLA declares formal ceasefire, after being on "no first strike" stance since 1993.

1999   *December*; after 18 months of unionist stalling, "power-sharing Assembly" (local government for Northern Ireland) finally established.

2000   *January*; after just eight weeks of operation, unionists exercise their traditional veto over reform and demand that the British government collapse the Northern Ireland Assembly because the IRA have not disarmed yet. *May*; IRA announce they will open their arms dumps to inspection and completely and verifiably put their arms "beyond use." Northern Ireland assembly re-established.

2001–4   Unionists delay peace process and prevent operation of the power-sharing assembly under pretext that the IRA have not yet disarmed; they refuse to sit in government—that is, "share power"—with elected Sinn Fein representatives until then. *October 2001*; after a sectarian campaign of bombings and intimidation of Catholic civilians, the British government declares the Ulster Defense Association (UDA) and Loyalist Volunteer Force (LVF) to be in breach of their ceasefire pledges. *December 2004*; Paisley states that even if the IRA disarmed the DUP would still boycott efforts to restore the power-sharing assembly. The situation at the end of the year was summed up by Irish Prime Minister Berte Ahern when he said "You are not going to get any change [in the deadlock] at the moment. Both sides are just dug in in their hard positions. There is not a glimmer of light."

2005   *April*; Sinn Fein president Gerry Adams calls on the IRA to end their armed struggle and commit themselves to purely peaceful democratic activity as an attempt to break the "downward spiral" of the peace process. Adams said he called on the IRA to end their armed struggle "because the peace process is in terminal decline. Without someone taking the necessary risks to break the spiral of decline we risk losing the progress that has been made in the last decade." *May*; local elections in Northern Ireland. The "extremist" parties emerged as the two main parties; Sinn Fein consolidated their position as the leading party on the nationalist side over the SDLP, and Ian Paisley's DUP eclipsed the Ulster Unionist Party (UUP) for the first time, becoming the major unionist party:[set following list as two tabbed columns with first column indented relative to the text above and below]

DUP   182 seats, up 52 (29.6 per cent, up 8.2 per cent)
Sinn Fein 126 seats, up 18 (23.2 per cent, up 2.7 per cent)

UUP	115 seats, down 40 (18 per cent, down 5.2 per cent)
SDLP	101 seats, down 16 (17.4 per cent, down 1.9 per cent)

Paisley announced that these election results represented the "burial" of the 1998 Good Friday Agreement, and ruled out a return to the power-sharing assembly. Opinion polls and the local elections confirmed that Northern Ireland was a completely polarized society where the two communities were drifting even further apart, with a hardening of attitudes as indicated in growing support for the most militant parties. *July*; IRA move to break this deadlock by announcing the end of their armed struggle and promise complete decommissioning of all their weapons. British government move to re-establish the power-sharing assembly, but unionists, despite IRA disarmament, continue to refuse to sit in government with what they term "Sinn Fein/IRA." In a highly skeptical response to the IRA disarmament, Paisley said his party was "underwhelmed" and unconvinced by the move. He accused the British government, Irish government, and IRA of duplicity, dishonesty, and a cover-up, and declared that it did not meet the requirements of proof the unionist people demanded. He referred to the guns in the hands of dissident republican groups, and said "The gun is not out of Irish politics," and made it clear that his party would still not form a government with "Sinn Fein/IRA." Instead he immediately produced a new red herring by demanding that the IRA must now be seen to "end criminality" before his party would enter any talks with Sinn Fein. *September*; disarmament commission confirms that the IRA has disarmed. *October*; the DUP revealed that they planned another series of demands before they would consider sharing power with Sinn Fein. Deputy Leader Peter Robinson said that even if they were satisfied the IRA had ended all activity, this on its own was not enough. The LVF ordered their units to stand down, and declared their feud with the Ulster Volunteer Force (UVF) over. This was described as a direct response to the IRA's decommissioning. (Despite declaring a ceasefire in 1998, the LVF continued its sectarian murder campaign under the guise of the Red Hand Defenders, a *nom de guerre* used also by its allies in the UDA. Following its formation in 1996, the LVF murdered 28 people, and ten members of the organization were also killed, mostly as a result of feuding with the rival UVF and UDA. Of those murdered by the LVF, eighteen were Catholics and ten were Protestants.)

Main Points of the Peace Agreement

The main points of the 1998 "Good Friday Peace Accord" or "The Northern Ireland Agreement Reached in Multi-Party Negotiations" are:

- Constitutional Issues: The British and Irish governments agree:
  1. To recognize the legitimacy of whatever choice is freely exercised by a majority of the people of Northern Ireland with regard to its status, whether they prefer to continue to support the Union of Great Britain and Northern Ireland or a sovereign united Ireland.
  2. But require a majority in Northern Ireland—"consent"—to achieve a united Ireland; if and until then, the union (status quo) will prevail.
  3. To recognize the birthright of all the people of Northern Ireland to identify themselves and be accepted as Irish or British, or both, as they may choose.
- Irish Government amends constitution, and removes Articles 2 and 3, which claim sovereignty over Northern Ireland—a major concession to unionists.
- Sets up a power-sharing democratic "Assembly" for Northern Ireland to replace direct rule from Westminster and
- Establishes a North/South Ministerial Council.
- Provisions for reconciliation and victims of violence;
- Economic, social and cultural issues, including "parity of esteem" for both the British and Irish traditions;
- Decommissioning of paramilitary arms;
- Security (demilitarization of security forces and emergency legislation);
- Reform of the police (Royal Ulster Constabulary becomes new Police Service for Northern Ireland—PSNI); and
- Release of political prisoners.

Decommissioning—Taking the Gun out of Northern Irish Politics

After the peace agreement was signed in 1998, the unionists violated it and stalled its implementation. They did this by demanding that the IRA unilaterally disarm *before* unionists would sit down and talk with Sinn Fein, let alone share power with them in local government. That this was an intentional "red herring" is demonstrated by the fact that since the IRA disarmament in 2005 unionists have continued to refuse to engage in the power-sharing assembly with elected Sinn Fein politicians, who represent the majority of the Catholic community. In drawing up the peace accord, the consensus on the issue of disarmament was that it was an essential part of the peace process that required an effort to decommission *all* the guns in Irish politics, including those held by the security forces and both the republican and loyalist paramilitaries. The agreement was that all armed parties would gradually and verifiably disarm simultaneously as the political institutions got up and running. An Independent International Commission on Decommissioning (IICD) was set up, headed by the retired Canadian General John de Chastelain, to oversee the disarmament process; but unionists chose to exploit this issue to prevent the implementation of the Good Friday Agreement. This demand for a unilateral surrender by the IRA violated the provisions of the agreement concerning disarmament, and effectively undermined the peace process for seven years until the IRA disarmed in 1995.

In September 2005, General de Chastelain declared that the IRA had cooperated with international inspectors and disposed of its arsenal in a massive decommissioning operation. Significantly, he stated that it remained for the disarmament commission to address the issue of unionist arms, and asked everyone with influence to use it to that end. Gerry Adams called it "a defining moment in the peace process"; but, as is described in the chronology above, Paisley and the DUP rejected it and presented a new series of unilateral demands, outside the provisions of the peace agreement, which they said still had to be met before they would consider sharing power with Sinn Fein.

Not-War-Not-Peace: Political Violence During the Peace Process, 1994–2005

In spite of the peace process, between the paramilitary ceasefires in 1994 and 2005 a reduced level of political violence continued in Northern Ireland. Not all the armed groups declared ceasefires, and even those that did were responsible for continuing violence. In particular, despite officially maintaining their ceasefires, the UDA and UVF were responsible for sectarian attacks in which Catholics were killed and injured, and loyalists killed and injured each other in inter-paramilitary feuds.

Deaths from Political Violence during the Peace Process, 1995–2005
(Fatalities only—does not include those injured or who escaped injury in politically motivated attacks. *Source*: Amnesty International annual reports and CAIN web service)

1995:	9 (4 killed by loyalists, 5 by republicans)
1996:	15 (4 killed by loyalists, 11 by republicans)
1997:	19 (14 killed by loyalists, 5 by republicans)
1998:	55 (19 killed by loyalists, 36 by republicans)
1999:	8 (4 killed by loyalists, 4 by republicans)
2000:	18 (15 killed by loyalists, 3 by republicans)
2001:	19 (14 killed by loyalists, 5 by republicans)
2002:	12 (8 killed by loyalists, 4 by republicans)
2003:	10 (8 killed by loyalists, 2 by republicans)
2004:	4 (3 killed by loyalists, 1 by republicans)
2005:	12 (9 killed by loyalists, 3 by republicans)

Total: At least 181 deaths (102 by loyalists, 79 by republicans), an average of just over eighteen per year from political violence since "peace" replaced "war" in Northern Ireland.

There also continued to be a large number of politically motivated "punishment" shootings and beatings by paramilitary groups of people within their own communities during the peace process years. While there was a gradual decline in the number of republican punishment attacks, this was offset by a large increase in the number of such attacks by loyalists:

Punishment Shootings and Beatings, 1995–2005
(*Source*: Amnesty International annual reports)

1995: Reports of shootings and beatings increased, but no figures provided.
1996: 151 by loyalists, 175 by republicans.
1997: 150 shootings and 72 beatings; breakdown not provided.
1998: More than 200 shootings and beatings; breakdown not provided.
1999: 138 by loyalists, 68 by republicans.
2000: Details not provided.
2001: 212 by loyalists, 119 by republicans.
2002: 206 by loyalists, 106 by republicans.
2003: 203 by loyalists, 101 by republicans.
2004: An average two shootings and two to three Catholic victims of sectarian assaults every week, but breakdown not given.
2005: Figures not yet available at time of writing.

Besides these killings, shootings, and beatings, there were hundreds of non-fatal sectarian attacks, nearly all against Catholics. The "everyday" forms of sectarian violence against Catholics in Northern Ireland continued, either in spite of or *because* of the peace process. This included lynchings and beatings of Catholics by loyalist mobs; vandalism, stone-throwing and hundreds of petrol- and nail-bomb attacks against Catholic homes, schools, churches, businesses, and sports facilities; "ethnic cleansing," where Catholics were intimidated from their homes; and attacks on Catholic children traveling to and from school. The traditional Orange Order "marching season" of riots and sectarian violence against Catholics in July and August continued each year, and even increased from before the peace process. The peace process years have been marked by *increasing* sectarian attacks against Catholics, apparently a sign of Protestant alienation from and anger with the peace process. This reached its peak in September 2005, when the loyalist paramilitaries orchestrated riots around Northern Ireland (described below).

Despite over twelve years of the peace process and ceasefires, all the armed parties to the conflict have continued to be active in some form. The security forces have only partially "demilitarized" their operations, and none of the paramilitary groups in Northern Ireland, with the notable exception of the IRA, have disarmed or disbanded.

Armed Groups in Northern Ireland, 1993–2005

All these groups—including the British security forces—are required either to demilitarize (security forces) or to disarm completely (paramilitaries) as part of the peace process agreement.

Republican (Catholic):
- Provisional Irish Republican Army: Decommissioned weapons and disbanded in 2005.
- Irish National Liberation Army: On ceasefire; have not disarmed or disbanded.
- Real IRA: Small breakaway group, nearly inactive, but responsible for disastrous premature bomb explosion in Omagh in 1998 that killed 29 and injured hundreds.
- Continuity IRA: Even smaller breakaway group, nearly inactive.

Loyalist (Protestant):
- Ulster Defence Association: On ceasefire, but violence against Catholics has continued, and feuds with other loyalist paramilitary groups have increased.
- Ulster Volunteer Force: Like UDA.
- Loyalist Volunteer Force: Like UDA, but claimed to have "stood down" at end of 2005 in response to end of IRA campaign.
- Their associated "death squads"—Ulster Freedom Fighters, Red Hand Commandos, Red Hand Defenders, Protestant Action Force, etc.: Like UDA.

Security Forces:
- British Army: By January 2006, the number of British troops in Northern Ireland had decreased from 12,500 to 9,000, its lowest level in thirty years; a number of military installations had been dismantled; and the last "roulement battalion"—troops on a six-month tour of duty unaccompanied by wives or families—was being removed (at one time there were six such battalions serving in the province).
- Royal Irish Rifles (formerly Ulster Defence Regiment): Locally recruited Ulster Protestant battalions are gradually being disbanded.
- Royal Ulster Constabulary (RUC) and Reserve; renamed Police Service Northern Ireland (PSNI); partly reformed and partly demilitarized.

Two major events are indicative of the increase in loyalist violence during the peace process years. In 1998, violence flared in Northern Ireland before and after the adoption of the Good Friday Peace Accord. In July, violence erupted during protests by the Protestant Orange Order and other groups over the Parades Commission's decision to re-route a Protestant march away from a Catholic neighborhood in Portadown, and three Catholic boys aged 8, 9, and 10 were killed when their home was fire-bombed by loyalists. In September 2005, another wave of rioting and intense street violence by Protestant mobs and paramilitaries swept Belfast and other towns in Northern Ireland as unionists expressed their anger over recent developments in the peace process. UVF units fired on the police, and their supporters threw petrol- and blast-bombs and hijacked and burned vehicles, after PSNI raids as part of an investigation into a UVF "show of strength." This occurred five days before a controversial Orange Order march in west Belfast, which the UVF insisted it would push through a flashpoint area despite its being banned by the Parades Commission. The violence was organized by the UVF and the UDA. Unionist politicians failed to condemn the violence, citing anger at perceived concessions to republicans following the end of the IRA's armed struggle. Following this, the British government declared that they still recognized the UDA ceasefire, but no longer accepted that the UVF were observing theirs.

Loyalist Arms

In Northern Ireland, there are 87,000 licenses for 140,000 weapons—virtually all of them in Protestant hands. These are not part of the decommissioning process. On top of that, there are thousands of illegal weapons in the hands of the loyalist paramilitary groups. Despite their "ceasefires," apart from some pistols from the LVF, no loyalist paramilitary group has decommissioned any of its weapons. They have frequently suspended their contacts with the IICD, and continue to be involved in murders, shootings, assaults, and organized crime. In particular, they have continued to kill and injure Catholics in sectarian attacks, and there has been a series of feuds within and between loyalist paramilitary groups in which dozens have died. In particular, in 2000 a bloody feud in the Protestant lower Shankill Road district in Belfast led to thirteen deaths and the forced removal of up to a thousand residents as the area sorted itself into exclusive UDA and UVF territories; and a feud in 2005 in which the UVF tried to wipe out the breakaway/rival LVF led to seven deaths.

After twelve years of "peace" in Northern Ireland, during which unionists stalled the peace process by imposing arbitrary deadlines on the decommissioning of IRA weapons, there had still been no significant movement on the decommissioning of loyalist weapons. In an obvious example of bias, this issue was rarely mentioned; instead the British and Irish governments and the media concentrated exclusively on the issue of IRA arms.

Conclusion: Peace or War, the Future of the Gun in Northern Ireland

From the beginning of the peace process in 1993 the unionists refused to live up to their side of the peace process agreement; they effectively stymied progress and locked the peace process in stalemate, generating a deepening crisis that was only broken by the unilateral IRA disarmament in the summer of 1995. The unionist parties used the IRA as an excuse to refuse to engage properly in the peace process. Their agenda was to stall, resist, and minimize any fundamental change, in the hope that, sooner or later, the nationalist agenda would collapse under the weight of its paramilitarism or "terrorism." Now that has not happened; and with the IRA decommissioning changing the face of Northern Ireland politics, political unionism is up the creek without a paddle. The likelihood is that they will continue to refuse to participate fully and equally—that is, democratically—with Catholics in the power-sharing assembly that the success of the peace process is entirely dependent upon. On every occasion when unionist leaders have walked away from or reneged on agreements to break the political stalemate, the British and Irish governments in turn have reneged on their end of the deal. This intransigence worked for over a decade, mainly because the governments chose to support each unionist demand in the hopes that this "appeasement" would bring them to engage fully with the peace process and not withdraw their "consent" or participation and effectively veto progress. On each occasion they have failed or refused to confront this *de facto* unionist veto on progress, with the result that they have had to suspend the power-sharing assembly four times and, in fact, it has hardly operated at all since it was established in 1998. These efforts to appease unionist demands have failed to gain their participation in the power-sharing assembly, and in the upcoming phase of the peace process the onus and focus will fall principally on the British and Irish governments, who will imperil the peace process if they allow the DUP to set the pace of political progress and continue to paralyze the process of change set out in the peace agreement.

The unionist parties have repeatedly declared their opposition to sharing power with Sinn Fein in any circumstances, despite the fact that Sinn Fein are the democratically elected representatives of the Catholic community. The unionist community have shown that they are not yet prepared to leave behind the sectarianism, bigotry, and intolerance that has marked the political life of the northern state since partition. The DUP is now the largest political party in Northern Ireland. It is based on a particular mode of Protestant fundamentalism, and is an extremist party that has consistently opposed the peace process. Politics and fundamentalist religion are deeply intertwined for the DUP, and especially for its leadership. They have never been able to truly accept the concept of Catholics as equals. The party leader is the charismatic arch-bigot the Reverend Ian Paisley, whose anti-Catholicism permeates his unique mode of Protestant fundamentalism. The DUP's oft-repeated position on sharing power with Catholics has always been and fundamentally remains "Never, never, never!" Their manifesto has been that there will be no assembly, no power-sharing executive, no negotiations with Catholics, and no change. Which, of course, means no lasting peace. It may be that the DUP is a party that, because of its sectarian history and inclination, cannot take account of the rights of nationalists. If Northern Irish society is to move forward towards a real and lasting peace, this anti-Catholic sectarianism must be confronted, because it dangerously continues to be the defining feature of the Northern Irish state. Unfortunately, all the signs are that that is not going to happen.

Sinn Fein and the IRA have adhered to the requirements of the Good Friday Agreement, and the unilateral IRA ceasefire in 1994 and their disarmament in 2005 represent the two biggest contributions to the peace process. In particular, the end of the IRA's "long war" represents not only a critical breakthrough in the peace process but a watershed in modern Irish political history, and created an unprecedented sense of optimism and expectation that renewed progress can be made towards a lasting peace. Only the leaders of the unionist parties responded negatively to this, and the September 2005 loyalist riots were a response to the realization that the status quo is not an option and to the uncertainties of a process of change that demands equality, human rights, justice, and inclusion.

In 2001, the Northern Ireland census revealed major changes in the demographic structure of the Northern Ireland population, with serious political implications for the future:

Northern Ireland Census 2001: Religious Background

Total population:	1,685,267	
Protestant:	895,377	(53.0 per cent)
Catholic:	737,412	(43.8 per cent)
Other and no religion:	52,478	(3.2 per cent)

Traditionally, a "Protestant majority" of 1 million made up two-thirds of the population and a "Catholic minority" of half a million made up one-third. Now, owing to the higher Catholic birthrate and increasing Protestant out-migration, Catholics are nearly *half* the population. In fact, by 1995 Catholics were already in a majority up to about the age of fifteen, and roughly level up to the age of nineteen (Coogan 1995: 514). While in 2005 Protestants were still a majority over the age of twenty years, the clear indication was that there will be a continuous rise in the number of voters supporting nationalist parties at the expense of unionist ones, and some demographers predicted that Catholics would be the majority and hold most elected positions in Northern Ireland within ten years.

Thus, the main reason for the *bitter conflict over the peace process* is that Catholics see it as a stepping stone towards a united Ireland—as a process that goes from peace, to power-sharing, to gradual movement towards a united

Ireland when they become a voting majority. This is anathema to Ulster unionists, and explains their deep distrust of and refusal to engage fully in the peace process. They want peace, but on their terms; they want to maintain partition, the union, and their dominance in Northern Ireland, and they cannot guarantee this if they share power with Catholics, who will soon be the majority. Thus the greatest likelihood is that the unionist parties will continue to erect obstacles and make unrealizable demands in order to prevent power-sharing and the establishment of the all-Ireland political structures; that the loyalist paramilitaries will not disarm or cease their violence while they perceive any threat to the future of the union; and that the peace process will remain in doubt for the foreseeable future.

The only way to remove the gun from Irish politics is to demonstrate that politics can work in addressing the problems faced by Northern Ireland society. That puts the onus on the British government and the Ulster unionists to show Catholics that they have been empowered by the agreement and assembly, and can pursue their political aspirations peacefully and democratically as equals, which is, of course, a condition that they have never yet enjoyed and whose absence was the most fundamental cause of the conflict in Northern Ireland to begin with. The fact is that Northern Ireland was never intended to be a democratic polity, but rather a one-party Protestant state dedicated to maintaining unionist domination. Thus, the challenge to peace in Northern Ireland is not the guns *per se*, but the same political causes that have also been responsible for bringing the gun into Irish politics in the first place—the mutually exclusive national aspirations of Irish-Catholics and British-Protestants, and the question of whether the north of Ireland should remain a part of the UK or be reunited with the rest of Ireland. The peace process is about equality and justice. It threatens no one, unionist or nationalist, Protestant or Catholic. It has already produced enormous benefit right across Northern Ireland society, with major improvements in both communities over the past decade of "peace." Most of all, it provides the basis for ending the endemic violence that has plagued the province since its inception, and of finally taking all of the guns out of the equation of Irish politics.

CHAPTER 6

Warriors and Guns: The Anthropology of Cattle Rustling in Northeastern Africa

Nene Mburu

The justification for the study of asymmetrical conflicts cannot be overstated, considering that they occur daily amongst pastoral peoples, they are not anchored to a specific military doctrine, they have no frontlines, the shape and size of the warring parties cannot easily be determined, and, although weapons of mass destruction are not used, casualties from single attacks are often higher than in some inter-state wars. Even so, for a serious study of human society, the escalation, or the attritional nature of a given form of conflict is a criterion inadequate for the justifying of scholarly analysis. Furthermore, as pastoral conflicts in general and livestock rustlings in particular fall under the internal security framework of the state, institutions outside the local African knowledge situation have a limited awareness of their existence and their devastating impact on the societies in which they occur; and hence the international capacity to regulate them is circumscribed.

It is important to acknowledge that my contribution's lack of statistical details for the current casualty rates, patterns of incidence, and constancy of raids for all the pastoral peoples of Africa inhibits any generalization of theories of limited warfare that could put the phenomenon of raiding into a more comprehensive theoretical framework. Although livestock rustlings and bandit skirmishes with security forces are often trivialized as incidents in military field reports and security intelligence summaries that are still not in the public domain, this study obtained first-hand information by cluster-sampling informants from a wide geographical area, mostly on an *ad hoc* basis, and triangulating their oral evidence with that of informed independent sources. The study defines the problem in the light of existing studies on pastoral conflicts, and then explores the anthropological and physical context of livestock rustling and predatory expansion among the Turkana, Pokot and Toposa of northeastern Africa. The degree of explicit conceptualization involved is therefore limited, as the evidence is mainly obtained from fieldwork, archival, and newspaper sources, which therefore lend themselves to an account that is more descriptive than analytical.

Problem Statement

In northeastern Africa, the lacuna in our knowledge of contemporary pastoral warfare is blamed on the general lack of scholarly interest in the phenomenon and specifically the paucity of authoritative studies on the centrality of firearms in the material culture of transhumant pastoral communities. This opinion is based on information obtained from fieldwork in northwestern Kenya and a review of studies on the subject, from which two categories of scholars emerge. Earlier scholars of pastoral societies, amongst whom Max Gluckman and his research in the 1950s and 1960s comes to mind, were advocates of the materialist and ecological schools of thought, who argued that pastoral conflicts are motivated by competition for livestock and scarce resources of nature, particularly water and pasturage. At face value, the periodicity of livestock rustlings under consideration seems to support this line of thinking, in so far as raids and predatory expansion increase during droughts and times of scarcity, and decrease during the rainy seasons, when there are alternative sources of livelihood. Nevertheless, is it not an oversimplification to ascribe the development of complex pastoral institutions to the rationale of dialectical materialism or purely to ecological factors? In any event, Paul Spencer's 1998 study of the Maasai pastoralists of eastern Africa discredits the Materialist and Ecological schools of thought by finding that it is possible for herders to accumulate as much animal wealth through peaceful animal husbandry as through organized rustlings.

More recent studies of fragmentary societies present contrasting arguments on the impact of modern firearms on warfare amongst east African herders, and generally fail to examine the symmetrical relationship between guns, livestock, and manliness, and further fail to anchor the proliferation of guns in the periphery of the state to changes in the region's political landscape. For example, John Lamphear has claimed that "firearms played little role in the military organization or tactics of many east African pastoral communities" (Lamphear 1994: 63–92). By contrast, Uri Almagor finds that "the introduction of firearms radically changed the pattern of intertribal warfare and raids. The number of casualties rose, livestock was looted in large numbers and small rifle-armed parties could, and frequently did, massacre whole unarmed villages" (Almagor 1978: 6).

Therefore my study attempts to fill the gap in the existing body of knowledge on the subject, positing that the culture of arms-bearing predates the modern state, but that its entrenchment is the tragic synthesis of various factors, the principal among them being that, by splitting ethnic communities into different countries, arbitrary delimitation of the state opened an opportunity for transhumant peoples to defy unpopular legislation such as disarmament provisions simply by crossing the invisible meridians that mark international boundaries. Secondly, I demonstrate that gun culture is nurtured by insecure social relationships where the traditional instruments of inter-community conflict management are degraded, the land is unproductive, and pristine traditions place a tremendous emphasis on the young male's rite of passage: hence rustling for livestock using guns is both the pastoral warriors' means of actualizing manliness and a coping mechanism. And, finally, by arguing that the proliferation of guns in the periphery of the state is the outcome of international vectors, particularly civil conflicts that began during the Cold War and the post-Cold War collapse of the state, but also a product of domestic manipulations by corrupt African leaders.

The Anthropological Context of Cattle Rustling

The Pokot

The Pokot (Pakot) people live in Baringo and Pokot Districts of Western Kenya, but spill over into eastern Uganda near Kitgum astride the porous Kenya–Uganda boundary. The community became *de facto* citizens of two countries in the twentieth century when Britain, the colonial power, having arbitrarily shifted the Kenya–Uganda frontier several times, finally delineated an international border in 1959 that slices through their ancestral homeland (CO 822/1559; KNA: PC/NFD1/1/2; Blake 1997; Hertslet 1909; interviews 1996 and 2005). The contradictions implicit in Britain's slapdash delimitation are that it exacerbates the marginalization of the Pokot in either country, where they are seen as ethnic minorities and foreigners, but also presents them with an opportunity to defy unpopular legislation such as disarmament provisions or taxation in either country by simply joining their kinsfolk across the unregulated state frontier. Those who live in Uganda are variously called Suk, Karasuk, or Upe (CO 533/380/13; interviews 1996 and 2005). Their kinsfolk who live in Kenya are known as the Pokot because, during colonialism, the name Suk denoted traitorous *askari* serving in the King's African Rifles (interviews 1996 and 2005). The community originates from the Kalenjin group, which derive their languages and social-economic and political customs and structures from both the Bantu and the Nilo-Hamitic ethno-cultural repertoires. Although Euro-Christian denominations have some followers amongst them, most Pokot worship *Tororot*, who is the supreme deity, and several of his intercessors, to whom they occasionally offer communal sacrifices, prayers, and dance. Community elders, diviners, traditional healers and medicine men have a significant duty during such rituals as organizers and participants. In this deeply superstitious community, sorcerers epitomize evil from which the people seek various forms of human and divine protection. For instance, to neutralize the ill omen of a sorcerer a family gathers and seeks the divine intervention of a particular spirit connected with death.

A minority of the Pokot cultivate millet and sorghum, for which they are considered physically feeble and sexually less virile and referred to, somewhat derogatorily, as "eaters of grain" (interviews 1996 and 2005). Nevertheless, the majority raises livestock, particularly cattle, around which many of the community's social institutions are organized. Nevertheless, for both animal-keepers and sedentary cultivators, cattle are significant in the material and spiritual sense. They are the means of measuring individual wealth and power, and widely used for daily nourishment, providing milk, cheese, and butter, as well as barter and payment of "bridewealth." In this patriarchal community, having many wives is a public display of sexual prowess, and so a man is allowed to marry as many wives as he can afford to pay for, which makes cattle the benchmark of power and social, political, and economic status (interviews 1996 and 2005). Cattle are valued so much that they are slaughtered only during special religio-political occasions. Even then, the norm is to spare special bull-calves for breeding, and it is taboo even for cattle thieves to kill a pregnant or lactating cow or to take from a mentally disabled person.

The Pokot society is governed through a series of age-grades whose membership is determined by the age at which one undergoes the initiation into adulthood. The ceremony involves the circumcision of boys and clitoridectomy for girls, performed in the bush by male and female traditional surgeons respectively. The initiates are expected to brave the pain to prove that they have come of age, so neither the boys nor the girls have the benefit of anesthetic during the operation or modern medicine during recuperation, which occasionally generates fatal consequences (Maero and Etsabo 2002). Young men are circumcised between the age of fifteen and twenty, while the girls are cut at around the age of twelve years at the onset of menarche. After initiation into adulthood, young people are allowed to engage in courtship, sex, and marriage and are expected to begin participating in local socioeconomic activities, which include raiding for livestock. Pokot initiates wear skillfully interwoven bodices of multi-colored beads both as ornamentation and to signal their membership in a particular age-grade. Young men and women form close horizontal bondings with other members of their initiation groups, and these bonds instill *esprit de corps* within age grades and serve for future political alliances. When a man or woman reaches old age in the Pokot society, he or she is accorded a certain degree of status and respect by the community.

At the local level, the opportunity, motive, and means of raiding are created by the socioeconomic marginalization of the Pokot community in a degraded land coupled with complex intra-ethnic relationships; externally, we look into shifts in the political landscape of the region. To put it in context, tribal elders traditionally presided over important community decisions, festivities, and politico-religious ceremonies, ordered cattle raids on specific ethnic groups and called a cessation of hostilities as necessary to resolve conflicts, resume transhumance and engage in social-economic intercourse with traditional enemies. However, Pokot elders significantly lost their authority in the nineteenth century after: (i) the introduction of guns transformed the nature and scope of pastoral warfare; (ii) colonial boundaries criminalized pastoral transhumance; (iii) Christianity destroyed the spiritual iconoclasm of community elders; and, (iv) bureaucratization of decision-making through the imposition of civil servants removed the ownership of resolutions from the people and alienated the community from the center. The elders' authority was further degraded in the 1960s when President Jomo Kenyatta of Kenya allegedly armed the community in a covert attempt to create a buffer on Kenya's border with Uganda (interviews 1996 and 2005). More guns went to the community in the 1970s because Kenyatta was apprehensive that General Idi Amin of Uganda had irredentist ambitions to absorb the western Pokot of Kenya so as to restore Uganda's eastern boundary to the 1902 frontier, which he intended to pursue through a military invasion similar to what he had attempted in the case of Tanzania. Thereafter the community took advantage of the prevailing political uncertainty to acquire more arms for themselves through raiding and barter, especially after the collapse in 1979 of General Idi Amin's dictatorial government in Uganda (interviews 1996 and 2005; Oketch and Lokwang 1999). The motive for their rearming was to protect their livestock from their traditional enemies, the Karamojong of Uganda, whom President Joseph Museveni failed to disarm after he liberated the country from Idi Amin's tyranny. From 1978 to 2002, it is claimed that cattle rustlers of the Pokot were covertly armed by President Moi's government to destabilize ethnic communities that did not support the ruling Kenya African National Union (KANU) party (Wanyonyi 1998; Warigi 2000). The problem was so severe that modest estimates in 2001 indicated that the Pokot and their Marakwet sub-tribe had more than 44,710 guns (Muggah and Berman 2001). Hence, by collectively arming tribal warriors for covert missions, the state compromised its moral authority, manipulated the institution of raiding, weakened the traditional instruments of inter-community conflict resolution, entrenched the culture of arms-bearing, and triggered an arms race amongst livestock keepers. Today, unilateral disarmament will only leave the Pokot vulnerable to neighboring cattle thieves, and so far it has failed because, being astride the porous Kenya–Uganda boundary where roads are impassable particularly during the rainy seasons, the community evades security troops by seeking refuge in Uganda (*The Standard* May and June 2005). Furthermore, livestock rustlers are not short of recruits, because most schools in Pokot district have closed owing to the general insecurity, and with easy availability of weapons from Somalia, Sudan, and the Democratic Republic of Congo, disarming cannot succeed until it is accompanied by sustainable economic reforms (Mburu 2002).

The Turkana

The Turkana are organized in territorial sections and the majority live in north-western Kenya around Lake Turkana (formerly known as Lake Rudolf), which, at 240 km long and 40 km wide, is the largest water mass in the region. A few Turkana families live in northeastern Uganda around Mt Moroto, where they are lured by reliable dry-season browsing for their livestock or to escape incessant resource conflicts, ticks, livestock diseases, and famine, and to allow exhausted land to recover (Kamau 1999; Ogola 2000). Their allies, the Matheniko community of Uganda, welcome their transhumance; but it places both communities in constant resource conflicts with the Pian and Dodoth herders, who feel vulnerable to a strong Turkana–Matheniko alliance. Other Turkana sections live in southern Sudan, across a disputed international frontier, where the community tends cattle, goats, and camels that are important in both their material and spiritual contexts. Other aspects of their economy include small-scale cultivation and raiding. Their relationship with their southerly Pokot neighbors is characterized by shifting alliances, in that they are allies after good rains and a bumper sorghum and millet harvest, or when there is a shared perception of threat from a better-armed neighbor such as the Karamojong of Uganda, the Dassanetch of northern Kenya and southwestern Ethiopia, or the Toposa of Southern Sudan (Onyang 1996). Conversely, each ethnic community becomes the enemy of the other during drought and periods of scarcity or after they acquire large quantities of the coveted Kalashnikov rifles from ethno-cultural affiliates or from their respective governments.

Turkana women wear around the neck and legs a variety of shiny brass and copper ornamentation that are plain, round, and smooth. Both women and men have spotless white teeth, probably due to their diet, which is rich in calcium; but also due to their habit of monotonously brushing them with *mswaki*, which is obtained from the root of a medicinal tree. The Turkana do not circumcise their men or women. The initiation ceremony that marks the *rite de passage* involves the smearing of a boy's hair with colored mud, which licenses the initiate to replace his wooden spear with a metal-tipped one. For women, marriage, which occurs between the age of 13 and 20, marks the passage into adulthood (interviews 1996 and 2005). After initiation, the young man is allowed to marry by paying an appropriate bridewealth, which ranges from 50 to 100 cattle or to a few Kalashnikov automatic rifles in lieu (interviews 1996 and 2005). The dowry places enormous pressure on young men, whose choice is between accumulating bridewealth through traditional animal husbandry, which could take many years owing to reduced animal productivity, or resorting to raiding as a quick fix. It should be reiterated that, despite the existence of monetary currency in the Turkana border region, a man's substance is still tellingly measured by the quality of his herd and the number of livestock he can count at daybreak and before last light. Consequently, the spirit of male chauvinism is firmly embedded in Turkana society, to the extent that the lack of animal wealth demotes a man to the status of a woman. Therefore the possession of a loaded gun and cattle is the primary means of actualizing manliness. This is particularly so during cultural festivities, when Turkana men proudly display their tattoos, whose significance depends on where they are located. A tattoo on the stomach is the handiwork of traditional medicine men or of spiritual healers exorcising demons that bring bad spirits. However, tattoos on a man's right shoulder indicate the number of enemy warriors he has killed during cattle raids, and Turkana men proudly display these, and any scars they may have on the face and chest, to women, because they epitomize machismo. In contrast, scars on the back are hidden from public view, because they suggest cowardice.

The traditional weapons of the Turkana included a spear, bows and arrows, and a sharp wrist knife and a handcrafted stool, which they used as a pillow, a seat, and a shield during combat at close quarters (see Figure 6.1).

Figure 6.1 Turkana stool used as a pillow (when tending livestock), seat (during peace talks) and shield (during close combat).

They also carried a stick to aid walking and for driving livestock. Before their encounter with Western colonialism in the nineteenth century the Turkana had large armies, which were led by charismatic leaders who were also diviners and spiritual healers (Mburu 2001). Their military-political organization was structured to suit territorial expansion and rustling for livestock. In the latter case the Turkana would carefully select their target, which they approached stealthily, and then engage the enemy in hand-to-hand combat for as long as was necessary to drive the stolen livestock to safety (interviews 1996 and 2005). Such conflicts were bloody, but paradoxically humane, considering that old people, female children, and the mentally disabled were spared. Through their community elders the Turkana were able to heal rifts and re-establish *rapport* with former enemies through marriage and barter for animals, grain and ironware, and through a system of social reciprocity for pasture and water.

It is important to sketch briefly how the state eroded the efficacy of the Turkana's instruments of conflict management and resolution. From 1913 to the 1920s Great Britain, then the colonial power in Kenya, Uganda and Sudan, disarmed the Turkana warriors and thenceforward prohibited customary cattle rustling across the international borders it had erected, mainly to delineate its sovereignty but also to protect the community from Ethiopian raiders, who used captives from transborder raids as unpaid domestic servants long after the international ban on slavery had come into force (CO 533/419/8; CO 533/421/4). Turkana warriors defied their elders, whose tribal authority had been undermined by arbitrary colonial boundaries, British military expeditions against them, and treaties the colonizer had entered into with gullible leaders. Armed warriors who chose not to disarm evaded disarmament by relocating into the safe havens of southern Sudan, and formed the *Ngoroko* as a clandestine resistance to Britain's colonial policy of administration generally and disarmament in particular, feeling that their community would otherwise be vulnerable to their heavily armed pastoral neighbors in Uganda, Sudan, and Ethiopia who were not disarmed or effectively governed. Thereafter the term *Ngoroko* came to refer to gun-toting livestock rustlers of no particular ethnicity or nationality.

Traditional authority was further undermined during the Second World War, when Turkana warriors were recruited in large numbers, trained, and armed for internal policing, partly to protect the British empire from nationalist militancy, but also to defend Britain's sphere of influence from possible incursions from Abyssinia (Ethiopia), which was at the time under the occupation of fascist Italy (CO/533/421/4). In the post-colonial period, most cattle raids were instigated by Kenyan politicians to create a diversion from their misrule by stirring tribal animosities within the state and across international boundaries. For example, it is alleged that during the 1980s and 1990s the Turkana were covertly issued with guns by the government of President Moi of Kenya without parliamentary debate or knowledge. It was not clear whether the guns, whose quantity remains a mystery, were intended for prosecuting ethnic cleansing in the Rift Valley province of Kenya, inducing the community to vote for Moi as a political bloc, destabilizing Uganda, or staking Kenya's claim to Elemi, a triangular territory disputed by Kenya, Sudan, and Ethiopia (DC/ISO/2/5/5). It is further claimed that the strategy was also to build a political coalition of the Kalenjin, Maasai, Turkana, and Samburu tribes, known by the acronym KAMATUSA, whom President Moi could later use to cleanse the Rift Valley region of sedentary Bantu cultivators, particularly the Gusii, Kikuyu, and Luhya ethnic communities (interviews 1996 and 2005). Whatever the motive, the guns obtained by the Turkana lacked ammunition, and they did not match the quality or quantity of what their Toposa and Dassanetch northern neighbors were getting from Sudan and Ethiopia respectively for pursuing similar political destabilization. Today the Turkana avoid disarmament by hiding in southern Sudan or Eastern Uganda amongst their linguistic 'cousins' or by serving under the warring factions and organized outlaws of southern Sudan or southwestern Ethiopia, because they distrust the polyethnic state of Kenya, which has in the past used them to fight its dirty wars and abandoned them when it was politically expedient (Ohito 2005; Ombati 2005).

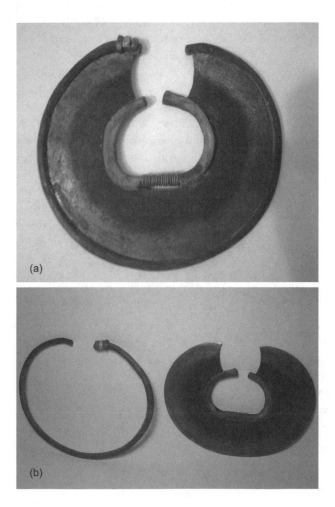

Figure 6.2 Turkana wrist knife (a) with the safety scabbard on and (b) with the scabbard off.

The Toposa

The Toposa (also called Topotha, Taposa, Dabossa) are a nomadic community predominantly resident around Kapoeta in the Eastern Equatoria Province of Southern Sudan (Beaton 1950). Some live in enclaves amongst the Turkana in northwestern Kenya close to the disputed Elemi Triangle, and being pastoral-ists, they trickle into the northeastern tip of Uganda amongst the pastoral Karamojong, where they can obtain good pasturage and water for their livestock (Mburu 2003). The Toposa language is Nilo-Saharan, and is mutually intelli-gible with the Karamoja cluster of languages (CO 822/3050). It sounds like Turkana spoken in a different dialect, and the two communities share many customs with their Karamojong and Jie neighbors of northeastern Uganda (CO 927/161/5). These include the smearing of an initiand's hair with mud, on to which they stick colorful plumes gathered from guinea fowls and rare birds. As part of their initiation into adulthood, young boys are sent to live in cattle kraals tens of miles away from home, where they learn to fend for themselves and to protect cattle, with their lives if necessary (author's interviews 1996 and 2005). In the context of ethnic culture such an initiation is a necessary spiritual enlight-enment, and from the practical point of view it prepares young men to face a life to which livestock is central; but it also produces a gunman who ignores the laws and behavior ordained by the polyethnic state. Cattle are the most significant measure of status and wealth in Toposa society, and the initiation rite into adult-hood centers on security of livestock, which involves the possession of a loaded gun. While their men spend long periods away looking after livestock, the women practice a sedentary lifestyle in temporary villages from where they cul-tivate a limited amount of grain along the river valleys. Toposa women proudly display the horizontal markings along their abdomens and faces, and these, along with filed teeth, symbolize their beauty.

The traditional weapons of the Toposa include a long throwing-spear and a shield. A warrior would run towards his enemy in a zigzag manner, using his shield to dodge and block weapons thrown against him, until he was close enough to use his spear. As soon as he reached the throwing distance, he would hold the shield with one hand and then crouch down on his rear leg, both to present a small angular target and to gain stability and leverage for a powerful throw. Having hurled his spear he would relocate to a rear battle position, rearm, and prepare to ambush an advancing enemy. Invariably such battles were fought at close quarters, but they were also fluid, and often covered long distances to and fro.

Among the Toposa, guns and livestock have a symbiotic relationship, as polit-ical power and economic security cannot be achieved without the possession of both. Hence the trend, which intensified in the 1990s, has been that some col-lectively acquire guns to increase and protect their animal wealth, while others barter their livestock to increase their arsenal of kalashnikovs. For example, after the collapse of Mengistu Haile Mariam's military dictatorship in Ethiopia, which had been heavily supported by the former USSR, the new Ethiopian government issued rifles to the Dassanetch, who are the Toposa's neighbors and traditional enemies, both as political appeasement and to form a frontier defense in the country's turbulent southwest. Similarly, the government of Sudan issued the Toposa community with at least 50,000 small arms (excluding landmines) as a political strategy to destabilize areas of southern Sudan that are controlled by the Sudan People's Liberation Army (AFRICANEWS 2001). The community has increased this arsenal to an unquantifiable degree through service as mercenaries with the Oromo Liberation Front, who are fighting to secede from Ethiopia, and who also provide them with refuge after they return from raiding their neighbors (Ombati 2005).

However, these firearms are not accountable, which makes disarmament unthinkable in the immediate future, and may explain why today many Toposa freely conduct banditry on remote country roads as a soft alternative to livestock rustling. They usually ambush halted or slow-moving private vehicles and convoys transporting international humanitarian relief from Kenya to southern Sudan that lack an adequate security escort. In any event, owing to the proximity

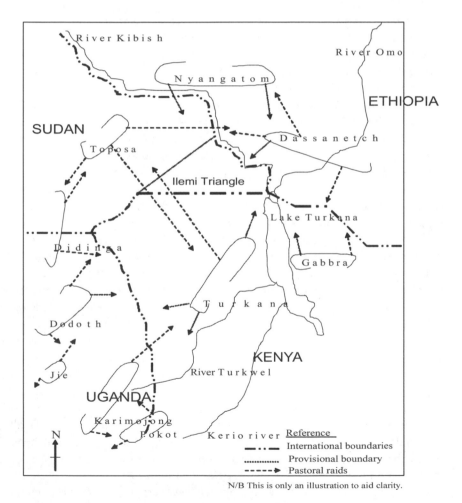

N/B This is only an illustration to aid clarity.

Figure 6.3 Map showing patterns of cattle rustling.

to the zone of civil war in southern Sudan and northeastern Uganda involving the Christian fundamentalist guerilla bandits known as the Lord's Resistance Army, the authorities of Kenya, Ethiopia, Uganda, and Sudan treat the habitat of the Toposa as hostile terrain. Thus, the incidence and scope of rustling has expanded, in so far as Toposa raiders are often state-sponsored tribal militias whom community elders cannot regulate.

The Ecological Context of Rustling in Northeastern Africa

Having briefly described the cultural context of rustling it is important to outline how the degraded physical environment contributes to raiding. All the above ethnic groups pursue pastoral nomadism, in that they constantly shift their habitat to conform to ecological and demographic imperatives and not, as has often been implied, because they prefer to live as vagrants and wanderers. Grazing for the herders shifts between different altitudinal zones, alternating between scarplands north of Lake Turkana during drought and the dry plains during the wet seasons. In this pastoral country the rains are short, localized, and few and far between, and cultivable healthy soils are only obtainable among the clayey deposits found along the riverine areas.

In these borderlands, people live in terms of primordial cleavages, and ethnicity, territorial sections, clans, and bond partnerships still demarcate their economic and political contexts. Generally, the habitat is extremely harsh, and in order to ensure survival, incessant contention and struggles between the above communities mark their transhumance migrations in pursuit of the scarce resources of nature. Homesteads for each ethnic community must therefore be simple to construct and easy to dismantle, as it is necessary to move every so often, which leads to significant population dispersal. Elsewhere, people live in fragmented pockets of low population density, because the availability of resources and need for physical security influences human settlements, making them characteristically impermanent. Hardly any of the pastoral communities develop sentimental attachments to specific localities, as do sedentary cultivators, although certain pastures and portions of arable riverbanks may be associated with a particular clan or ethnic community. A similar informal code of practice applies to rights over water, which is claimed by a particular group only when there is scarcity. The importance of water cannot be overstated, considering that drilling is a laborious and time-consuming task, as people can only use basic hand tools to dig and scoop out the soil. Most of the wells are on dry riverbeds, where the water is near to the surface; but whereas the sand is easy to dig out, the walls also tend to crumble easily. Their maintenance through desilting is critical: hence such boreholes, water pans, and dams temporarily become the property of the ethnic community, territorial section, or clan that built them.

Persistent drought in the region since 1996 is certainly a natural phenomenon, but also the outcome of raiding that has led to overcrowding on the safe pastures, and to burning charcoal for sale as a more secure livelihood than herding, which nevertheless damages the ecology through deforestation, reduces the rainfall, and further degrades the productivity of the land (*Weekly Review* September 1997; *Daily Nation* August 1999). Environmental conservation for the region has not featured prominently in the Kenyan government's economic policies, whereas Sudan has no control of the south where some territorial sections of the Turkana and Toposa live. To exacerbate the situation, raiding becomes a coping strategy, because Sudan's southern periphery is too dry for sedentary cultivation, roads are impermanent, and the periphery lacks infrastructure that could generate foreign exchange or create employment to support the local pastoral economy. In 2000, the severity of environmental stress forced 60,000 desperate Turkana into international humanitarian relief camps, while those too proud to live on handouts took up the gun and became cattle bandits (Clayton 2000).

The ruggedness of the terrain and the lack of all-weather roads is an obstacle to disarmament, in that security forces can only be deployed in small foot patrols, which lack heavy weaponry that could neutralize the firepower possessed by the bandits, and their inability to carry much in the way of logistic support limits the sustainability of large-scale military operations. Paradoxically, victims of bandit raids in Uganda and Kenya often run away from areas of counter-bandit operations, because there is no bond of trust with the state (Quam 1997; *The Standard* May 30 and 31, 2005). For this reason, the governments' appeals to the bandits to disarm go unheeded, because forcible disarmament using soldiers has limited chances of succeeding. Local tensions are common, especially along the unregulated Kenya–Sudan border regions of Lokichokio and Kakuma, among hungry people who are neither in the bush as bandits nor environmental refugees in famine relief camps, but who nevertheless get frustrated seeing convoys and planeloads of food and medical supplies bypassing them on their way to southern Sudan. Another obstacle to disarmament is that each border community described above has a fragment of its people living in enclaves across international boundaries in at least one other country. Actually the nationality of each person cannot be defined with certainty, considering that pastoral borders expand and contract to correspond with the proximity of water and good pasture; hence herders often criss-cross the international boundaries, unaware of their existence or relevance. In addition, whereas traditional raiding was an altruistic "redistribution" of the neighbor's livestock, today the pastoral way of war is fuelled by the proliferation of illegal firearms and the domino effect of international instabilities that began during the Cold War.

Summarizing Remarks

The indifference of international society to organized violence perpetrated by the cattle bandits of many African states suggests that there is limited understanding of the environment in which the phenomenon thrives. On the surface, the periodic character of the organized violence described in this study supports the materialist school of thought, because raids increase during drought and famine, and diminish during the wet season, when milk and wildlife are easily obtainable and people can supplement their diet with wild fruit, tubers, vegetables, sorghum and millet. Nevertheless, the dynamics of livestock rustlings and predatory expansion are too complex to be explained only by the rationale of dialectical materialism or ecological factors. Hence the phenomenon has been anchored to: customary traditions that enmesh killing and stealing with the *rite de passage*; the lack of empowerment of gerontocratic authority and other traditional inter-community instruments of maintaining order; the degradation of the quality and quantity of livestock through both preventable and natural factors; internal manipulation of the institution of raiding by corrupt leaders; and, externally, the domino effects of failed states.

Part II
Locked and Loaded

Race, Sex, and Gender

CHAPTER 7

Arming Desire: The Sexual Force of Guns in the United States

C. Richard King

Near the start of the motion picture *Jackie Brown* (1997) Ordell Robbie (Samuel L. Jackson) and Lewis Gara (Robert De Niro) talk about the gun trade, black identity, and the media, while watching *Chicks Who Love Guns* with Robbie's girl-friend, Melanie (Bridget Fonda), who lacks a last name and remains off camera for a major portion of the scene. The video, inspired by a real-life production, *Sexy Girls, Sexy Guns*, consists of quick cuts of bikini-clad women shooting various high-powered weapons, interspersed with personal narratives and commentaries about the firearms. The first begins with a white woman with blonde hair, dressed in an American flag bikini: "Hi, I'm Sidney, a personal trainer and Miss Orange County finalist. And this is my Tec-9." A profile appears, listing her stats: 5'6", 100 pounds, 26 years old, 36-25-36. Sidney continues, "I love my Tec-9," and proceeds to shoot it. Robbie, ordering Melanie to refill the drinks, fast-forwards through scenes, offering commentary on various guns, their power and price. For instance, he describes the AK 47 enthusiastically, "The very best there is. When you absolutely, positively have to kill every motherfucker in the room. Accept no substitutes." Repeatedly the telephone rings; Robbie refuses to answer it himself, barking instead when Melanie baulks, "Girl, don't make me put my foot in your ass." While Robbie is handling his business, Melanie flirts with Gara and criticizes her boyfriend for being fake, stupid, and incompetent.

While seemingly innocuous, especially for Tarantino, this scene highlights the key themes of this chapter: the (male) pleasures of watching, objectifying, and sexualizing; the threat in word and weapon to enforce order and silence dissent; the power to take life and control others; and the subversive play of flirtation and inversion. On the one hand, it proposes a rather simple formulation: men dominate gun cultures and gun cultures extend male domination. On the other hand, it suggests something more complex: guns amplify sexualized power, projecting masculinity and violence, which encourages dehumanization and degradation, while also allowing the possibility for subversion and negotiation.

It almost goes without saying that guns and gun cultures are phallocentric. They center on men: pursuit, predation, precision, dominance, aggression, toughness, conquest, and immediacy. They have always pivoted around men's power and men's pleasure. And although exceedingly homosocial, heterosexual difference and desire animate gun cultures as sexual cultures. In addition to a thriving video niche market and an active internet subculture (see http://www.girlswithguns.org), examples range from mainstream marketing ploys, as in the Splat Girls, who make promotional materials (like calendars) and media appearances for a paintball magazine, and softcore pornography of girls in bikinis or less holding or firing guns, to sex toys fashioned after pistols and hardcore pornography featuring actual guns as fetishes or phallic substitutes. Less obvious perhaps, but no less crucial, are the various discourses on women as other (lover, spouse, object) animating these subcultures. Mark Pitcavage's (1996) tour of a gun show nicely illustrates one such discursive field. Here, he found bumper stickers and tee-shirts reading:

> Wife and Dog Missing. Reward for Dog.
>
> I just got a gun for my wife. It is the best trade I ever made.
>
> My wife yes. My dog maybe. My gun never.

All these juxtapositions of "girls and guns" are best read as articulations of sex and power, potent, if sensational, reminders of the sexual force of guns. Importantly, sexual violence correlates better with guns and gun cultures than it does with pornography.

> The availability of sexually explicit materials in adult theaters and bookstores does not correlate significantly with rates of reported rape. But other variables do. These include alcohol consumption, the percentage of poor in a region, and the circulation of another type of magazine, 'outdoor' publications such as *Field and Stream* and *Guns and Ammo*. (Green 1992: 124)

This is not to excuse pornography, but rather refocus inquiry and reflection (as I do here) on the ways in which guns amplify phallocentrism.

Oddly, although sex is central to gun cultures in the United States, popular and academic readings of firearms rarely discuss it. In fact, the sexualization of guns often gets lost in struggles over individual entitlements, state power, property and its protection, violence, security, and constitutional intent. In this chapter, I push beyond instrumental and moral panics over access to, ownership of, and use of firearms, unpacking the sexual meanings of guns in American culture. I offer five readings of the sexual force of guns in the United States, assembling an initial and suggestive overview rather than an exhaustive survey. First, I listen carefully to how sex talk, particularly metaphors and language play, entangles the erotic and the ballistic, amplifying the velocity, violence, and trajectories of predatory sexualities. Second, I detail the making of men in and through rituals in homosocial spaces centered around firearms and heteromasculine normativity. Third, I attend to the place of the firearm in contemporary cinema and heterosexual pornography, suggesting that they typify the contradictions of post-feminist constructions of gender and sexuality. Fourth, I consider an effort to unsettle the established linkages between masculinity, guns, and hunting through parody and play. Fifth, I trace the centrality of the sexual force of guns to the post-9/11 world order. Throughout, I set aside easy, individualistic assessments that might favor the language of the unconscious and the logic of fetishism, opting instead to integrate post-structural, queer, and feminist theories to highlight the ways in which the sexualization of guns arms deeper desires, namely hegemonic formulations of masculinity, heterosexuality, and domination.

Sex Talk

Guns provide a language for talking about sex, offering a set of cultural metaphors, similar to those made available by other symbolic domains, such as sport or animals, that inscribe power and conscribe pleasure. Indeed, for several hundred years, firearms have provided a fecund sexual vocabulary, noteworthy for its flexibility and productivity, which describes bodies, acts, and relationships.

Although it has become common of late to hear men, particularly those who workout, describe their biceps as guns, more frequently over the past few centuries firearms have referred to explicitly erogenous zones, specifically the male genitals. In fact, guns have offered simple analogies and playful metaphors for men seeking to arm their desires. Some examples include:

Gun	Rifle	Piece
Pink Pistol	Sex Pistol	Love Pistol
Meat Pistol	Pocket Pistol	Love Gun

Here, the body is imagined as a weapon, an instrument of power and control, and apparatus of appropriation and penetration, even if softened by notions of love. In addition, sperm have long been referred to as bullets. More recently, the language of guns has moved beyond men to speak of women and their bodies. In particular, large breasts frequently are referred to as guns, and porn stars with large breasts often have stage names that play around with this nomenclature, including Colt 45, Montana Gunns, and Letha Weapons. One transhistorical explanation for this may be, as Shirley Ardener (1987: 135) has suggested, that women's breasts and men's penises constitute symbolic parallels—external and easily accessible body parts that produce life-giving fluids; and thus it makes perfect sense that as women and their bodies more centrally enter public spaces as (sexualized and empowered) agents, the result of this parallelism in the changed situation thus brought about should be linguistic seepage and slippage.

A grounded account, to which I return shortly, directs attention to the shape and struggles of post-feminism, underscoring the unique contradictions of gender and power in the contemporary United States.

Firearms have also lent themselves to the naming of sexual aids. In Hong Kong, an acquaintance suggests, condoms are referred to as "bullet-proof vests." And closer to home, a popular vibrator is dubbed "the silver bullet."

In addition, the language of guns has afforded a nuanced lexicon of sex acts. While select terms, particularly rifle and gun, have become terms to speak about sexual intercourse, many more metaphors have been fashioned to refer to masturbation. In fact, no fewer than fourteen terms have been spawned to describe male masturbation:

> Assault on a friendly weapon
> Buffing the rifle
> Clean your rifle
> Cock the magic pistol
> Cocking the rifle
> Emptying your sex pistol
> Firing the flesh musket
> Firing the love rifle
> One-gun salute
> Shooting enemies
> Shooting the pump-action porridge gun
> Skeet shooting
> Target practice (with white ammo)
> Unloading the gun

In contrast, my search of dictionaries and websites revealed only one term for female masturbation: oiling the holster, which itself places women in a receptive and secondary role. This disparity reminds us of the power dynamics central to sex and sexual discourse, highlighting the fact that men not only create but also center much of mainstream sexual discourse.

Indeed, the vocabulary for sexuality imagined through guns is a phallocentric discourse that at the same time enacts masculine agency and identity and dehumanizes women and inferior men. This lexicon speaks of men who lack appropriate or adequate size as having a snub nose pistol, while stigmatizing those who are infertile as shooting blanks. It lends itself to practices in gun cultures as well. The sexualized language of guns becomes the language of hunting in many cases. Hunters' discourse, according to Marti Kheel (1995; see also Kalof et al. 2004; Luke 1998), hinges on sexual allusions, wherein bullets are balls; shooting is discharge; hitting a target is penetration; a weapon's potency is its penetration power; and shooting too quickly is premature discharge: controlling discharge in conjunction with penetration power ensures a kill. As playful as it may be, the sexual vocabulary offered by guns reiterates the entanglements of sex and violence, highlighting the importance of force, domination, and humiliation to much of what passes as normal sexual relations. Or more, as one current slang term encapsulates it: "I shot all over her face with my gun."

Rites/Rights

Guns transform subjects and spaces, encouraging (often nuanced) stagings of self and society. Not infrequently, guns anchor and animate rituals replete with sexualized meanings in subcultures devoted to hunting, policing, and killing. And while local and intimate ceremonial occasions, like a boy's first blood, or solo kill, reiterate the place of firearms in the crossing over/toward manhood, the more formalized and institutionalized rites of passages central to the perpetuation of homosocial spaces offer vivid illustrations of the power and possibility of guns in making men. Importantly, the anti-structural play central to these ritual moments/movements turns on the cultural work of sexual categories. Stanley Kubrick's 1987 film *Full Metal Jacket* highlights the sexual force of guns in the manufacture of men as citizens and soldiers. This harrowing rendering of the Vietnam War follows a group of young US Marine recruits through basic training and then into the depths of combat. Whereas automatic weapons center their tour of Southeast Asia, mediating their (often dehumanizing and deadly) relationships with others, it is in boot camp that they form new selves through guns. To be sure, the disciplinary, technical, and mechanical aspects of basic training teach them much about being soldiers, but the ritual melding of guns and sexuality instructs them on how to be good Marines and better men.

Early in basic training, following their receipt of their rifles, their drill instructor, Sgt. Hartman, advises the new recruits to forge a conjugal bond with their new weapons, a monogamous relationship to the exclusion of all others:

> Tonight you pukes will sleep with your rifles. You will give your rifle a girl's name. Because this is the only pussy you people are going to get! Your days of finger-banging Mary Jane Rottencrotch through her pretty pink panties are over! You are married to this piece, this weapon of iron and wood. And you will be faithful!

No longer will the soldiers in training engage in the awkward and immature pursuits of boys back home, but henceforth they will remain committed to their weapons. And while he reminds them of their manly role and relation *vis-à-vis* their feminine firearms, shortly thereafter, he reminds them at the end of the day that they are not yet men, much less soldiers, "Lights out. Good night, ladies."

Throughout basic training their instruction returns to and relies upon the sexualization of guns and their relationships with them. In one noteworthy scene, the recruits march in two columns, clad in tee-shirts and boxers; with rifle in hand, they repeatedly chant in call-and-response fashion:

> This is my rifle! This is my gun!
> This is for fighting! This is for fun!

The emerging men have two weapons: a rifle and a gun (or penis), and the possession and mastery of the former reinforce the control and potency of the latter. Later, dressed in fatigues they again march in formation, chanting:

> I don't want no teenage queen.
> I just want my M-14.

Once more, no longer boys, their desire and focus is not on sex but on the weapon, to which they must remain committed and faithful.

Near the end of basic training the recruits have nearly become soldiers, the boys transformed into men. A testimony to the transformation and the centrality of guns to it is an inspection of the assembled recruits:

Sgt Hartman: What's this weapon's name, Private Pyle?
Leonard Pyle: Sir, the Private's weapon's name is Charlene, sir!
Sgt Hartman: Pyle, you are definitely born again hard. I may even let you serve
        as a rifleman in Beloved corps.

Pyle has not only been *born again hard*, but his relationship with Charlene propels his transformation from awkward and incompetent recruit to skilled, tough, and polished rifleman, from weak and fat boy to hard, respectable, and worthy man.

Negotiations and Negations: Post-Feminist Articulations

By all accounts, something profoundly important has happened to representations of women in contemporary media: women have become warriors as strong, tough, and assertive as the conventional male action hero (Early and Kennedy 2003; Heinecken 2003; Innes 1999, 2004; McCaughey and King 2001). In films, television programs, and video games from *La Femme Nikita* and *Aliens* to *Charlie's Angels* and *Tomb Raider*, these women—born again, like Private Pyle without the ritual or the manhood—often use firearms, troubling in many respects the established associations between gunplay and the work of gender. When read out of context, one might be tempted to suggest that such imagery empowers women or unsettles sexual hierarchies; however, when placed in a broader social field that includes heterosexual pornography, it becomes apparent that the sexual force of guns still amplifies phallocentrism, albeit in a more perverse and polymorphous fashion.

In content and form, mainstream cinema shares much in common with soft-core pornography, both of which might be usefully read as efforts to renegotiate or play around with the meanings of masculinity/femininity as well as the trappings of social power (the gun as phallus once more). At first blush, films featuring women warriors and photospreads centered around women stripping, shooting, and otherwise in action both complicate femininity, as they heterosexualize gun play. Such representations hinge on transgression, namely the breaking of gendered expectations, allowing women to embody toughness, assertiveness, skill, and authority. As meaningful as this multiplication of femininity may be, all such imagery also demands the assertion of hyperfemininity, most often expressed through bodies that exaggerate cultural ideals of feminine beauty. This contradiction opens a space of ambiguity in which authors and audiences can play around with notions of gender, power, and desire. Significantly, however, the male gaze contains and constricts this liminal space, undermining the capacity for subversion.

Hardcore pornography centers (on) the male gaze as well, but in contrast with softer sexualizations of guns, it reveals itself to be openly misogynistic and quite overtly affirms domination. In this representational field, guns direct male power and authority, applying it to the bodies of women. They compel (sexual) action, coercing conformity. They force the subject on the object, transforming violation into vindication. Firearms allow for violent fantasies and dehumanizing narratives of pursuit, capture, appropriation, assault, and satisfaction to be played out, giving permission to transgressive desires. They appear most often in rape porn, visual enactments of real or imagined sexual assaults, and in sadistic features, in which another's pain induces pleasure. And in an odd blurring of hunting as sport and hunting as the logical extension of heteromasculine sexual norms—as in "to be on the prowl"—one "reality" series of porn tapes, *Hunting for Bambi*, incorporates (paintball) guns into the predation—a snuff film without the gore (Luke 1998).

Whether soft or hard, mainstream or extreme, popular sexualizations of firearms do little to trouble conventional understandings of gender, power, or guns. Instead, in the present, neo-conservative moment, they offer contexts for negotiation that ultimately negate the redirection of the sexual force of guns. Consequently, they do not undermine or rework sexual hierarchies.

Parody: Post-modern Politics

The sexual force of guns has not simply encouraged post-feminist struggles over the power and pleasure of gendered meanings, but has also occasioned critical interventions shaped by postmodern sensibilities. Indeed, following Frederick Jameson's (1991) reading of the emergent political landscape, critics increasingly use parody to subvert established associations between guns, masculinity, and culture. A recent media campaign orchestrated by People for the Ethical Treatment of Animals (PETA) nicely illustrates the parodic edge of current cultural politics, while underscoring the centrality of sexuality to the (re)articulation of gender and power.

On April 1, 2005, PETA announced that researchers had identified a new syndrome, Diminutive Male Genital Disorder (DMGD) and linked recreational hunting to abnormally small penis size. In a press release, the animal rights group summarized the findings of a two-year study that had isolated an "abnormality" on the twenty-first chromosome that had two linked effects: smaller penis size and an increased drive to experience the thrill of killing in non-threatening situations such as recreational hunting—what they dubbed "controlled victim aggression manifestation" (see http://DMGD.org). PETA trumpeted the study: "These findings confirm what we have believed for a long time: hunters just don't measure up. They are apparently overcompensating for their failure to hit the mark in the bedroom by blowing small animals away in the woods" (PETA 2005). Clearly, PETA sought to play around with popular conceptions of hunting, problematizing the power and masculinity that the practice of hunting often confers on men.

Although it was meant to be funny, not everyone (as evidenced by chatter in electronic forums) found the satirical press release and the connections or condition it imagined to be a laughing matter. Hunters and their supporters bristled at the effort to emasculate them, frequently offering retorts that celebrated their size and prowess. For example:

HarbringerHouse: Wouldn't aggressive hunting behavior correlate with higher levels of testosterone, and therefore more "size"?

Global_Domination: Does this mean that now I have to sell my rifles and never go hunting again? Because looking down ... seeing Big Jim and the Twins ... I mean ... Damn!

Snarkie: This research is inherently flawed, because I usually end up clubbing the wounded deer to death with mine.

Not surprisingly, the sexualized violence central to gun cultures, here, animates assertions of masculinity through the phallus (at once the penis and the gun).

Worse, some readings of the media campaign have suggested that it actually reinforces dehumanizing sexual and corporeal hierarchies. Most notably, intersex individuals—those born (1 in every 20,000 births) with hormonal and genital differences that fall outside traditional notions of male and female and typically have resulted in unnecessary and emotionally and physically scarring surgeries—and their supporters were put off by the prank. In particular, the advocacy group Bodies Like Ours critiqued PETA for its perpetuation of popular and hurtful understandings:

A bizarre and hurtful fantasy of PETA implies that those with certain types of Intersex ... are not fully men, cowardly, and possibly murderers ... The announcement further implies men with micropenis are unable to have adequate sex lives with their partner ... Micropenis and absence of a penis often result in healthy boys undergoing sex reassignments without their consent on the assumption that a small penis lessens their masculinity and they would be happier as girls. (http://www.bodieslikeours.org/forums/printthread.php?t=1232)

Consequentially, as PETA reformulates the problem, finding that hunting with guns produces sissies not men, it inadvertently embraces the norm and the processes of normalization it so desperately seeks to trouble. Together these critiques from those who support hunting and those who advocate on behalf of the intersex expose the limitations of the postmodern cultural politics employed by PETA: its parody has negligible effects, precisely because it unsettles neither the logics nor the structures of phallocentrism, but in fact reinscribes as it plays with guns and hunting the linkages between bodies, sexualities, and (symbolic) violence.

Neo-Oriental Incursions

The war on terror along with the invasions and occupations of Iraq and Afghanistan have intensified the sexual force of guns, exposing the deep entanglements of difference and power in hegemonic gun cultures. Immediately after 9/11, pundits, politicians, the press, and much of the public in the United States revived and retooled classic Orientalism. A rhetoric of essential, racialized differences rapidly crystallized between us and them, East and West, Christianity and Islam, civilization and barbarism, the rule of law and the chaos of insurgency. And as guns (as well as bombs, missiles, tanks, helicopters, and so on) emerged as not only the logical but the only means of addressing grief, securing borders, and purging the new world order of evil, gun cultures associated with policing, counterinsurgency, combat, special ops, and nation-building displaced democracy and its ideals of inclusion, dialogue, and deliberation. Not surprisingly, gender and sexuality proved fundamental to the channeling of the sexual force of guns and gun cultures against demonized others and in pursuit of a pure nation and a safe state: the valiant American soldier (almost always cast as male), the imperiled female soldier (Jessica Lynch), the urgent need to liberate the women of Afghanistan, the vile sexual abuse inflicted upon prisoners in Abu Ghraib, the disproportionate harms endured by women in the wake of invasion, and the persistent campaign against gays and lesbians at home (see Bloodsworth-Lugo and Lugo-Lugo 2005; Chew 2005). In this context, then, guns and gun cultures have a heightened capacity to enforce racial and sexual hierarchies (symbolically) within war zones to be sure, but perhaps less obviously and more importantly in the everyday practices and precepts on the home front as well.

Humor, pornography, and gender play anchor the most recent uses of the sexual force of guns. A satirical representation of Osama bin Laden graphically illustrates these rearticulations. Bin Laden's familiar face has been placed in the body of female model, dressed in fetish wear, with breasts exposed and an assault rifle pointed toward the sky (http://www.phaster.com/phaster_playmate_bin.html). Under the title, "Centerfold Playmate with a Gun Fetish," one of several parodies that feminizes and mocks politicians and celebrities, the image-text (like the videoclip in *Jackie Brown*) features measurements (36D-27-35) and vital statistics, and in common with *Playboy* lists ambitions ("to find peace of mind, stay focused, and to keep what's important to me close"), turn-ons ("weapons of mass destruction, leather fetish bars, pork ribs, and oh yeah GUNS!"), and turn-offs ("democracy, humor, carriage rides, and people who are cruel to animals.") The accompanying caption further underscores the desire to deride and dehumanize, reading in part that the "terrorist and aspiring lingerie model" wants "to create an Islamic religious state where everyone ... listen[s] to Barry Manilow and smoke[s] crack."

More disturbing, is nowthatsfuckedup.com, a website, originally created to profit on the sharing of pictures members submitted of their wives and girlfriends, that began offering free membership to US soldiers serving in Iraq and Afghanistan in exchange for posting pictures from "over there." Although the site administrator welcomed images of soldiers "hangin' out, or saying hi ... something like you would be sending home to your family and friends," he encouraged more graphic images: "Let's see some tanks, guns ... some dead Taliban." Members of nowthatsfuckedup.com applauded the move, regularly voicing support for the troops, asking questions about the photos and marveling at the soldiers' exploits. As one moderator put it, "you guys are giving everything for us, it's the least we can do for you guys. theres [sic] been guns for toys programs, but wheres [sic] the AK's [AK 47 assault rifle] for DDs?" (http://www.nowthatsfuckedup.com/bbs/ftopic4132.html). Comments on the photos expose a troubling disregard for those killed in war. Photographs of dead bodies bear captions like "What every Iraqi should look like" and carry titles such as "Die Haji Die" (Thompson 2005). In accompanying texts, soldiers elaborate this dehumanizing discourse: "They need to be taught a lesson, a lesson hard enough that they will think twice before waging a jihad against us" (Thompson 2005); or "the bad thing about shooting them is that we have to clean it up" (Zornick 2005).

The parody of bin Laden and nowthatsfuckedup.com starkly clarify the interpenetration of pornography and war and the manner in which the sexual forces of guns and gun cultures mediate their intersections. At the very least, following Robert Jensen, we can glimpse in these iterations that "pornography and the wars of empire are based on the idea that domination is natural and inevitable" the idea that the power and privilege of men and (white, Christian) Americans is commendable and necessary—and a reminder, moreover, that the gun and the camera work together to take life and dignity. An interdependence that is perhaps best captured by one of the postings on nowthatsfuckedup.com in which a photo shows a woman, her vagina exposed, receiving medical care after losing part of her leg to a land mine, while what is left of her foot is exhibited for the viewer. The caption reads, "Nice puss—bad foot" (Thompson 2005).

Conclusions

To close this chapter, I offer a final example of the entanglements of guns and sexuality. Although neither as playful nor as painful as many of the foregoing iterations, it nicely returns us to the key problematics.

In 2000, the University of Oklahoma professor David Deming (2001: 43) read with horror an editorial column in the student newspaper that advocated gun control, arguing that "easy access to a handgun allows everyone ... to quickly and easily kill as many random people as they want." In response, he wrote a letter in which he "pointed out that [the columnist's] 'easy access' to a vagina enabled her to 'quickly and easily' have sex with 'as many random people' as she wanted [and] that her possession of an unregistered vagina equipped her to work as a prostitute and spread venereal disease" (ibid.).

While Professor Denning uses this incident, and the public reception of it, to highlight (what he sees) as a lack of protection for free speech and conservative dissent on campus, to my mind it better illustrates the sexual force of guns in social worlds emergent at the intersection of post-modern sensibilities, post-feminist contradictions, and post-imperial conquests, social worlds in which firearms amplify and extend existing inequalities, affirming established associations as they shoot down subversion. Indeed, the ludicrous comparison of guns and vaginas not only objectifies and sexualizes women, but bills them as deviants that must be policed and controlled (by men) in the name of order, tradition, health, and respectability. And here we return to why the articulations and amplifications of guns and sexuality matter so much. On the one hand, the sexual force of guns produces pleasures, populations, and possibilities through images and actions that feminize and dehumanize. On the other hand, although it encourages play (humor, subversion, and even critique), it routinely stabilizes social hierarchies, enhancing the effects and acceptance of phallocentrism, heteronormativity, and misogyny.

CHAPTER 8

Drawing a Virtual Gun[1]

Katherine Gregory

This chapter examines how members of pro-gun chatrooms reproduce gun culture on the internet by constructing their online group identity around commonly shared beliefs they ascribe to the gun. Specifically, I want to understand how online spaces are used to build a community around gun culture, so grounded in the physical artefact. Although gun culture has been the subject of much debate, little is known about how online chatrooms operate as a source for community engagement and cohesiveness outside material culture. This study begins with observations made in a chatroom and concludes with a content analysis of pro-gun websites. Drawing on links between firearms, nationalism, and methods of activism intended to mobilize online supporters in the promotion of gun-owner rights in the United States, I analyze the many ways the discourse obfuscates the power associated with firearm ownership and production in the United States. Ultimately, I ask whether the internet reproduces the existing social structures or whether it contributes to the designing of a new social order.

Our popular concept of community has been historically associated with a sense of place. In the last twenty-five years, however, notions of community and identity-formation have shifted away from physical geography with the advent of BBS (bulletin board systems) and the internet. As a result, social groups are no longer confined to their geographical location or social position to establish their social bonds (Wilson and Peterson 2002). This relatively new method of social interaction is fostering social inclusiveness and community-building based on common interests and identity claims that were either in earlier times limited to one's social location or concealed owing to their stigmatizing characteristics. Social groups no longer solely defined by extrinsic social characteristics or bound to a tight social network are replaced by loose social networks based on common interests (Gold 2003). This "fluidity of community" may have positive aspects that produce a sense of exclusivity for members; however, it continues to raise questions about how online communities are shaped and controlled, and whether they simply replicate the existing social order or evolve in new ways. This leads to unanswered questions about who initiates and shapes online discussion; who has access and entry to the chatroom; and who or what voices are excluded from the discourse (Denzin 1999; Dicken-Garcia 1998).

Online service providers make available chatrooms, subdivided into different topics, where visitors may post, read, and respond to textual messages in real time. In most cases, there is a limited number of visitors who may visit any one chatroom at a given time. In the virtual space, moderators sometimes have the ability to expel or log out recalcitrant interlopers or members. The pro-gun chatroom where I observed for this project was no exception. The space enforced in its members a cultural logic, in the form of shared experiences, political values, moral rectitude, veneration for rural living, and, of course, a passion for gun-ownership rights in the context of the United States. Their ideological cohesiveness moved them to the center of this space, dictating what was considered a normative discourse around guns and relegating any dissenting positions to the margins in the form of silencing by methods dictated by a moderator.

Even as national and international barriers fell away with access to the internet, the pro-gun chatroom remained an Americanized space, as prescribed by the dicta of pro-gun interests. Text, audio capabilities, and profile photos reinforced the culture of the chatroom. On occasion, during late nights when most North Americans across the continent are asleep, the site was occupied by Arabic- and Farsi-speakers who had Arabic and Farsi screen-names and wrote in Arabic script. Meanwhile, others used the audio feature to speak in Arabic for public listeners to hear or to shout out pro-Iraqi comments in English. As I do not speak or read Arabic, I do not know what was written on the screen for visitors to read. Most regular members ignored the onslaught of foreign speakers; however, on more than one occasion a senior member referred to the interlopers as "towel heads" and interpreted the use of the Arabic language in the chatroom as a possible method for communication between "terrorists planning their next attack." With the exception of pro-gun and/or pro-hunting Canadians and Australians, the American group found themselves amongst American pro-gun enthusiasts. This shared passion for hunting as it tangled with the construction of rural whiteness coalesced into a community under the umbrella of a national cause.

Methodology

Establishing an ethnographic approach to online research requires facing a variety of methodological challenges unique to virtual observation and participation in chatrooms and on websites (Sharf 1999; Mann and Stewart 2000; Brownlow and O'Dell 2002; Sade-Beck 2004). In particular, the field site raises question of how correspondents in "virtuality" force the ethnographer to grapple with disembodied voices that have been de-historicized and lack cultural communication markers provided by a "real life" environment. Warding off ambiguity in the encoding of new forms of digital communication is developing through repetitive textual and graphical use on the internet. Emoticons play a role in imbuing a message with a tone. Even with emoticons suggesting intentions, however, textual communication on the internet calls into question how words, stripped of their context, become destabilized signifiers in online communication.

Privacy and the vulnerability of the human subjects (Brownlow and O'Dell 2002; Sade-Beck 2004) and the researcher was a concern at the onset of this project. This was brought on after I observed audio-based "gun talk" in the chatroom. The content threw up a red flag for me as strong anti-government sentiments about gun-control laws melded with articulated sympathies for folk legends revered among many US militia groups. These attitudes made it necessary to ensure the anonymity of all parties concerned. Hence steps have been taken to protect their identities by not revealing the chatroom's host site and by changing the screen-names of members from the chatroom.

Overall, I spent 50 hours in the chatroom over a three-month period and conducted a content analysis of numerous political sites, resulting in a snapshot of an ever-changing virtual landscape. I was not, however, without my initial bias when first entering the chatroom. It was this bias that created my fears around disclosing my identity as a researcher to members of this social group. Before proceeding, I sought the advice of numerous qualitative cyber-scholars regarding self-disclosure in the chatroom. The response regarding my obligation to disclose my intentions there was mixed. To ensure my safety as the author, I did not use my university email account, but instead used an email ID that did not reveal my name.

Had I chosen to ask questions of members, another bias might have emerged. Questions from a researcher might have disrupted the "natural flow" of dialogue in the chatroom—and possibly the outcome of my findings. In a student project[2] conducted for one of my courses, the student entered a similar chatroom, where she "flamed" the room by asking incendiary questions about gun-ownership rights. The members, who were at the time having a conversation about unrelated matters, quickly "rounded up the wagons"[3] and took the student's questions as an attack on their beliefs. During the course of this exchange, a member threatened to "stab" the student with a "virtual knife" and called her gender-specific pejorative names. At the risk of creating such a disruption to the chatroom for this study, I opted only to observe and not disclose my intentions. My screen-name did remain visible, however, to the 25–45 users who visited the room at any given time. In some respect, my presence, like that of a dozen other such "silent" visitors, could have been considered as "lurking." Hence I treated the chatroom as a public forum and did not seek consent from members for this study.

Would my relationship with the regular members of the chatroom have changed had I told them that I represented the academic establishment or that I was a right-wing gun enthusiast? For some pro-gun members my academic title translates into "the east coast establishment," deemed responsible for any infringement on their right to carry a gun. I might have gained the confidence of some of the members had I disclosed my childhood experiences of growing up in a household where hunting rifles were present, or that my maternal grandfather's family were gunsmiths in Albania, and later manufactured highly prized collectors' firearms; but these signifiers are not central to my "core" identity, and so presenting them as "legitimate" markers for entry into the group would have been false representation on my part.

In the Chatroom

Most of the argumentation expressed in the chatroom that supported the right to own, and in many cases to carry, a firearm in the United States revolved around the Second Amendment, which states that US citizens have a right to organize as "a well regulated militia" to take up arms against the tyranny of a corrupt state. This "right to bear arms" debate circulated amongst members who shared similar values around gun-owner rights. What was never articulated or excavated in the historical context of gun-control law, however, was that whites had an exclusive right to own and carry a gun dating back to pre-colonial times, when, in the absence of consistent protection and control by the law, a weapon served as a practical form of self-defense (Bellesiles 2000; Roth 2002). Never was it mentioned that discharging a firearm was the method used by white settlers, who continued to populate what is now the Continental United States, as a means to protect themselves against and to inflict their will upon American Indians. This implicit relationship between gun usage and colonial expansionism across territories that later became part of the United States makes it impossible not to associate early gun-control issues to America's history of racism and whites' fear and control of American Indians and black slaves and freemen (Bellesiles 2000). Hence suppression of the probable link between white privilege and gun-ownership in American history continues (Roth 2002).

Often online identity politics makes it possible to transcend physical signifiers that define individuals and groups in real life. Mutual interests, therefore, become the cohesive force behind many communities emerging from the internet without cultural artefacts or practices to bind them. Of all the regular members who frequented the site, except for the occasional visitor, most identified themselves as white either on the basis of their screen-names or their profile photos, or through coded discourse about multiculturalism, crime, or liberalism in America. Although the group members present in the chatroom changed over the course of any given day, the same twenty "regulars" appeared again and again during the three-month period of observation.

Group membership was affirmed on the basis of visual and textual signifiers. Screen- names used in the chatroom were often metaphors for members' relationship to a gun or to rural living. Members incorporated hunting or weapon motifs in their screen names, such as *Gun Holster, Hunting Hound, Deer Hunter,*

Sniper, and *Texas Pistol*. In many cases, a primary identification with gun culture could be supplemented by a photo profile, in which a member could display an image of him-/herself handling a gun or holding a carcass shot after a hunt, further solidifying their gun-stance and legitimacy in the group. Most images reinforced a direct relationship to gun-ownership and/or nature, and identified the member as white. However believable the profile may have been, it is highly possible that the photos used to represent the member may have been fabricated. Images of regulars were enhanced with textual self-descriptions, further reaffirming direct interests in gun-collecting, hunting and fishing, or target practice, or in connection with the mastery of other weapons such as knives or bows. Gun usage in some cases reflected the person's livelihood as a hunter in a rural region or as a rancher. In many cases, however, gun usage signified a leisure interest in target practice or collecting rare weapons. Whether as a form of economic livelihood or as a hobby, gun culture was identified as a central identity claim for members.

Often the room served to provide advice and information about guns on the market. Usually there was at least one "expert" present during any given time to field questions. In most cases, the authority was a working-class member who put forth his or her acumen during the course of a multi-threaded conversation with regular members. Their presence in the room deflects attention from the issue of who "controls the discourse over any period of time" (Denzin 1999: 109), but asserts rather *how* they controlled it. Only then, as Denzin posits, can researchers provisionally answer how "power is socially distributed in terms of 'race, class, and gender'" (1999: 109).

On a few occasions members of the US armed forces joined to talk about military armor or a need to practice using a pistol before their deployment to Iraq. Under such circumstances, the soldier held an elevated status in the context of "knowledge holder." White women were also a strong presence in the community. They imparted their knowledge of gun culture and used the forum to express their political sentiments about gun-ownership. And although the space sometimes descended into sexual banter, with regular females as the objects of desire, heterosexual flirting did not defect from female participation in discussions of politics or how to dress a deer.

Most members were well informed about state bills that could infringe upon their right to carry a concealed weapon. Framing these and other political unknowns meant describing their cause as a constant struggle to secure their rights permanently. However, it is difficult to understand how they presented themselves as marginalized in the face of existing "structures of power," when their interests were already represented by a powerful lobby. Were members an extension of the existing power structure, or was there a real "threat" of "losing their rights" to bear arms, as some chatroom members alleged? Some members positioned themselves as "underdogs," suggesting group interests were under siege by the Federal and State governments that have regulatory control over gun-ownership. Needless to say, if this group socially positioned itself as on the margins in the face of institutional bureaucratic powers (Hill and Wilson 2003), the enemy in this instance was any politician or political body that framed them or firearms as the cause for violence in the United States.

Big Bad Government

If the pro-gun chatroom was initially set up to serve as a site where issues pertaining to gun control could be debated, the space had long lost its diversity of opinions. Pro-gun chatters were rarely, if ever, challenged in terms of their viewpoint. It was a space that, for most part, reinforced their held beliefs. Most of the talk about guns was one-sided, and many members, it appeared, preferred it like that. Occasionally, there were interlopers, but rarely were they the centerpiece of the multiple threads of conversation that took place there.

During one audio-based exchange, the tenor of the discussion hinted at more radicalized ideas associated with fringe groups, or US militias. The discussion centered on the retelling of Randy Weaver's shootout with US marshals, told from the point of view that Randy and his family were set up and ambushed by a Federal agency. Central to the reconstruction of the narrative was the manner in which the Alcohol, Tobacco, and Firearms (ATF) US Marshals were described as trespassing on private property, killing Weaver's wife, son, and dog, and justifying the exchange of fire. The two chatroom parties who were conversing over the hum of sexual banter were *Hunting Retriever*, a senior member who spoke with a West Texas drawl, and *TargetPracticeTeacher*, whose profile would lead me to conclude he was a police officer, since his photo was a freeze frame taken from a video camera mounted on a police car during a routine car search. Reading aloud from Weaver's autobiography, *Hunting Retriever* relayed to his audience how the discrepancies in Weaver's hearing date were a set-up that triggered a chain of deadly results. My impression was that the conversation was a thinly coded method for "sussing" out potential allies with similar views.

This dialogic exchange may have been scripted or erupted spontaneously; however, what was apparent is how well the two members knew each other and how they appeared to be rehashing prior knowledge about the legendary Randy Weaver. They were constructing an alternate narrative valorizing Weaver to iconic status. Moreover, embedded in Weaver's mythology was a deep distrust of the Federal government, a promotion of isolationism that supports rural self-sufficiency and indirectly rejects what is absent from that landscape, namely any notion of a pluralistic American society.

Registration and gun-permit laws enacted by city and state politics across the United States give states the jurisprudential basis to accept or reject gun-permit applications. This, too, fostered a disdain among pro-gun members for state and local governments, conjuring up a collective contention between chatroom members and government regulation of gun-ownership. Members maintained their "autonomy" from government regulations, perpetuating the notion of self-sufficiency and ways to circumvent any impending restrictions. Information of Governor Schwarzenegger's possibly signing a bill that could force bullet manufacturers to inscribe each bullet with a serial number quickly traveled around the chatroom. The discussion led to members' conjecturing whether or not bullet manufacturers would boycott selling their products to California police departments, resulting in a lack of bullets and consequently of protection for law enforcement officers. This characterization of various measures as "governmental repression" was a common theme circulating round the chatroom, and met with a call to direct action to be taken by citizens and their allies in weapons manufacturing.

"Liberal bashing" rhetoric was often communicated to establish insularity amongst the group members in the chatroom. They were quick to label outsiders as "hippie losers," despising everything the anachronistic "hippie" represented, real or imaginary. This exclusionary practice reinforced the group's cohesiveness by identifying who or what was their common enemy. It was also standard practice to associate "gun controllers" with "communist liberals." The philanthropist George Soros was labeled a "leftist peckerhead" for "picking up the bill for a lawsuit" related to a gun-control bill. In some cases the label extended to any sovereign nations that imposed restrictions around carrying a gun. As expressed by a white female member who made the following statement during a discussion about traveling to the Canadian border with a concealed weapon: "Canada is a great case in point. I don't bring my gun to Canada. I stop at the state police post on the US side and I give 'em my .44. 'Would you guys hold this for me while I go to this communist country?'" The rhetoric suggests any form of "state control" regarding gun-ownership is a negative throwback to the Soviet era, and contrastingly links the jargon of "freedom" with this notion of deregulation.

In attempting to associate "liberal" government representatives with a lack of concern for citizens' safety, regulars used an argument associating gun-ownership with protection rather than criminal activity. "Gun controllers," they claimed, "would rather see a woman raped, beaten and murdered, than hear her explain why she defended herself with a firearm." This line of reasoning was mostly made by males, inferring that "liberals" were out of touch with the mood of the nation and more concerned with controlling gun-ownership than "protecting" women against would-be attackers. This assumption implicitly suggests that if a woman were armed with a gun, she could deter an attack. The results of this discourse leave "victims" of violent crimes victimized by a callous government that does not care for their welfare. Hence, "government policy" was indirectly blamed for a woman's inability to fend off a rapist.

Associated with this notion of big government infringing upon individual rights and sovereign states was a unanimous contempt for the United Nations. Members chided the governing body for its "inability to make a decision based on consensus." This value, though not directly related to gun-ownership issues in the US, reflects another stance also held by many members, who felt that the United States should withdraw from the United Nations to protect its sovereignty.

Holding the Knowledge

Regular members who held a historical or mechanical knowledge of gun culture possessed the greatest amount of status in the group. This hierarchy of credibility often positioned white, working-class males as "senior" by stratifying other members. On occasion, female members exhibited a substantial amount of gun knowledge, and partook in the production of education and safety awareness. Regulars sometimes referenced one of these experts as a way to bolster their own status. In effect, the knowledge-producers became something of icons in the virtual space, perhaps repositioning the role they were otherwise assigned in society on the basis of their formal education, their occupation, or their rural location. White-collar workers clearly had to defer to them about hunting, gun models, or dressing a deer, thus reconfiguring the balance of authority in the room. The question remains whether or not the elevated status of working-class whites in the chatroom undermined the hierarchy of social class in US society, or simply allowed them to reclaim their white privilege?

The presence of *Ms Boise* in the chatroom clearly interrupted manifestations of gendered authority in the chatroom. Her profile consisted of a photo of a white woman who lists "kittens and assault weapons" as among her interests. In many female profiles, hyper-feminine gender codes were married to hyper-masculine interests. This female member stood out because she was also an "expert" who spoke eloquently about gun-control issues and gave detailed instructions on how to cast bullets. For hand-loading, she explained, one would need brass, a powder scale, a dispenser, lead slugs, a lead pot, shell holders, a powder "trickler," and "b" sizing dye. *Ms Boise* always reminded her audience not to "cut corners" and to "be conscious of your safety." The brass casings, she promised, would last a long time. Her recipe for bullets did not end there, however.

Ms Boise's instructions were usually peppered with remarks about wanting to "limit government's nose in my affairs … because they can mess with you until your heart's delight." This was the basic stance shared between *Ms Boise* and regular members around the issue of carrying a concealed weapon in states such as California and Wisconsin. Another senior member, *Gunslinger*, went on to add that "being a Californian isn't a crime, being a liberal mindf— Californian should be a crime." Whether this instruction was intended to assist isolated libertarians on how to outsmart future regulation of bullet casings, or to instruct "militia sympathizers" is only a guess. Nonetheless, it promoted direct action and countered any assumptions about who was an authority with weapons.

Separating "gun enthusiasts" from members who had killed in combat distinguished the glorification of the ability to kill another human being or animal and the real horrors of what a powerful weapon can do to human flesh upon impact. During a multiple-thread conversation, a young, white male gun enthusiast looking for "high capacity rifles" and bullets that could put "holes" in someone commented that "there are a lot of women at this site who don't know anything about guns." As it was, his audio-based comment ran simultaneously with the continuation of a textual dialogue between two older female members about "dressing a deer."

The young gun enthusiast quickly relinquished his "superiority" in the chatroom when a "real" soldier inquired about the performance of a Barretta pistol. The soldier anticipated his redeployment to Iraq, where he had previously served in the artillery and now expected that house-to-house combat awaited him. The nature of the war in Iraq made his .43 rifle obsolete for this type of warfare, forcing the soldier to develop the skill of shooting at close range with a hand-held pistol. His comments to the effect that "government doesn't care about the soldiers who are fighting over in Iraq" went unchallenged because of the soldier's firsthand combat experience and his willingness to serve his country and to risk his life performing military service.

Glorification of White, Rural Living

The pro-gun chatroom collectively celebrated the gun as a product of the mechanical age. Many threads of conversation suggested that owning a gun was a means of preserving a rural way of living by surviving off the land and maintaining self-sufficiency. Members who had a gift for language sometimes crafted narratives idealizing rural life. Their storytelling celebrated working-class white culture by providing rich descriptive language about farming, animal husbandry, herding, hunting, or just sitting on the porch. The lifestyle was connected to nature and a slower passage of time often equated with a pre-digital world. Nature in this sense meant an understanding and respect for the elements, in particular the weather. Daily salutations shared by regular members usually included a regional weather update that determined good or bad crops, herding patterns, and potential driving danger. Sometimes truckers shared in the exchange of weather information.

A counterpoint to the just-mentioned description of a glorified rural America was the group construction of a dystopic urban world. Some of the distortion about urban life appeared to come straight out of a 24/7 cable newscast. Meanwhile, the contrast fed online members' interpretation of urban life as a dangerous place where "criminals" could force their way into one's home, requiring one to take the law into one's own hands. The topic of "urban crime," I believe, became a thinly veiled coded language for racial pluralism and immigration, fueling fantastical discourse about "managing" one's property by "shooting first, and then calling 911." As one member stated, "you're not going to wait until the police arrive," making the home both a site of refuge and place of permeable intrusion.

Virtual intruders sometimes entered the chatroom, lashing out with negative epithets for rural stereotypes. The screen names of the interlopers often reflected an association with skateboard culture. When crashing the chatroom, flamers would shout textual messages or occupy the audio component, calling the group "stupid" or "rednecks" and claiming the pro-gun members needed a gun in compensation for their erectile insecurity. This stereotyping falsely depicted regular members as "uneducated" and inarticulate. Members who identified themselves as working-class through education or occupation were often found articulating viewpoints and argumentation that was well formed and clearly communicated.

Vernacular discourse often attributes a "location" to the speaker (Sweet 2005). In this case, members using the audio feature often imbued the space with their southern or southwestern drawl. Their cadence could be described as possessing a slower rate of speech; however, this characteristic should not detract from the commentary imparted in the chatroom. The content that was communicated in a deep vernacular countered many seated stereotypes and assumptions circulating in popular culture about rural white America. Perhaps some of those assumptions made by intruders were the same stereotypes that surfaced during the 2004 presidential election, when pundits underestimated the perspectives of white, rural voters by dismissing them as ignorant.

Pro-gun Websites

The most visible national gun lobby in the United States, the National Rifle Association is believed to be the most influential non-profit lobby promoting gun usage. With an estimated 3 million members, this lobby considers itself to be the "first civil rights organization," holding gun-ownership in the United States as a civil right (www.nra.org). Their website is easily accessible and provides updated local and national gun-related media coverage, keeping members abreast on issues such as a "right-to-carry" a concealed weapon and anti- or pro-gun mandates about to be signed by state officials. The passage of a bill will often serve as headline for the site as a way of announcing their victory to members.

The "Action Center," found in the top right corner of the website, functions as a source for online political action. Whether or not methods such as letter-writing and petitioning have become "domesticated" or translate into online effectiveness is questionable. Either way, buttons link members to a variety of political tactics. A letter template allows visitors to send a pro-gun message to their state representatives. Other links provide ways to register to vote or become politically active in local gun-related issues. This form of activism has an effective one-click infrastructure regarding up-to-the-minute issues, and provides an easy way to elicit public involvement. It is difficult to measure its effectiveness owing to limited research in this area.

The NRA links to sister sites are specifically set up to defeat anti-gun propositions or bills coming up in any state legislature. This effective method addresses the most pressing issues with an instant "link to action" at the website. Two examples included stopping the expansion of a list of "unsafe" guns and blocking the "imprinting" of serial numbers on bullets sold in the state of California. The press release suggested grave concern for an "anti-gun" bill about to head to Governor Schwarzenegger's desk, framing the "correct" stance for members and urging them to send email directly to the governor's office (http://www.nraila.org/CurrentLegislation/ActionAlerts/Default.aspx).

Banners found on the homepage function to set the ideological tone of the site, linking visitors to issues or services related to the site. In step with the militarization of everyday language used in America, the site "salutes" Democrat and Republican Senate members who wrote a bill exempting "gunsmiths" who produce fewer than thirty guns per year from having to pay a "'manufacturing'" tax on "modified" guns produced elsewhere. Through the NRA's efforts, this law was passed as part of a larger highway construction package bill signed by President Bush. Saluting governmental bodies may suggest the NRA holds institutional powers in high regard; but this sentiment is not bestowed upon politicians who oppose their interests. The site mocks governing bodies that challenge their position in the form of a banner singling out Democrats who authored the "Clinton Gun ban" bill. A photo of Senators Kennedy, Feinstein, and Schummer and a slogan telling "Mr. and Mrs. America to turn them all in," suggests that "liberals" are the real enemies to gun-owners and will erode gun-owner rights through legislative means. What is concealed, however, is how the NRA deployed its power to prevent the "reauthoring" of the 1994 automatic-assault weapon ban bill.

To counter such implications, the organization presents itself as pro-law enforcement. The layout of the banner depicts a police training session with a white female officer holding the focal point of the photo with her gaze into the camera. To her right is a black male officer peering away from the screen, to his right. His face and body language are positioned at an angle, and he does not hold the gaze of the viewer, making him non-threatening to viewers. It could be an attempt at showing "diversity;" however the white, female law enforcement officer holds the power in the picture. With the lifting of the automatic-assault weapons ban, this visual campaign distances the NRA from any implication of having put automatic-assault weapons back on the streets, further risking the lives of law enforcement officers.

The NRA web site also provides links to journals published by the organization. Issues thematically focus on hunting stags or becoming an armed citizen. Newer publications have expanded their reach to other niche markets such as *Woman's Outlook*, targeting women's firearm needs, and *InSights*, targeting "junior" members. It's fair to surmise that this recruitment tactic clearly normalizes gun-ownership for women and teens.

Local Movement

Motorists will learn that "Guns Save Life" while driving across central Illinois *en route* to Urbana-Champaign. The message blurs the line between online activism and a real-life campaign found along fences of private property buttressed along the freeway, thus reinforcing an association with gun-ownership and rural living. The website is part of the Champaign County Rifle Association and is strewn with animated US flags fluttering and a "POW MIA" flag symbolizing soldiers missing in action. The site serves a dual role of also announcing a "fallen" local marine who has died while fighting in Iraq.

Besides refuting purportedly skewed data on gun violence and death claims made by the medical establishment as "medicinal poison," the site takes a direct-action approach towards "no carry" zones, defined as local business establishments that prohibit gun-owners from carrying their weapons. The site "respects your wishes" but intends to boycott those establishments. A graphical image depicting the proposition that a red circle and line over a gun equals a red circle and line over a US dollar symbol signifies their economic weight. Hence, if small business owners do not support their cause, gun-owners will not economically support them.

Other sites capture the symbolism and discourse linking the personal web-pages of the "bravest fighting men who ever walked the earth" to the interests of gun-owners (www.gunroom.com). Connecting the Navy Seals site to pro-gun interests reinforces the link between the preservation and protection of the United States and gun-ownership. The message further blurs political interests with identities, melding into a single militarized force that legitimizes a link between the White House and gun-owners who are personally "charged with the protection of our Constitution," and perhaps the well-being of the US President as well. This is intended to be understood as "our fight" to protect a nation; but it is also two clicks away from listings of area shooting ranges. Overriding the political effectiveness of a website's ability to mobilize members is the question of who is winning the propaganda wars. Clearly, the pro-gun sites dominate the rhetoric of patriotism, righteously telling visitors who the "real" Americans are and how the rest of us are somehow less than that because of our stance on the war in Iraq or gun control.

Conclusion

In the pro-gun chatroom, affective group identity (Grossberg 1992) coalesced around shared interests in the material phenomenon of the gun. In the formation of this online community, the gun effectively functioned as a cultural signifier stabilizing a "co-construction of meaning, self-identity, group identity, formations of power and authority, and place" (Sweet 2005: 240). As a result, the "self-management" of the ideological architecture of the chatroom left limited space for dissenting views around gun-ownership rights and the social meaning attached to firearms, however it solidified the group's identity.

By using text, images and audio soundbites, pro-gun chatters produced a cohesive culture around gun-production knowledge, idealized rural living, and

perceptions of who or what is a threat to their survival. These practices and perspectives are normalized as cultural icons such as Ted Nugent become their
mouthpiece on corporate media. Hence the discourse on gun-owners' rights will
continue to obfuscate power relations embedded in the possession and discharging of a firearm, or the influence of a lobby that represents their interests.
This type of online/offline community and political activism, therefore, reproduced the existing power relations found in society rather than contested them.
Hence pro-gun identity claims framed through a prism of "struggle" against
federal and state legal structures and positioned as "grassroots" still remain
mostly fiction but are also a fabric of American identity constructed in "real life"
and reproduced in cyberspace without the means of material culture.

CHAPTER 9

"Gun Rights Are Civil Rights": Racism and the Right to Keep and Bear Arms in the United States

Christy Allen

Over 40,000 gun-owners and gun-rights enthusiasts from across the United States were making their way to Reno, NV, in April of 2002—answering the call put forth by the National Rifle Association (NRA) in its 131st Annual Conference theme, "I'll Fight For Freedom!" Settling into the taxi on my way to the convention center, I envisioned a sea of middle-aged white guys in faded jeans and T-shirts sporting the red, white and blue of the American flag. It was my first venture into the field for my research on gun-rights activism, and I was preoccupied with thoughts of how to minimize the differences between me, a left-wing woman in her twenties studying at a British university, and the right-wing activists I was sure I would meet. Though I grew up in the Midwest, I never interpreted the Second Amendment the way these activists do—as an individual right to keep and bear arms not only against criminal attack but also against government oppression. As if he could read my mind, the taxidriver, a middle-aged black man, shifted in his seat at a stop light so that he could look at me. "You're not here for the NRA Convention, are you? I have to say, you don't look like a member."

Looking back, it's easy to see the common assumptions the taxi driver and I had made about each other when he told me I didn't "look like a member"—we both imagined we knew what a gun-rights activist looked like. Just that morning I had seen the then NRA President Charlton Heston on CNN, telling the news anchors: "Those old dead white guys who wrote the Bill of Rights knew what they were doing." Associated Press polls consistently report that black Americans are much more likely to support gun control than white Americans (Lester 1999; McClurg et al. 2002). Traditionally, sociological accounts of the American gun-control debate describe a fundamental division between the urban, cosmopolitan Northeastern Americans, with little experience with, little use for, and often outright disdain for, firearms and Southwestern Americans, made up of rural traditionalists who grew up with firearms and see them as tools to which they have a constitutionally protected right (for example, see Bruce-Briggs 1976; Hofstadter 1971; Kennet and Anderson 1975; Tonso 1989).

Recent studies demonstrate more fully how American gun culture is associated with a certain "character" defined by gender, race and class—most likely a working- or middle-class white man who fulfills the role of hero, or "good guy." This image, or, as Williams calls it, "populist myth," of the Second Amendment is indeed entrenched—as Abigail Kohn's ethnographic book *Shooters* shows, we identify with the heroes of the American gun culture in the Minuteman citizen soldier, the western pioneer, and the cowboy (Kohn 2004; Williams 2003). The setting of gun-rights activism is often a world of "us" against "them," where personal responsibility is paramount; the hero knows with moral certainty when to use violence and sees the role of government as "subordinate and supplementary to individual personal efforts" (Leddy 1987).

My interviews and participant observation at gun-rights conferences and activist workshops over the course of nearly three years have confirmed that though the white, libertarian male is still cast in a central role, the stage of pro-gun activism is becoming crowded with other characters. In particular, there is the emergence of smaller, identity-specific gun-rights groups, such as Mothers' Arms, Second Amendment Sisters (SAS), Pink Pistols, and Black Man with a Gun. Most of these activists hold membership in and work with older gun-rights organizations like the NRA, but maintain their own specific right-to-keep-and-bear-arms agenda. This chapter will focus on this phenomenon with relation to the issues of race and racism in the gun-rights movement in the US. How does a version of American history that acknowledges white supremacist oppression and violence fit into the gun-rights narrative that emphasizes a moral advocacy of gun use by the heroic white male? Have black Americans joined the contemporary gun-rights movement in any meaningful way, as was predicted by a national commission on violence and firearms policy over twenty years ago (Zimring 1985)?

"Gun Control is Racist"

On that first fieldtrip, I became intrigued by an argument not only raised in some of the panel sessions but also overheard on the Gun Expo floor. I was at the Institute for Legislative Action (ILA) booth, signing up to receive "action alerts," when a middle-aged white man approached the counter with a specific request: "I'm wondering if you have anything about this—I'm under the impression that the dismantling of Jim Crow laws ensured the individual right to keep and bear arms." This may have gone unnoticed had it not been reinforced by a panel session I attended the following day called "Media Commentators Speak Out!" A black conservative with a syndicated radio talk show spoke, stressing the value of responsibility. He offered a "colorblind" appeal to the audience, saying: "This is not a black and white issue, this is not a left and right issue, this is a life and death issue!" and later, to applause: "They see I'm African-American, but I have to remind them I'm American first!" It wasn't until he was prompted in the Question and Answer session that this was challenged.

A thin man with long blond hair wearing a Harley Davidson shirt approached the microphone and started talking about the 14th Amendment (equal protection before the law). He was impassioned and articulate:

> Denying conceal carry permits is denial of equality under the law ... If you support discretionary permits,[1] you support discrimination. Think about it. In New York, you can't get a permit in Harlem. In LA, in Compton, no way in hell. It's a civil rights issue. Even Martin Luther King applied for the right to carry and was denied. When I lay this down, people go: "That makes sense. That's how we go to blacks and Latinos."

I was struck by so much in this brief presentation—it was the second time in a short period that I had heard white men raise the issue of racism and civil rights, and he had brought the idea of "going to" blacks and Latinos into the conversation. His remarks prompted the radio talk-show host to respond: "You know, I live in D.C.[2] where the cops don't want blacks to have guns—these are racist laws! This is an issue of race! They are afraid of the black kids and don't want them to have guns. We've got to get this message out, we're in the same fight!"

My earlier assumptions about what a gun-rights activist looked like and what made up his or her concerns were complicated by this new idea—*this is a civil rights issue. Gun control is racist.* As it turns out, this is a familiar strand in pro-gun literature and websites and in academic scholarship on the Second Amendment. The construction of gun control as racist policy appeared in William Tonso's article "White Man's Law" in the mid-1980s. While much gun-control literature maintains that the most comprehensive piece of federal firearms legislation (the Gun Control Act of 1968) passed through Congress in response to high-profile assassinations (see Spitzer 1995), Tonso departs from this view, proposing that Congress was so panicked by the protests and riots of 1967 and 1968 that it passed the Act to "shut off weapons access to blacks, and since they probably associated cheap guns with ghetto blacks ... they decided to cut off these sources while leaving over-the-counter purchases open to the more affluent" (Sherril 1973; Tonso 1985).

One of the most thorough historical and legal examinations is to be found in Robert Cottrol and Raymond Diamond's article "The Second Amendment: Toward an Afro-Americanist Reconsideration" (Cottrol and Diamond 1991). Cottrol and Diamond argue that questions raised by the Second Amendment—those of self-defense and relying on the state for protection—take on a unique urgency when viewed through the lens of the black American experience. The article examines statutes in colonial America prohibiting "Negroes," slave and free, from carrying weapons, through to the Antebellum experience of the black codes of the Southern States, and finally, turning to the twentieth century, bringing into focus lynching and terrorism of black communities by groups such as the Ku Klux Klan (KKK). The article raises the notion that "gun rights are civil rights" in its recollection of the Deacons for Defense and Justice, a group who obtained firearms and accompanied other civil rights workers for protection. The Deacons had approximately sixty chapters across Southern states, and demonstrated that "while non-violence had its adherence among the mainstream civil rights organizations, many ordinary black people in the South believed in resistance and believed in the necessity of maintaining firearms for personal protection" (Cottrol and Diamond 1991; see also Hill 2004).

Cottrol and Diamond's article remains a decisive scholarly work regarding gun control as "people control," and is referenced at length in the academic literature that followed. Articles such as "Gun Control and Racism" (Tahmassebi 1991) and "The Racist Roots of Gun Control" (Cramer 1995) look at similar colonial statutes, slave codes, and evidence of the need for blacks to arm themselves for self-defense during the Civil Rights era. These articles constitute academic "evidence" for many gun-rights activists, some of whom put up links to the articles on their websites. Some of the articles are re-published in the Second Amendment Foundation's (SAF) own publication *The Journal of Firearms and Public Policy*. At more than one conference, I have received handouts from various activists on "useful web pages about race and gun control" and "the racist roots of gun control." Is this eagerness to expose gun control as racist really a sign of solidarity with black Americans and other minorities? With the sentiment that "gun rights are civil rights" put forward in this fashion, it is useful to examine whether this resonates with the black gun-rights activists who have engaged in the pro-gun cause in leadership roles.[3]

Black Man with a Gun

If evidence were needed that "gun control is racist" is a salient issue in the pro-gun cause, one could find it in the activist who calls himself "Black Man with a Gun." Though Kenn was comfortable with firearms after joining the Marines and working in law enforcement, it wasn't until learning about the connection between the civil rights movement and pro-gun activism that he made the transition from gun-owner and firearms instructor to full-time gun-rights activist. In his book *Black Man with a Gun: A Responsible Gun Ownership Manual for African Americans*, Kenn describes his journey. On the advice of a friend he began doing research on how to build a career imparting his knowledge of firearms to more people in his community.

> I decided to crash an annual meeting of the National Rifle Association that was being held in my area ... Before that time you couldn't have gotten me to have anything to do with them because the people I saw with the "NRA" stickers on their trucks weren't the kind of people that I thought I wanted to be around. I was wrong. (Blanchard 2000)

Intrigued by Kenn's story, I arranged to meet him for an interview in September 2002. He described the impact of "sneaking into" the NRA meeting several years earlier. It wasn't just that the people he met defied his expectations by welcoming him warmly.

> They gave me, like, a history lesson for the next 3 hours. I was so—ashamed and overjoyed at the stuff I didn't know and had to find out. They put me on this whole path ... and the best story I ever heard is a group called the Deacons of Defense and Justice. And I was shocked that they even existed. 'Cause I hadn't even heard about it, until an old white guy here told me about it. And I thought, this is messed up! When you don't know your own history. (interview, September 29, 2002)

Learning about the Deacons galvanized Kenn, and his activism took on many forms—it was clear he understood his mission as multi-dimensional: he must convince black Americans that the right to keep and bear arms is a civil right, and he must also influence traditional gun-rights organizations to adopt recruitment strategies more appealing to those who do not fit the conventional profile of a white, middle-aged rural gun-owner. In the beginning, he was the CEO of African-American Arms Enterprises and Instruction, speaking at gun-rights conferences and working as a consultant for the NRA, testifying for the passage of concealed carry legislation in various states. All the while, he was studying.

> The folks who know are like, the old brothers. I grabbed all my old uncles, anyone I thought was a hunter or knowledgeable, to impart me with some key stuff, and I'd write it down. It took me about six years. I was like, wow, I didn't know that this law in 1640 prevented slaves from doing this, and I didn't know that ... it just kept going till I thought I could use this stuff, for other people. (interview)

While Kenn discusses gun control as racist because of the legacy of gun control laws, he says the contemporary manifestation is that black Americans are conditioned by white supremacists to associate owning firearms with threats of violence.

> They still have the philosophy that it's better they don't tell anybody, because they're going back from those laws. When you've been conditioned that if you show that you have a firearm, that you even have a bullet in your house that you could get seized by a paramilitary militia, get pulled out of your home—you keep it on the down low. And that's been pushed through all our generations. So when I made my title, Black Man with a Gun, it was almost like, "How can you be so bold?! Isn't something gonna happen to you?" (interview)

One of Kenn's initiatives, sparked by a conversation on a radio talk show, was to help "break the silence" by forming a black gun club. His first "Gun 101 Class" attracted fifteen people—and with them he founded the Tenth Cavalry

Gun Club (TCGC) in 1993, named after the African-American army units also known as "buffalo soldiers." The TCGC now has chapters in Georgia, Maryland, New Jersey, New York, and Virginia, and states its purpose as giving "support, education and encouragement of safe/responsible firearms ownership to people who have not traditionally participated" (www.tenthcavalrygunclub. org). In the interview Kenn spoke excitedly of one of the annual events of the TCGC, "Minority Day at the Range," celebrated on June 17th to commemorate the day in 1866 when slavery came to an end in the US. He laughed, telling the story: "Oh, they were like the United Nations of Guns, and I was like, someday, this is how the world's gonna be!"

This idealistic vision and success from being "Black Man with a Gun" does not come without its tensions. Over the years, I would observe Kenn fulfilling many roles—at a gun-rights activist training conference held in Texas in 2003, he was not only the keynote speaker at the evening banquet, but also ran workshops on effective communication and appeared on a panel on "Racism, Gun Control and Civil Rights Laws." While this speaks to Kenn's talents, it also points to traditional gun-rights groups' needing the "black perspective," momentarily giving attenders an overall impression of "diversity." Some of the ways in which Kenn describes his work make it sound almost akin to that of a translator; for example:

> I get a lot of questions, nationwide, on my site ... So, I might send a prayer to one guy, and I catch the hunter who's been divorced, and he wants to give his guns to his kid, and he wants to know the rules, and I have to actually call somebody in here [Gun Rights Policy Conference]— 'cause these guys know all the laws. ... So I'll send an e-mail to one of these guys, what's the law in Arkansas? And he sends it back to me. Then I write this nice note, you know, saying, yo, brother, this is the way it works, this is the law ... So that's my job, I soften the stuff. And it's a constant. It's a constant. (interview)

The "constant" of "softening" the gun-rights message goes beyond communication over gun laws in different states. It raises the difficulty pro-gun blacks may feel making common cause with large pro-gun organizations because of the perception that the pro-gun leadership remains insensitive to racism and to gun violence affecting black Americans.[4] This perception is not without reason; one late famous rifleman, who won a Lifetime Achievement Award at the 17th Annual GRPC (Gun Rights Policy Conference) I attended, once wrote in his *Guns and Ammo* column, "the consensus is that no more than five to ten people in a hundred who die by gunfire in L.A. are any loss to society. These people fight wars among themselves. It would seem a valid social service to keep them well-supplied with ammunition" (Cooper 1991; quoted in Seligman 2000).

While this kind of statement is repudiated by most gun-rights leaders and activists, it is a sentiment I have heard expressed by some white speakers and activists in the field. When I present Kenn with scenarios like these from pro-gun magazines during our interview, he acknowledges them but does not necessarily blame it on racism, saying, "if you have a homogeneous population—you can't think outside your group. It doesn't make you bad, just maybe not ... learned, not diverse." Kenn speaks eloquently about the staggering rates of black gun violence, going beyond the intense individualism of pro-gun rhetoric when discussing issues like poverty, drugs, and family. He tells me that when he turned 25, he celebrated, pausing before saying quietly: "That is a true number. One out of four black guys does not make it past the age of 24 without being dead, locked up, in the justice system, where you can't vote, you've already been nullified as a person." Being grounded in these experiences means he's had to be thoughtful about how to support himself as a fulltime activist. While he has testified for traditional gun-rights groups on a consultant basis, he explains his decision to remain self-employed thus:

> It's hard ... [they] don't have, again, a division of black thinkers or whatever. ... I came real close to being hired; I had addressed this a million times to them. But I basically figured out, if I actually worked for them, I'd lose. I'd become, oh, you just work for them, so everything I'd say would be negated. (interview)

Thus, while Kenn gives credit to NRA activists for teaching him the connection between gun rights and civil rights, he knows that many traditional gun-rights activists have to make more space for pro-gun civil rights activists if, together, they are to reach more African-Americans. One image that endures is of Kenn leading a workshop in Dallas, holding up familiar pro-gun paraphernalia, images of white Revolutionary soldiers: "This isn't going to speak to everyone."

The Farmboy

I'm introduced to Gary Davis at a Gun Rights Policy Conference (GRPC)—an annual gathering of activists, academics, firearms manufacturers and politicians in the gun-rights world organized by the Second Amendment Foundation (SAF) and the Citizens Committee for the Right to Keep and Bear Arms (CCRKBA). They gather at GRPC every year to discuss their legislative battles, to network, to plan strategies for the future. Gary stands out in this gathering of predominantly white men; he's a tall man who towers over the breakfast crowd, and his eyes remain hidden behind black tinted glasses at all times. I do my best to explain my research questions, acknowledging we might not have much in common. "Well, I don't think our angles are so different," he tells me. "My hero is Malcolm X and he talked a lot about human rights and self-defense." He agrees to an interview.

Gary grew up in rural Missouri, where fishing and hunting with his father on the weekends was more than just recreation: it was also the way they put food on the table. He's married, a bus driver by trade, and a lifetime member of the NRA, who knew firearms as tools before he knew them as weapons serving in the Vietnam War. He describes himself as a single-issue voter who got involved explicitly in gun-rights activism in 1994 when President Clinton signed the Assault Weapons Ban, saying: "That pissed me off. They trusted me with M16s in the jungle and I haven't shot anyone since Vietnam, and they're telling me they don't trust me at home as a responsible citizen?" Since then, Gary has served as president of the Western Missouri Shooters Alliance (WMSA), advocating and testifying for concealed carry in his state and also getting out the vote for pro-Second Amendment candidates in Congress. When pressed for more information, he says, "Let's just say I'm good at organizing Good Ol' Boys around a cause," with a chuckle. He will say more on the topic of Good Ol' Boys and racism. Growing up, Gary says he loved Martin Luther King, but didn't feel that the message of nonviolence spoke for him.

> As a child growing up in the Civil Rights era in this country, every day you would see when Civil Rights workers were shot, lynched, beaten to death. And, I told my father—and he was of the same like mind—I said, when I get older, I'm gonna defend my family. I'm not gonna just sit there and be a pacifist.

Gary points repeatedly to Malcolm X and the North Carolina National Association for the Advancement of Colored People (NAACP) spokesperson Robert Williams as heroes for being prominent black leaders who encouraged blacks to form gun clubs, to learn to shoot, and to defend themselves against white paramilitary groups like the Ku Klux Klan (KKK). While acknowledging that the KKK isn't as powerful as it used to be, he states the necessity to remain vigilant and to view things constantly from a historical perspective. It's the first time I've heard of Robert Williams, and Gary recommends his book *Negroes with Guns* as essential reading (Williams 1998 (orig. 1962)).

For Gary, considering gun control from a historical perspective means acknowledging its explicitly racist roots in black codes in the South. "Blacks could not own guns, they couldn't vote, and they couldn't own property. So it was and it is about people control." He also cites laws that may not appear to be racist in intent, but end up racist laws in effect. For example, he refers to an 1879 Tennessee law that prohibited any pistols that were not "Army or Navy" models—expensive models that most blacks could not afford. Denying blacks access to inexpensive firearms left them more vulnerable. Though the laws he cites aren't current, Gary says all gun control laws are racist, and stresses the importance of learning from history: "That's why I feel these so-called black leaders don't represent me, as they're anti-gun. I'm the type of person to look at things from a historical perspective of what was, and how the Klan has lynched and murdered and burned at stakes thousands of us. And I just refuse to let history repeat itself."

While Gary speaks about racism and the right to keep and bear arms as a necessity for fighting state-sponsored oppression, he grimly notes that the population he currently feels black men may need to defend themselves against is other black men. Within two minutes of our speaking, he mentions that he thinks that not only would Malcolm X encourage responsible, law-abiding people like himself to defend themselves against racist whites, but also "he would disapprove of these young black guys who are committing genocide in the black community. And he would encourage people to defend themselves against them." Gary doesn't quote the statistics I'm familiar with ("gun violence is the leading cause of death of black men aged 15–24" (Bureau of Justice Statistics 2002). He tells me that on December 22, 1991, his youngest brother was shot to death. Unlike many other survivors of gun violence victims, Gary sees himself as an advocate of "self-control, not gun control."

> My mother and grandmother, you'll never hear them blame my brother's death on the gun. They blame the black fools that did it. I don't blame the gun. I blame the thugs that did it. And one of 'em got out on bond, and two weeks later robbed and shot another guy, went back to jail. Before the first week of March was over, 1992, he robbed and killed another guy.

He cites a familiar pro-gun argument, that it was the brain going to the trigger, that what should be of concern here is the individual's actions, not the gun that, if "left on the table for a hundred years and nobody touched it, would never go off by itself." Gary seems slightly bewildered by the idea that what plagues young black American men is a gun problem; he thinks it's a cultural problem that's killing them. He can't relate to some of the young black men who ride his bus. Instead of having Civil Rights workers for heroes like he did, Gary says they are immersed in a culture of gangsta rap.

Gary knows the pain and sorrow caused by gun violence. But arguments from the NAACP's lawsuit against firearms manufacturers to hold them responsible for the disproportionate firearms-related deaths of minority males don't make much sense to him (see "NAACP v. A.A. Arms et al." 1999). When he hears them blame pro-gun groups like the NRA and firearms manufacturers for targeting minorities, he wonders what evidence they have for this assertion. He hasn't seen ads for firearms in black magazines or on Black Entertainment Television (BET), he says, nor has he heard firearms manufacturers on black radio stations, concluding that the NAACP is in denial. "You'll hear them blame the NRA but you'll never hear them criticizing any of these black rappers for being irresponsible and advocating violence."

It's clear that Gary feels more at home with individualistic NRA slogans ("guns don't kill people, people do") than he does with black leaders who want to regulate the accessibility of guns and to compromise the immunity of firearms manufacturers in respect of the safety of their products. His work in Missouri was recognized when he was the first African-American to be awarded the Jay M. Littlefield Memorial NRA-ILA Volunteer of the Year Award. Sometimes other black people will tell Gary he's being used by the firearms manufacturers, by the NRA and by the WMSA. I mention that he is one of only two black people I've seen at this conference, that the right to keep and bear arms to me often seems like such a *white* thing. He responds: "You know what? The white guys know they cannot walk this alone. They need us as well, and I'm glad of that. When somebody black says 'they're using you,' well, I tell them to use me as much as they want to."

It's enough for Gary to know he's fighting for a cause he feels is just—one that is, for him, explicitly linked to the legacy of Civil Rights era heroes and to the cherished American values of self-reliance and individual responsibility. He complicates the image of the typical NRA member, both in his avowed admiration of Malcolm X, and in his willingness to extend the gun lobby's well-known fear of the government into activism that is based on inclusion of minority groups and explicit declarations that "gun rights are civil rights." Gary was also the first activist to tell me to read Robert Williams' *Negroes with Guns*—but he wasn't the only one.

The Professor

In an article he wrote titled "A Liberal Democrat's Lament," Robert Cottrol points out that his background is not what one might expect from someone with a high profile in the gun-rights movement—for one thing, he didn't grow up in a gun-owning household or the rural Southwest. Rather, he was a young boy living in Harlem, New York, when he first became at all aware of the connection between racism, self-defense, and guns (Cottrol 1999). Leaning back in his chair in his office at a large university, he considers my questions about when and how he first began to consider the Second Amendment as an individual right—one that he would spend much of his life defending in academic literature and in his role on the Board of Trustees of the NRA Civil Rights Defense Fund. Looking at the ceiling, he nods and says:

> I grew up in a time when we were witnessing racial violence unfolding in the South. In that time, I read Robert Williams' book *Negroes with Guns*, and that made a very strong impression on me. I also saw *The Diary of Anne Frank*, and soon after read an article—"What if Otto Frank had had a gun?" I also recall my boyscout handbook had a section on the Bill of Rights, some sort of discussion of the Second Amendment—that it was meant to prevent tyranny. So, I had all these things coming at me, so it must have occurred to me, hey, the right to keep and bear arms is actually a good idea. So, in junior high, when most students were in favor of gun control, I was saying, gee, if I lived in the Mississippi Delta I'd want a gun, especially since the sheriff is probably a member of the Klan.

Listening to Bob reminisce about his childhood, it's easy to imagine the sense of comfort and strength the thought of self-defense would bring to a precocious young boy "witnessing racial violence unfold in the South," especially in light of his reference to Robert Williams. By the time I interviewed Bob, in September 2003, I had read *Negroes with Guns*—I had met Bob earlier that year at an NRA conference in Florida, when he echoed Gary's book recommendation. Williams' biographer Timothy B. Tyson calls *Negroes with Guns* "one of the most telling and important documents of the African American freedom struggle," and documents the "roots of Black Power" in Williams' controversial activism (Tyson 1999). Williams became president of the Monroe, North Carolina chapter of the NAACP in 1957, boosting its dwindling membership. Though Monroe was a small, rural county of about 11,000, Williams' NAACP chapter drew national attention for the causes it championed and Williams' advocacy of armed self-defense in the face of violent attack by white racists. His presidency was suspended by the national office of the NAACP, but he continued its involvement in local desegregation issues, often resulting in intimidation and violence in a county with as many as 7,500 sympathetic to the Klan. After a confrontation with an angry white mob and knowing he was wanted by the FBI, Williams fled, first to Canada, and later to Cuba, where he wrote his treatise, *Negroes with Guns*. In his book, Williams stresses that he does not advocate violence for the sake of violence, nor even reprisals upon white people; indeed, he understands and agrees in principle with the strategy of passive resistance endorsed by Dr Martin Luther King, Jr. and much of the civil rights movement. But he states that:

> the majority of white people in the United States have literally no idea of the violence with which Negroes in the South are treated daily—nay, hourly. This violence is deliberate, conscious, condoned by the authorities ... That is why, one hundred years after the Civil War began, we Negroes in Monroe armed ourselves in self-defense and used our weapons. We showed that policy worked. The lawful authorities of Monroe and North Carolina acted to enforce order only after, and as a direct result of, our being armed. (Williams 1998)

This kind of reasoning appealed not only to people like Bob; according to Tyson, it was the most important intellectual influence on Huey P. Newton and the Black Panther Party for Self-Defense in Oakland, CA. Founded in 1966 by Newton and Bobby Seale, the BPP's original purpose was to patrol black ghettos to protect residents from police brutality. In their "Platform and Program" in October 1966 the Party listed what they wanted and what they believed; calling in item number 7 for the end of police brutality and the murder of black people, they stated that "the Second Amendment to the Constitution of the United States gives us the right to bear arms. We therefore believe that all black people should arm themselves for defense" (Black Panther Party for Self-Defense 2004). The BPP eventually developed a Marxist influenced ideology, and its membership peaked at around 2,000 people; in June 1967, they sent an armed contingent to the state capitol in Sacramento, CA, to protest against a proposed gun-control law and to assert their Second Amendment rights to bear arms against their oppressors.

Throughout all the gun-rights conferences and training workshops I've attended where the claims that gun control is racist are made, no one has ever embraced the BPP action in Sacramento. As Lance Hill writes: "in this narrative Martin Luther King Jr. serves as 'moral metaphor' of the age while black militants—advocates of racial pride and coercive force—are dismissed as ineffective rebels who alienated whites with Black Power rhetoric and violence" (Hill 2004). I was intrigued that Bob so openly admitted being influenced by Williams, as, in my fieldwork experience, the only civil rights leader evoked at gun-rights conferences is Dr King. Though he admires Williams, this does not necessarily extend to those Williams influenced. When I asked Bob about the BPP and whether he considered their activism as an example of an oppressed minority legitimately making gun-rights claims, he says: "No. The Black Panthers are the wrong example. They were a species of street theatre, going around spewing Marxist rhetoric, saying we should kill cops."

Bob's response echoes what I've heard before when I've tried to raise the example with other gun-rights activists. Some powerful intellectuals and lawyers in the gun-rights movement trace their involvement to their days as civil rights workers in the South. They talk bravely of needing protection in the face of the Klan; yet when I ask: "What would you say about a group like the Black Panther Party for Self-Defense?" they shake their heads. A white law professor who first bought a gun for protection as a civil rights worker told me: "The way I think about the Black Panthers is this. Are you standing in your neighborhood with an M16? Look around you. Is everyone in your neighborhood out there with you? No? Well, then go back inside and put your gun away" (fieldnotes, April 26, 2002). According to Bob, the correct example of an African-American claim to the Second Amendment can be found in the Deacons for Defense and Justice. Bob states the Deacons "defended their communities, they defended civil rights workers, with no Marxist rhetoric. And the Klan got the message, which was, if you mess with us, you will find yourself face down in the sugar cane field—and they were turned off by this." Bob's dismissal of the Black Panthers owing to their Marxist ideals and the civil rights lawyer's criticism reveal that, while there may be a salient strand of the gun-rights narrative that states that "gun rights are civil rights," it can only be taken so far.

The repetition of concern over "Marxist rhetoric" reaffirms that the gun-rights cause goes beyond disdain for gun control to wanting to define the proper role of government in Americans' lives, and that this vision is overwhelmingly socially conservative and economically libertarian. For example, at the 2003 GRPC in Houston, Texas, one of the keynote speakers called for the abolition of all federal forms of social security and welfare. Some gun-rights supporters may have some difficulty finding enough common cause with the right-wing leadership of the movement. As Bob, a self-professed liberal democrat, said:

If you translate the pro-gun position to—if being pro-gun means anti-government, or anti-welfare state—well, the federal government has been the fairest employer in my and my parents' lifetime. I'm not against a powerful federal government, so long as it respects civil rights laws. So, the gun-rights movement picked up some baggage that's not always central to the issue, and it may give some people pause. (interview)

Some people wary of the pro-gun lobby might also say that the "gun-control is racist" argument is not relevant today, but Bob is not ready to concede that the struggle is relegated to the past. "I don't blame the duck hunter for not framing the issue in a more sophisticated manner. I blame intellectuals for not asking the question—what in this century makes one think the state should have the monopoly on force?"

Conclusion

Writing in 1985 for the Update of the National Commission on the Causes and Prevention of Violence, Franklin E. Zimring noted that one of the most striking characteristics of the pro- and anti-gun lobbies in the US was their "lily-white leadership." Perhaps more striking, reading it today, is what he wrote next, that "this will change" (Zimring 1985). Applying this to the study of the gun-rights movement means that it is important to ask whether or not the leadership of the gun-control debate, including powerful pro-gun organizations like the NRA and meetings like the Second Amendment Foundation and the Citizen's Committee for the Right to Keep and Bear Arms Gun Rights Policy Conference (GRPC) are indeed still "lily-white." This has been absent from most literature on the gun-control debate, which usually focuses on the efficacy of gun-control provisions rather than on ethnographic research that can explore the various reasons why so many Americans champion the right to keep and bear arms. Though it is well known that pro-gun Americans associate firearms with tools of wholesome sport, recreation and resisting government tyranny (Tonso 1982), many assume that "government tyranny" to be imaginary, a spectre conjured up by racist white men who join anti-government groups. Ethnographic research reveals that while those "angry white men" certainly have their place in the pro-gun cause, they are not the full story. For some, the notion of resisting government oppression is decidedly anti-racist—and not so imaginary, nor so distant.

The profiles presented here of three pro-gun activists illuminate how a version of American history that acknowledges white racism can fit without incongruity into a pro-gun world that usually emphasizes the heroics of the white male—by focusing on the intersection of armed resistance and the Civil Rights era. The issues of race and racism are salient in the gun-rights movement, not only for the black activists I've met, but also for white activists who got involved in gun rights after receiving threats when they were civil rights workers in the South. As unexpected as it may seem, the "myth of nonviolence" surrounding the civil rights movement means people like "Black Man with a Gun" learn black history from the NRA, that activists like Gary still feel alienated from groups like the NAACP, and an academic like Bob urges pro-gun activism based on the strategies of the Civil Rights movement. Thus, the claim that "gun rights are civil rights" is problematic.

On the one hand, by emphasizing individual responsibility to the point of obscuring collective responses to racism and violence, the pro-gun construction of civil rights does not truly embrace the full history of the black freedom struggle like the Black Panther Party for Self-Defense. On the other hand, it challenges those of us who do not champion gun rights with a compelling question: When Americans face systematic racist oppression by the state and fellow citizens, what is their recourse?

CHAPTER 10

"Man to Man": Power and Male Relationships in the Gunplay Film

Robert Arjet

Anyone seeking the essence of the gun-based action film would do well to begin with the last few minutes of 1988's *Die Hard*. Beginning a swift procession of central themes, John McClane, the bruised and bloodied working-class hero, emerges from the destroyed Nakatomi Plaza, the skyscraper headquarters of a Japanese-owned multinational corporation. McClane has just saved his estranged wife from the clutches of a cultured, foreign anti-hero through a spectacular and highly improbable feat of gunplay. Despite the ostensive primacy of the boy-loses-girl, boy-kills-villain, boy-gets-girl-back plot, the heterosexual relationship is immediately overshadowed by a series of male–male interactions as the white McClane and his African-American buddy Sgt Powell finally consummate their relationship with a hug; the arrogant yet astoundingly incompetent Deputy Police Chief angrily confronts McClane; and Karl, the villain's presumed-dead right-hand-man, appears from the rubble to menace McClane with a sub-machine-gun (at which point McClane literally pushes his wife out of the action). Sgt Powell then kills Karl, thus completing his transformation from feminized, twinkie-eating, overweight, non-gun-using man to (under McClane's influence) a steely-eyed, unflinching man-with-a-gun.

Die Hard is a classic example of what could be called the "gunplay film," a type of film that is often derided as "just stupid." In these films, neither guns nor the people who wield them behave realistically, plots are simple and predictable, and the largest part of the appeal appears to be in watching men killing each other and blowing things up.

Yet, while all these observations are true, three important points argue against the judgment of "just stupid." First, gunplay films make a great deal of sense when understood as a form of modern mythology—ideological allegories in the service of violent masculinity. Second, the behaviors of the characters in these films make a great deal more sense when viewed with the understanding that these movies are primarily about male relationships—violent, homosocial relationships mediated predominantly through gunplay. Finally, while guns do not behave in movies in the same ways that they do on the streets, they do in fact behave in certain predictable and revealing ways in gunplay films. They behave in ways appropriate to their role as tools with which men negotiate violent, homosocial relationships.

In fact, studying the discrepancies in behavior between guns in movies and firearms in real life warrants the use of two entirely different terms for two functionally separate objects—one physical and empirically understandable and the other constructed of imagination and fantasy.

"Firearms," then, are material objects that can be bought, sold, carried and fired. These items are used to produce around 130,000 deaths and injuries in the United States every year, and behave in fairly predictable ways bounded by physics and probability.

"Guns," however, are totemic symbols that movies exalt and men desire. They are objects of fantasy—ideas. Men can think about, desire, and imagine guns, but what they can actually purchase, carry and/or use are firearms.[1]

And while guns are at least theoretically gender-neutral, the truth is that over 90 per cent of the people who kill with firearms are men (US Department of Justice 2006). In mainstream entertainment narratives, a man with a gun is a given[2]—a movie about a woman with a gun is remarkable.[3] In the journals of the gun culture (*Combat Handguns*, *Guns*, *Guns and Ammo*, etc.) and in the stories and images of guns that perfuse US culture, women are virtually non-existent.

Yet the relationship of masculinity to violence—including movie violence—remains somewhat of a cultural blind spot. The violence researchers Zimring and Hawkins argue that "Firearms use is so predominantly associated with the high death rate from violence that starting with any other topic would rightly be characterized as an intentional evasion" (Zimring and Hawkins 1997). Evading the question of men—and their attitudes towards guns—would seem to be at least as negligent.

Men, Movies, and Myths

If we take "mythic" to mean those qualities of a story that predispose hearers and viewers to understand that story as a description of the world, an argument about how it works, and a prescription for what to do about it, gun narratives are without a doubt important myths of our time. Laden with ideological baggage, these films enact parables of a world in which masculinity and violence conquer all.

Like the myth itself, violence can be understood "not as a given function of human nature, but as an artifact embodying ideological assumptions" (Sharret 1999). Like actual violence, representations of violence always mean something—there can be no such thing as "senseless violence," just as there is no such thing as "senseless tourism" or a "senseless hairstyle." Violence is a signifying practice, whether or not its perpetrators want it to be. People undertake violent acts at specific times, in specific ways, for specific reasons. It is the job of the observer to ask: "Why this violence, in this story, in this way?" "Why these particular weapons?" "Why these responses?"

Even more than real-world violence, representations of violence are artefacts of ideology. They are far more under the control of their creators, and they will always bear the traces of the ideology that guided their creation. If "violence itself is a means of signifying, ordering and understanding" (Slocum 1995), it is incumbent on us to decipher the ways that violence structures particular narratives, and to understand the reasons why those narratives, in which violence plays that particular role, have become so popular in our time.

To begin with, action films play out the fantasies of masculine power that underlie US gun culture. Gunplay films both explicitly and implicitly construct male behavior and relationships that are based on dominance, homosociality, and violence. In so doing, they dramatize the relationships that are at the root of the majority of actual firearms violence. Gunplay films spend a great deal of time and energy constructing and representing male relationships in particular ways, usually overshadowing the heterosexual relationships of the films. Because gunplay films make such a central concern of male relationships, they can be seen as mirroring—and perhaps influencing—changing beliefs about men and guns in the US.

A Brief History of Gunplay

As a subgenre, the Hollywood gunplay film rose to its height in the 1980s and early 1990s. It remains one of the clearest and most emphatic manifestations of the "cultural crises" about both masculinity and violence itself, having undergone a remarkable series of changes in the years between the 1960s and the 1990s. From the revolutionary violence of *Bonnie and Clyde* and *The Wild Bunch* to the semi-Fascist posturings of *Dirty Harry*, the post-Vietnam wish-fulfillment of Rambo's adventures in Indochina and Afghanistan, and the racial politics of *Die Hard* and *Lethal Weapon*, gunplay films have always portrayed brave men with guns engaging in struggles that speak to the fears and anxieties of their relentlessly male audiences.

The social turmoils of the years between 1967 and 1971 are well documented, and often commented on in relationship to profound changes in the ways that Americans thought about and experienced both violence and masculinity.[4] Race riots, the anti-war movement, assassinations, women's liberation, and rising crime rates fueled a general sense of uncertainty and anxiety in the mainstream and a new breed of film in which the streets were mean, power corrupted, and the triumph of good over evil was ambiguous at best.

Any discussion of gun violence in movies must make reference to two films of this period: *The Wild Bunch* and *Bonnie and Clyde*. These films receive virtually universal credit for revolutionizing the portrayal of film violence, and on their heels came a string of films that further signaled a watershed in the ways that the

United States looked—both thematically and stylistically—at violence on film: *Dirty Harry*, *Sweet Sweetback's Baadasssss Song*, *Shaft*, *The French Connection*, and *Straw Dogs* (all 1971).

By 1973, *Magnum Force* had repeated the success of Dirty Harry, the original "renegade cop" character. By 1976, *Death Wish* and *Taxi Driver* portrayed vigilantes who struck out against mugging and child prostitution in decaying inner cities. The white US mainstream was in the grips of an identity crisis, and old ideologies of just and legal violence were beginning to look weak and falsely optimistic. This "post-Vietnam" era—named literally for what was lost—would give rise to a new generation of gunplay films during the years of America's ideological reconsolidation under Ronald Reagan (Slotkin 1992).

The 1980s saw the height of the gunplay film. The backlash against all that the Vietnam era had come to signify was in full swing, and the revitalization of the white male as both victim and hero was well under way. The year 1982 saw *48 Hrs*, the first comedy-action interracial buddy film. By 1983, *Uncommon Valor* began the re-fighting of the Vietnam War, and *Scarface* once again upped the ante on film violence.

In 1985, *To Live and Die in L.A.* made an unabashed appeal for style as substance, *Commando* created the blueprint for male rivalry and gun fetishization, and *Rambo: First Blood Part II* turned a somewhat thoughtful film about the plight of veterans (*First Blood*) into a celebration of destructive force, masculine rage and the bitter, unconnected, tragically ennobled "new warrior."[5] In 1986, films like *Raw Deal* and *Cobra* showed that the genre had stabilized enough to produce relentlessly predictable films that can still draw an audience on cable over a decade later. In 1987, the beginning of the tremendously popular and influential *Lethal Weapon* series ensured that gunplay films would be part of the landscape for years to come.

These films showed independent, "clear-thinking" men who valued action (violence) above words, and, we can assume, would never have lost a war in Vietnam, tolerated a race riot, or allowed the (limited) legal, social and economic enfranchisement of millions of women, ethnic minorities, and homosexuals to challenge the dominance of the white patriarchy. The gunplay films of the 1980s gave a mainstream still reeling from the Iran hostage crisis, the energy crisis, and any number of profound social and economic changes a vision of the kind of men it would take to put America "back on track."

By 1990, however, the cultural wing of the "Reagan Revolution" was beginning to unravel, and at least some of the films that portrayed gun violence began to reflect (and perhaps shape) a growing sophistication and/or discontent.

Films like 1991's *Boyz N the Hood* and 1993's *Menace II Society* insisted on the squalor, fruitlessness, and banality of firearms violence. Gunplay in these films is—realistically—short, ugly, and between African-American teenage boys. This type of gunplay does not restore social order, punish the guilty, or validate masculinity. As in real life, it kills the guilty and innocent alike while perpetuating a dysfunctional social order based on male violence.

At almost the same time, a trio of films by two up-and-coming white directors would challenge the representation of violence that had solidified since *The Wild Bunch*. Quentin Tarantino's *Reservoir Dogs* and *Pulp Fiction*, and Oliver Stone's *Natural Born Killers* argued for a new understanding that violence was always subject to manipulation and that even the most shocking acts of cruelty could be filmed in such a way as to render them entertaining.[6]

Finally, in the late 1990s, the Hong Kong influence that had paved the way for martial arts stars-turned-gunplay heroes (Steven Segal, Chuck Norris, Jean-Claude Van Damme) found a mainstream audience in films like *Face/Off* (1997), *The Matrix* (1999) and *Mission: Impossible 2* (2000). These hybrids celebrated the beauty and dynamism of choreographed violence over its effects, and suggested that the gun did not have to be the central trope of violence in the US film. To a large extent, the era of the gunplay film was over.[7]

Guns, Power, and "Working Stiffs"

Gunplay films, in which guns are indispensable to masculine identities and relationships, depict explicitly what must be understood implicitly in other forms of US gun culture. Within the world of the gunplay film, guns act as tools not primarily for affecting the world around the user, but for negotiating violent, homosocial, power-based relationships with other men.

The power that flows through guns in action films has particular forms and expressions. However, any power that a man wields in a gunplay film—whether sexual, familial or legal in origin—must eventually be proved or defended by engaging in gunplay with other men. This is the central truth of the gunplay film, and one vigorously propagated by the gun culture at large: nothing that a man has—not his possessions, not his family, not his power—is truly his unless he can defend it in gun combat with other men.

Not only a tool for channeling power, however, the gun is depicted as having physical power in and of itself. In purely physical terms, the power of an actual firearm can be described accurately in terms of foot-pounds of force released by the rapid expansion of combustion gases caused by the burning of the propellant in the cartridges. These are reproducible measurements, ones that testify to the concrete reality of the firearm.

The physical power of the gun, however, is portrayed through its effects: its ability to knock people down, shatter windows, detonate gas tanks, destroy furniture, and otherwise affect the physical world in spectacular ways. While these visual and auditory signs of the gun's power are often wildly exaggerated, it should be noted that they are almost as often wildly downplayed. When the plot and or theme call for it, weapons that possess great destructive potential in lived experience are proved completely ineffectual. Heroes run through withering fire that would cut down entire platoons, incapacitating bullet wounds to the shoulder are effectively healed with improvised bandages (or ignored entirely, as in *Die Hard*), and car tires show astounding resistance to puncture. The physical power of the gun serves only to magnify and channel the ideological power of the gunplay hero.

Thus, in order to understand power in the gunplay film, it should be remembered that these films rose dramatically in popularity at a time when mainstream white men in the US increasingly shared a sense of helplessness and impotence, a belief that the privileges and comforts that had belonged to their fathers by right were beyond their grasp (Savran 1998). A large part of this change in expectations came from economic shifts that de-skilled entire industries and shrank what little autonomy the average worker may have had in the 1970s. In apparent response to this lack of agency, gunplay films prominently feature white men—very often coded as "working stiffs"—struggling against an overwhelming bureaucracy, an unsympathetic boss, or duplicitous government agents—sometimes all three.

In films like *Dirty Harry*, *Rambo II*, *Die Hard*, *Raw Deal*, *Above the Law*, and *Hard to Kill*, unpretentious, working-class-identified heroes must struggle against power structures that are incompetent at best, and corrupt at worst.[8] Personified by grinning, cultured villains and bumbling, rule-bound bosses, these authority figures must be either convinced of the hero's righteousness through heroic gunplay or killed in the same manner—the power to confront oppressive authority must be channeled through gunplay.

The overwhelming forces facing these "regular guys" also frequently take the form of the vast numbers and impossible armaments of their adversaries. In *Boyz N the Hood* and *Menace II Society* men either attack each other one at a time, in small, fairly evenly matched groups, or in ruthless and one-sided "drive-by" assassinations. This is the way that modern criminal firearms violence has regularly occurred, even at the height of Los Angeles "gang warfare." In most gunplay films, however, the hero—alone or accompanied only by his buddy— must take on anywhere from ten to several dozen enemies in the course of the story. With a gun in his hand, the gunplay hero faces down the impossible odds, and by sheer dint of his heroic mastery of the gun, performs the impossible.

In one particularly extreme example, *Above the Law*'s Nico Toscani (Steven Segal) sits in his car as assassins, armed with fully automatic weapons, march five abreast towards him. In a sequence that is equal parts Odessa Steps and the *Wild Bunch*'s "long march," they advance on him, emptying their guns into his car. Nico—armed with only a pistol—not only emerges from the car unscathed, but, by outflanking the enemy, captures all five of them. Gun in hand, the gunplay hero lives out a fantasy of total power and total invulnerability. His enemies are powerless to harm him, his power to harm them unlimited. In this way, scenes of gunplay present a counter-narrative of competence and efficacy in the face of overwhelming odds.

The significant strides of women's rights during the 1970s are reflected in the roles that women play in the gunplay films. Although these films are replete with scenes in which men exert their power over women, the homosocial structure of the relationships within these films requires that power over women always translates into power over other men. The heterosexual relationships in films such as *Cobra*, *Magnum Force*, and *Hard to Kill* generally have very little to do with a mature or even credible heterosexual relationship, and everything to do with the hero's definition as (hetero)sexually potent (*Year of the Dragon*, *Hard to Kill*, *48 Hrs*), the denial of desire in the homosocial relationship (*New Jack City*, *To Live and Die in L.A*), and/or the negotiation of a male rivalry over or through a woman's body (*Scarface*, *Raw Deal*, *Terminator*, *Mission: Impossible 2*, *Menace II Society*, *Cobra*, *Lethal Weapon II*, *Die Hard*, etc.).[9]

One particular dynamic between men and women in these movies aptly demonstrates the homosocial nature of gun violence, and could be termed the "Now will you listen?" scene. This is the scene in which gunfire erupts in such a way as to show a resistant woman the futility of arguing with men who wield guns. One of the best examples comes from *Hard to Kill*, in which Mason Storm has awakened from a coma and tries to convince his attending nurse that they are in mortal danger. She doubts his word and tries to calm him, until the gunmen burst into the ward, firing wildly. He orchestrates an escape, and, in a moment of relative safety, he demands of her, "Now will you listen to me?"

The power that men wield over women must always be supported by resort to gunplay, because the power that men wield over women in a homosocial structure is only a measure of their power in relation to other men; and in gunplay films power between men always devolves to the level of the gun. All the myriad forms that vanquished assailants take, all the many, many ways that gunplay heroes demonstrate their competence all boil down to the same proposition: the hero has power over other men. With this power, all other benefits are possible—wealth, prestige, comfort, public vindication, moral redemption, sex with beautiful women, a happy family life. Nothing is beyond the capabilities of a man who can defeat other men in gunplay. Without this power, there is only death at best, humiliation and feminization at worst.

Guns, Power, and Male Relationships

The gun's exaggerated power to affect physical objects (bodies, cars, windows, helicopters, etc.) and to influence relationships with women notwithstanding, the most important power these films depict is the gun's ability to affect male relationships.

The gun's importance to male relationships in these films cannot be overemphasized. Guns—and only guns—allow men to enter into significant relationships and negotiate those relationships during the course of the action. Without a weapon, men simply don't count. Because gun violence is the method of negotiating male relationships, the unarmed man is simply cut out of the relationships, relegated to the group that includes women, children, hostages, suitcases of money, and other inanimate objects.

A disarmed man is virtually voiceless in the gunplay film. The disarming of a common gunman is the narrative equivalent of killing him, and the disarming of the hero creates a tension and anxiety that can only be relieved when the unarmed hero re-acquires a weapon and begins to use it again. These "disarmed hero" scenes are ubiquitous, and some of the more notable can be seen in *Rambo II*, *True Lies*, *Above the Law*, *Under Siege*, *The Last Boy Scout*, *Die Hard*, and *Lethal Weapon*. The moment when the disarmed hero re-acquires a weapon is narratively akin to that resounding moment when Popeye opens a can of spinach or Clark Kent pulls aside his drab suit and tie to reveal the scarlet, blue, and gold of his Superman costume. It is an assurance that a violent but righteous man is again in the action, and that he will prevail in the end. A hero with a gun can enter into and negotiate relationships with other men, and that is the essence of the gunplay film.

As in the gunplay film, men in real life negotiate and re-negotiate their relationships constantly. Deliberate firearms injury (excluding suicide) almost always results from a failure of two men to negotiate a relationship non-violently. That relationship may be between friends, relatives, or bar-room adversaries, but the relationship between the two men determines, at least in part, whether and how firearms will be used. Gunplay films take this to the extreme: not only is virtually all gun violence the result of male relationships, but men construct and illustrate their relationships almost exclusively through the use of guns.

This particular type of gun-mediated masculinity owes a large cinematic debt to the story of Travis Bickle. After *Wild Bunch*, but before *Rambo*, *Taxi Driver*'s crazed loner and his obsession with gun violence coined a new set of clichés about how men relate to and through guns—unfortunately, while *Taxi Driver* appeared to be critiquing these relationships, the gunplay films that followed chose to valorize and celebrate them.

Even a superficial comparison of *Taxi Driver* to a film like *Hard to Kill* shows that Mason Storm in 1990 was following closely in Travis Bickle's 1976 footsteps. Both men train in montage, acquire guns, and slowly prepare themselves to wreak havoc on other men. The difference, of course, is that *Taxi Driver* portrays Travis Bickle as a pathetic and disturbed man whose violent relationships with other men exist primarily in his mind, while *Hard to Kill* portrays Mason Storm as the kind of upstanding citizen who can uphold the law, dish out retribution, ferret out corruption, and walk off into the sunset with a reconstituted nuclear family.

Of particular interest is the fact that *Taxi Driver* appeared immediately after the United States' final defeat in Vietnam, but a few years before the beginning of the gunplay film boom. Travis Bickle offers a thoughtful and troubling representation of white male violence at the opening of the post-Vietnam era. Soon to be eclipsed by Rambo and the Terminator, Travis Bickle shows the dark side of fantasies of male violence. Much of *Taxi Driver* is given over to the complex acts of self-construction through gun-performance that gunplay movies would soon come to valorize.

The most famous of these acts of self-construction is of course, the mirror scene. Bickle culminates his transformation into gunplay hero with a performance in which he confronts/constructs himself as enemy, audience, and performer. Standing in front of the mirror, he asks himself, "You talkin' to me?" and answers "Well, I'm the only one here, who the fuck do you think *you're* talkin' to?" before he draws his pistol and dry-fires at his reflection. Bickle performs a bizarre act of self-construction through which he bootstraps himself into a valid existence via an imagined male relationship—mediated with a gun—in which he is both hero and anti-hero, aggressor and victim. That famous scene is not just about the insanity of mass-murderers: it is a diagram of the way that guns and relationships interact to construct violent masculinities.

Why Straight White Men Use Guns

The special relationship between guns and masculinity comes further into focus if we look at who uses guns and who doesn't. Despite the real-world prevalence of any number of alternative weapons, the gun is the only truly fit weapon for the mainstream white male action hero. The horror film, on the other hand, is clearly the province of the knife, with other edged weapons falling in behind. Scissors, shards of glass, pitchforks, and razors have all seen great use in horror films; but it is virtually impossible to find a horror film in which a monstrous "other" stalks and kills his intended prey with a gun. Despite the relative efficacy of the gun to the knife (or shard of glass, etc.) the truly horrible, the feminine monstrous, almost invariably uses an edged weapon.[10] Almost any other tool is acceptable—the chainsaw, the meat hook, the electric drill; but not the gun.

The reason may well be that the gun is symbolically the province of the masculine white male. Knives are the province of monsters (*Halloween*), sexual "deviants" (*Psycho, Cruising*) women (*Fatal Attraction*), and feminized ethnic minorities (*The French Connection*). From at least the mid-nineteenth century, however, the physical ability to handle a firearm has been connected with masculine power in the popular imagination of the United States. Simply put, straight white men use guns.

Seeing what makes the gun so suitable for the channeling of male power requires a look at the ways in which the knife (ice-pick, shard of glass, etc.) is inferior. To use the knife, the attacker must come into physical contact with the victim. This doesn't just mean that a knife-wielding attacker must cross the room and approach to an extremely close distance. It means that the attacker must physically bring the knife, an extension of his hand, into contact with the victim's body, and then into the body itself. Even without the other forms of bodily contact that might ensue (punching, grappling, torso-to-torso contact, etc.,) the knife generates a certain anxiety because it requires that the attacker become physically intimate with the victim in a way that boils down to one man touching another man in an attempt to penetrate his body.[11] This would seem to present difficulties for the constructions of homosocial masculinity that are at the heart of the gunplay film.

Another way of phrasing it is that the intimacy required by the knife (shard of glass, ice pick) doesn't allow for the projection of the attacker's power. Guns are terrifically important as a means to channel and project the power of men across distance. If the attacker must physically cross the room and touch his victim, the essential masculine traits of singularity and hard boundaries are threatened. Evidence of this are the innumerable scenes where knifes are employed as missile weapons, spinning improbably through the air to kill the victim from a considerable—and decidedly non-intimate—distance.

Another failing of the knife is that it requires a much more visible penetration of the victim's body by the attacker than does the gun. However much can be said about the desire to penetrate displayed by gun users, there is a strong—and squeamish—resistance to the idea of a hero who thrusts a steel phallic symbol into his victim (Grossman 1995). While a bullet must certainly penetrate the body of the victim in order to cause harm, it does not do so in a manner visually similar to that of the knife. Although squibs are used to show their effects, the bullets themselves are not shown striking the body and penetrating the victim's flesh. There is a spray of blood, the body recoils, and the victim falls.

Knives, however, do not disappear like bullets—they are not invisible phallic power. Bullets are too fast to be seen, too deadly to be resisted, they can't be blocked, parried, or dodged. Knives, by comparison are much cruder in their visibility. Where bullets deny both visibility and tangibility, knives make masculine power tangible and visible, and force a visual depiction of masculine penetration that seems perhaps too graphic and explicit for the homosocial logic of the gunplay film. Like homosocial relationships themselves, the knife makes explicit and messy what the gun keeps implied and "clean." Asking the Terminator to use a knife[12] is akin to asking Batman and Robin to have an open and frank discussion about their relationship. The prevailing logic seems to be: "We all know it, we just don't talk about it."[13]

Guns prevent the intimate contact between male bodies required by knife fighting. The gun stands in for all the power of the male bodies in close proximity and then adds powers of its own. Gunfights remove the male body from the center of the narrative, and displace the homoeroticism and homosociality yet another step.

The gun's unique suitability as a channel for white male power can be further examined by asking the question: "Who has the gun?" While the answer might seem to be "everyone," a careful answer reveals the peculiar connection between masculinized white males and guns.

48 Hrs and *Die Hard*, for instance, both feature African-American men who are disarmed, either literally or figuratively, and are then re-armed by their white police buddies. In *48 Hrs*, much of the banter between Hammond and Cates concerns whether Cates—a white police officer—will allow Hammond—an

African-American convicted felon—to carry a gun. *Die Hard* reaches its putative climax when John McClane rescues his estranged wife from the anti-hero; but there is more tension, heroic music, and a greater sense of resolution moments later when the African-American Sgt Powell finally finds himself able to draw his gun and kill Karl, the anti-hero's right-hand-man, in order to save McClane's life.

The question of who will be allowed to bear arms in time of cinematic crisis goes all the way back to *Birth of a Nation*, and appears famously in *Stage Coach*.[14] Although outlaws and convicted felons may be allowed access to firearms, women—and feminized men—rarely wield guns effectively. Although there are clearly exceptions, they are few and far between, and like *The Long Kiss Goodnight* or *GI Jane*, many of them become films that are very much *about* the fact that a woman has effective access to a gun. On the rare occasions in gunplay films when women carry guns, they generally either fail to use them effectively (*True Lies*) or are conveniently incapacitated well before the narrative climax (*Above the Law, Rambo II, Falling Down*).

Unarmed feminized men, however, are abundant in the gunplay film. The lone Chinese-American (virtually always a feminized ethnicity) in the police team in *Year of the Dragon* is not only introduced on the firing range, where he demonstrates his ineptitude with a gun, but dies unarmed and running away, living only long enough to whisper his crucial information to the white, male hero. In *Lethal Weapon 2*, Riggs and Murtaugh team up with the mob informant Leo Getz, but make it clear that the short, stereotypically Jewish, and extremely feminized Getz has no business with a gun. Getz does the men's laundry, appears in an apron to vacuum Riggs's mobile home, and—perhaps most damning—insists on hugging the two partners. The men's refusal to provide Leo with a weapon is a running source of homophobic and misogynist humor in the film.

The corrupt federal prosecutor in *Raw Deal* does receive a gun from the hero, but he cannot use it effectively, and dies quickly. After the wrathful former FBI agent Mark Kaminsky has rampaged through the mob headquarters killing everyone in sight, the prosecutor gives himself away by crying—an exceedingly rare display of emotion in these films. Kaminsky realizes that the prosecutor has been working for the mob, and offers him the traditional option of killing himself to escape further dishonor. The prosecutor, however, is not manly enough to take the honorable course, and attempts to shoot Kaminsky. Of course he fails, and Kaminisky kills him immediately.

Hard to Kill goes even farther. Mason Storm's final confrontation with the corrupt (and feminized) Senator Vernon Trent is not a gun battle, a *kung-fu* match, or a knife fight, but a humiliating game of hide and seek. Storm stalks through the senator's house, taunting him with a sing-song "Oh, Vernon, Verrrrnon ... ." When Storm finds him, Trent is wearing a dress-like bathrobe. Storm effortlessly disarms him, and then violently shoves a sawed-off shotgun into his mouth. Storm pretends to castrate Trent with the shotgun, taunts him about the size of his testicles, but does not kill him. Instead, Storm concocts a punishment far worse, a punishment that mobilizes racism and homophobia to torment the captured senator with an extravagant feminization:

> I'd like to kill you so bad I can barely contain myself. But I've been thinking, death is far too merciful a fate for you. So, what I'm gonna do is put you in prison. Nice petite white boy like you, in a federal penitentiary, well, let me just put it this way: I don't think you'll be able to remain anal retentive for very long.

Gun Violence as an Emotional Shortcut

In the end there is one purpose of the gun in male relationships that stands out as possibly the most harmful. Dysfunctional, homosocial, and misogynist as they may be, many of the relationships depicted in these films are intimate ones, relationships in which men embrace, profess their love, care for each other, and find trust, respect, and sympathy. Repeatedly, however, gunplay stands in for the real emotional work that actually produces intimacy in relationships. As different as the *Lethal Weapon* series may seem from films like *Crimes of the Heart, Steel Magnolias,* or *Terms of Endearment,* they do share a common concern with the working-out of important relationships. In gunplay films, however, the gun and its use usurp the place of the hard emotional work that "chick flicks" so painstakingly portray.

In place of confession, tears, arguments, and emotional confrontations, films like *Lethal Weapon 2* use gunplay. At the end of the film, a voice-over of Riggs calls the names of some seven people whose deaths he is avenging as he empties a (seemingly endless) clip of ammunition into a hapless thug. In the few days that the film covers, Riggs and Murtaugh lose five work buddies to the villains, and Riggs not only loses his new lover, but also learns that the villains were responsible for his wife's death years earlier.

The emotional toll of this kind of loss would be disastrous to characters in most narratives, on a par with the tragic carnage of *King Lear* or *Hamlet.* In tragic narrative, this kind of loss causes emotional devastation and intense grief, and is shown to have terrible consequences. Yet *Lethal Weapon 2* does not end like a Greek or Shakespearean tragedy, with Sgt Riggs ending his own life or tearing out his eyes in desperation. In fact, the film ends on a cheerful note, with the buddies making good-natured homophobic banter about the tender embrace that they share in the closing shot.

This is only possible because Riggs and Murtaugh have used the power of the gun as a shortcut to emotional work. Both the emotional work of grieving for overwhelming losses and the emotional work of bonding between partners is performed through gunplay.

The narrative/emotional logic is clear. All the emotional repercussions of seven close losses are cleared away by the purifying deaths of the anti-hero, his right-hand-man, and his thugs (in reverse order, of course). No extended period of deep grieving, no psychological counseling is necessary, because all the villains are dead and the two heroes are alive. The score has been settled, and because it comes out in favor of the heroes (even if just barely), there is no thought given to the empty desks at work that Riggs and Murtaugh will face in the morning.

Even the horrifying truth about Riggs's wife can be swept under the carpet by the emotional power of the gun. The premise of the first *Lethal Weapon* is that Riggs's grief over his wife's death in a car accident is so overwhelming that he is on the brink of suicide and actively seeks out opportunities to die in the course of his police work. In *Lethal Weapon 2*, the right-hand-man tells Riggs with sadistic glee that his wife was not the victim of a drunk driver, as had been believed, but that he had personally killed her in an attempt on Riggs. As devastating as this news might be, it is cancelled out in the orgy of killing that makes up the film's third act. Starting with the thugs who tried to kill him, Riggs works his way through the villains until, together with Murtaugh, he finally kills them all. His wife's death thus avenged through gunplay, Riggs' deep emotional suffering—so integral to the first film—is canceled out. It would seem that the greatest overstatement of the power of the gun is not, after all, in terms of physical power—detonating gas tanks, blowing holes in walls, etc.—but in terms of emotional power—the power to cancel out grief, bind men together, and heal deep psychological wounds.

In the end, gunplay films tell us that the world of men (the only world that counts) is a world of homosocial relationships negotiated through violence; that guns are the only way to enter into and negotiate these relationships; and that people without firearms are of no consequence to these relationships. The "senseless violence" of gunplay films is anything but. Violence is never "senseless"—people understand it both as having an effect on the physical world and as producing social meaning. Gunplay films harness the power of mythology and fantasy to the very real dangers of firearms violence in US society to craft fables of simple-but-violent masculinity triumphing over wealth, power, treachery, femininity, weakness, and doubt. In clear and predictable ways, gunplay films create the fetishized object called a "gun" to channel the hero's masculine superiority over his rivals and to cement his relationships with his buddies.

Exactly how these processes work merits a great deal of further study. As studies of pornography have greatly enriched our understanding of the ways in which women are constructed (and commodified) as sexual objects, gunplay films and other "action" genres have much to teach us about the ways in which men are constructed as inherently violent beings, as well as helping us to understand the peculiar power that guns have over men—both in this US society and around the world.

Part III

Playing, Dancing, and Thinking with Guns

CHAPTER 11

Aiming for Manhood: The Transformation of Guns into Objects of American Masculinity

Amy Ann Cox

While the debate continues over the actual use of guns during the first few centuries of American development, questions regarding the cultural meaning of gun use and ownership continue to be neglected (Bellesiles 2000, 2002; Gruber 2002; Lindgren 2002; Main 2002; Rakove 2002a,b; Roth 2002). Understanding the cultural messages attached to guns provides a window into comprehending more fully firearm ownership and use. It might also assist in explaining changes in gun-ownership rates during certain periods, and firearm purchasing patterns. Many contemporary gun-owners associate certain values with their own gun ownership, many of which they view as arising from American history (Kohn 2004: 17, 103–6). Also, the values and meanings attached to guns affect readings of the second amendment (Dorf 2002; Finkleman 2002; Rakove 2002a,b; Schwoerer 2000; Spitzer 2002). This chapter specifically examines the transformation of guns from a multipurpose tool that assisted in the performance of masculine tasks to a cultural symbol of masculinity by examining how these changes affected New England men from the colonial period to the mid-nineteenth century.

A recent study of American gun culture probed the cultural meanings attached to guns today and discovered that gun owners view many of the ideals strongly associated with guns as having historical roots. These shooters believe that: "guns signify American core values: freedom, independence, individualism, and equality," and that "being a gun owner means being a good American" (Kohn 2004:17). Also, male shooters see "familiarity with guns as the status quo for American manhood." They portrayed gun use in terms of a rite of passage into manhood and keeping a gun for defensive purposes as a partial fulfillment of their male responsibility as fathers and husbands (Kohn 2004: 17, 105–6).

Using guns to assist in the fulfillment of masculine duties certainly has roots in the colonial period, a time when guns—serving as tools to accomplish manly endeavors—implicitly contributed to colonial ideas about manliness. However, many of the manly tasks that guns supported might also be accomplished using other tools. As conditions in the colonies began to change, particularly with the rhetoric of the Revolution, gun use became increasingly symbolic, associated with a wider range of often masculine values, especially liberty, freedom, and independence. Still, guns did not uniquely symbolize these values, as swords continued to be especially popular as a representation of military might (Olson 1991). The gun first becomes explicitly and uniquely tied to American notions of manliness and freedom after the War of 1812, when popular narratives celebrated the triumph of the common man with his gun. This change is particularly evident in the creation of American mythology and national character. Changes in the construction of masculinity allowed this shift in gun meaning to occur as earlier views of "family and community centered manhood" gave way to a manliness that turned on the individual and his accomplishments. This newer construction allowed for objects to have a much greater role in creating masculine identity, and this, along with a historical setting that celebrated gun use, created an atmosphere in which guns might confer manliness upon their owners and users.

In the colonial period the meanings that we attribute to guns today were implicitly expressed, as guns functioned in men's lives to support activities that contributed to their understandings of manliness. Manly worth in New England was derived from family relationships and responsibilities, best demonstrated by how well a man controlled himself and those under his care (Lombard 2003: 9, 18; Wilson 1999: 2). Masculinity was framed by relationships with others, and a man without power in a home, an "insufficient husband," also became an "inadequate member of society" (Wilson 1999: 97). In fact, in order to achieve manhood, a man was expected to pursue the acceptable course of marriage and parenthood and supervise a disciplined household, and thus to uphold the prevailing notions of a well-ordered society. A good society featured "rational, moral husbands at its core, ruling over, providing for, and planning for women and children, who lacked control over their appetites and passions" (Lombard 2003: 119). Only within the framework of the family, a context interwoven with manliness, might men become masculine through their successful provision, leadership, and constant utility. For men, creating a family represented not only an important prerequisite for achieving manhood, but also the development of the vehicle from which all manliness originated (Lombard 2003: 3–4, 97).

Within the context of manliness constructed by the completion of duties within family relationships, guns could only serve as a tool or a prop for achieving manliness. With manliness conferred within communal relationships, few material items could serve to bestow male identity, with the exception of the clothing that differentiated the sexes. Thus guns were not critical to the male quest to protect and provide for family and community, although they certainly remained very much a masculine tool, as the functions guns served fell solely under the purview of men.

Provision of food might utilize guns, as New England men hunted, especially fowl, to feed their families. Yet with the exception of the earliest periods before the establishment of animal husbandry, men did not rely on hunted animals as a main source of meat, but rather used them as a supplement (Baker 1984: 109; Coe and Coe 1984: 42; Derven 1984: 55; Hooker 1981: 54; McMahon 1985: 26–38). Thus hunting may have been an enjoyable activity that produced useful benefits. Whether or not men shot animals because they needed, rather than desired, the birds or deer they brought home, hunting allowed them to put even more food on their tables. A seventeenth-century writer reported "some have killed a hundred geese in a week, fifty ducks at a shot, forty teals at another, it may be counted impossible though nothing more certain" (Benson 1937: 23). Such quantities of birds would certainly have added greatly to tables in the earliest settlement efforts. In 1736, John Jenks of Lynn shot six wild turkeys that he found among his corn. The account of Jenks's killing "five [turkeys] upon the spot" and wounding another indicates he had with him the scatter shot most effective for use in killing birds for sport or pest control (*Boston Evening Post:* October 11, 1736). He came to the field prepared to shoot, even if he did not arrive at work intending to do so. In any case, guns assisted men in providing their households with a nutritious diet and allowed them to add some variation to the standard fare derived from farming and animal husbandry.

Accounts of gun use in the colonial period demonstrate that men kept guns to aid in farming and to protect their property, another key factor in determining their abilities to provide for their families. The Boston newspapers carried stories of men facing off against wild animals to protect their livestock. In 1730, a man awakened during the night to the cries of his swine. He found a wild animal among them and, with his dogs, chased it up a tree. He then built a fire near it, and left two women to watch it while he went and fetched a gun-owning neighbor. They used the gun to bring the animal, a large panther, down from the tree and to kill it (*Boston News Letter:* February 19, 1720 and July 4, 1765; *The Boston Gazette:* January 29, 1739). Guns also assisted in protecting crops from birds or squirrels, either by scaring them off or by dispatching with them altogether (Benson 1937: 168, 249). In fact, protecting livestock appears to have been a major reason for owning a gun. In James Lindgren and Justin L. Heather's (2002: 1806) assessment of gun-ownership in early America, they found that "60% of estates that list livestock also list guns, compared to only 22% of estates not owning livestock—owning livestock being a strong indicator of current (rather than past) farming activity." Clearly people who husbanded animals and cultivated crops found guns to be very useful, everyday tools.

Men also utilized guns to protect their families and communities from physical harm, another important masculine duty. Burglars and other intruders posed a threat to colonists, who often had to rely on their own defenses in such cases. In February of 1680, Dyer, a man in Braintree, shot and killed an Indian "as he was breaking his window and attempting to get into his House against his will." By shooting the Indian he not only protected his property from an intruder but likely saved his own life or the life of one of his family: the Indian's gun was "found charg'd, cockt and prim'd in his Hand" (Robey 1972 Vol. 2: 15). A man's obligation to defend his home and family went beyond mere protection from threats within his property borders. In the aftermath of a robbery, a man, joined by members of his community, utilizing firearms, might chase down the perpetrators and bring them to justice. The freedom to use a gun in this way continued the English tradition of protecting family and private property (Malcolm 1994: 2–3).

Following a robbery in 1685, a group of "Neighbors" went out to search after the robbers. Not representing an organized police force or militia unit, they enacted the civic responsibility of every man to protect his community from harm. When they found the robbers a "showdown" of sorts occurred, and "one of the 5 snapt and missed fire, another shot, then one of our shot so as to shoot one of their dead: another of the five fought one of ours with his sword, till another of ours knockt him down" (Robey 1972 Vol 1: 86). Expecting a violent end, the robbers started the shooting, ensuring the retaliation of the search party. For individuals living in close proximity to would-be victims, the ownership of arms was viewed as critical to a rapid neighborhood response to robbers and to local security.

The principle of protection was carried out on a larger scale when men used guns to protect their families in organized campaigns against threats (real or perceived) from neighboring Indians, the French, and ultimately the British. Service in a militia unit intended for the defense of a man's immediate community remained an obligation throughout the entire colonial period (Rawson 1672). During times of official war men formed companies that might leave a region to go and fight offensively. For example, during the 1720s, skirmishes occurred between the New Englanders and local Indians known as Captain Lovewell's War, or Drummer's War (Penhallow 1726). Captain Lovewell marched a company of forty-six men to fight the Indians. Both sides used guns and fired at least four rounds each before the English retreated, once Capt. Lovewell and a number of others were killed. However, "the fight continued very Furious & Obstinate" until nightfall, when fifteen men had been killed or wounded. They supposed that they killed more of their enemy than they lost, and the fight was celebrated in the newspaper. The pamphlet written recounting the events and a sermon lamenting the dead sold "in a few days" and required a second printing (*Boston News Letter*: 8 July 1725). Symmes (1725: 2) wrote in his memoir that the "Courageous" soldiers "nobly play'd the man for their Country," and the fighters received accolades for their service.

Although guns proved critical to a man's ability to fulfill his obligation to provide food and protect his family and property, not all men owned guns. Lindgren and Heather's multivariate assessment of gun-ownership, based on purchasing patterns in the colonial period, determined, that "guns were not a luxury good, but rather a relatively expensive staple that only a third of the poorest estates could afford, but that a solid majority (70%) of middle and upper class estates owned" (2002: 1806). Many male tasks could be accomplished through other means. Supplementary meat could be trapped, bought, or done without. A man might protect himself from an intruder or defend his livestock by using a sword or other edged weapon (*Boston News Letter*, February 26, 1730). For most of the seventeenth century, only two-thirds of the militiamen carried a musket and the rest carried pikes (Radabaugh 1954: 3–4). But as warfare evolved into "a shooting affair" during King Phillip's war, even the pikemen had to carry firearms and ammunition. By the end of the seventeenth century both the infantry and the new cavalry units used guns exclusively. Thus warfare represents one of the few areas where guns became more useful to men than other tools. Generally, though, while gun use for hunting and protection of property, family, and community conformed to early ideals of manliness, none of these tasks requires a gun, and guns remained less significant to achieving manhood.

Throughout the Revolution and into the beginning of the nineteenth century, the construction of manliness generally stayed the same. In fighting the Revolution men acted in a way consistent with their long-held patriarchal beliefs: "though they overthrew a system of monarchy, both leaders and backers of the American Revolution communicated an understanding of gender that was entirely consistent with the patriarchal manhood ideals around which New England men had built their identities since the seventeenth century" (Lombard 2003: 169). Throughout the eighteenth century men had protected their property against encroaching neighbors using violence, sometimes with guns, a pattern of behavior that prepared them to fight battles against England when they felt their property threatened. These men fought as property-owners to maintain their independence as landowners—an issue intrinsically bound up with their ability to provide for their families and fulfill their duties as men. In this way, men's actions during the Revolution did not represent a break with the old order, but rather a continuation of their long-held beliefs regarding the construction of real manhood. Inasmuch as men used guns during the Revolution so as to defend home and property, their perceptions of guns did not change.

While fighting in the Revolution, men utilized personal firearms, along with various artillery and edged weapons, to defend their property and families. Accounts of the Revolution frequently linked gun use with values that fit into traditional ideas about masculinity. A 1774 letter received by a man in Boston from a friend living further inland emphasized that guns were the common tools of regular men who chose to fight to defend their country. When reports reached the inland town that Northampton had been attacked by regulars, men "seized their guns, their horses and provisions, and set off, with a determination to attempt, risqué, and force all in defence of their innocent but distressed fellow-countrymen." He continued, "The united language of almost every man is, that he has a right to be happy; that he is determined to be free," these rights "ought not to be surrendered but with their heart's blood" (Willard 1968: 9–10).

When urging men to muster in defense of New York in 1776, Colonel Samuel Selden of Connecticut emphasized the importance of fighting to defend family and property, saying, "Rouse the People to see their Danger Stir them up by all that is dear in this life our Wives our Children our property our Liberty is at stake" (Ryan 1979: 31).

The events of the Revolution directly imperiled the colonist's manhood. It threatened not only masculine obligation to family and community, but also liberty and independence, two key components of male value (Kann 1998: 1). Many considered the manliness of the Americans to be dependent on the outcome of the rebellion. This represents a shift, as fighting became more than simple fulfillment of manly domestic duties, but a concentrated defense of manliness. In this case, weapons, most commonly firearms, afforded men the only way to protect and maintain their masculinity by fighting the British. This belief is evident in the widely read and highly influential pamphlet, *Common Sense*, in which Thomas Paine explicitly links fighting with the preservation of manliness, and declares war the only way to prevent the British from stripping Americans of their manhood (Kramnick 1976: 8–9). Paine labels all of those who desire compromise to avoid fighting "unmanly" and, in contrast, calls Independence a "manly principle" (1976: 81, 88, 113). He urges men to fight a defensive war against the British aggressors who threaten their homes, property, wives and children (1976: 88). Interestingly, he frames the fight as a defensive one against "Highwaymen and Housebreakers," placing it within the purview of male protection, and thereby requiring all men who desire to uphold their masculine duties to fight the invader or fail in their duty to family and community (1976: 123). Thus, the Revolution becomes one sphere of men's lives in which they are forced to utilize *guns* to uphold their manliness. Unlike other manly duties that might be fulfilled without a gun, very few fighting men could avoid picking up a gun to complete their service.

The explicit link between fighting in the Revolution and manliness carried over from the national rhetoric into the words of ordinary men. Samuel Holden Parsons, a New England Colonel, discussed both manly behavior and fighting in a letter to his nine-year-old son Thomas, whom he admonished to "be virtuous & manly in your behavior" and "behave with decency & manly fortitude" (Ryan 1979: 59–60). He then outlined what such behavior consisted of, including specific instructions in the event of Parson's demise: "if I fall in this War, I shall expect you & all my Sons to Arm in defence of the glorious cause of Liberty & lay down your Lives in defence of your Country & to avenge my Death if necessary" (ibid.). Although Thomas was too young to fight at the time, these words from his father would certainly influence the youth to view fighting as an important component of masculinity.

Immediately following the Revolution, manhood continued to be intimately connected to the relationships that a man shared with others, and particularly his ability to maintain control of those family members over whom he had authority; in this way manhood was established through a diligent adherence to social order. The founders "advanced a coherent conception and language of manhood on the consensual norms that enjoined males to establish independence, start families, and govern dependents to achieve manhood and procreate new generations" (Kann 1998: 29). This construction of manliness maintained many similarities with colonial ideas about family responsibility and community service. Within this framework guns might function as a tool of manliness in the same way that they had prior to the Revolution. The language of the Revolution concerning manliness and fighting continued to live on, as Americans embraced celebrations of independence and their brief united history. However, the continued use of swords as the general representation of military might and resistance, and the absence of narratives clearly delineating the symbolic use of guns in the transition from boy to man, signal that although guns had gained in significance as a cultural symbol, they had not yet reached the position that they hold today.

Remembrances of the Revolution continued to draw on the language of manliness and use of guns and their relationship to American freedom, though not exclusively. In an oration delivered at Concord, Massachusetts on July 4th, 1801, Samuel P. Fay declared: "The conduct of our patriots was dignified and firm. They spoke in the manly and impressive tones of injured right and determined resentment; while conscious rectitude gave strength to the voice of honest indignation." When this failed, he stated, Britain forced America to argue "in the conclusive logic of iron and gun-powder" (Fay 1801: 10). However, guns were not the only symbol of this fight, as Paul Allen's poem "Celebrating Revolution" highlights the "manly virtue" of those who fought for American independence, but uses the sword to describe the destruction wrought on Great Britain: "That sword which oft, in many a doubtful day, / Broke through the ranks, and scatter'd wild dismay— / Which made stern tyrants shrink with conscious dread, / And tore the plume from proud Britannia's head" (Allen 1801: 6). Thus American society continued to merge the use of guns with ideals of manliness, but only in a limited way that still fell under the purview of community and family-bound ideas of manliness.

The early nineteenth century signaled a transition period for manhood during which the entire paradigm of masculine construction shifted, from a vision of manhood reliant upon performance within familial and community relationships, to one based on the actions of the individual related to the world (Rotundo 1987: 36–9). As this construction of masculinity took shape, men became men "because of what they were up and doing": they were active, egalitarian, and individualistic, and these qualities made them masculine (Pugh 1983: xvi, xv). Whereas in the colonial period a man could not achieve manhood without a family, in the nineteenth century masculinity could be obtained by solitary figures operating outside of family or community. Even a man with a family who built communities, such as Daniel Boone, became transformed in legend to a lone hunter, detached from both family and society (Leisy 1923: 12). While in reality the lives of New England men continued to be grounded in relationships, they nevertheless envisioned themselves as obtaining manhood as individuals, and within the outer sphere of a man's world (Lombard 2003: 178). This shift from a community-bound view of masculinity to one based on achievement paved the way for guns to become objects imparting manliness to their user. Owing to events such as the war of 1812, the prominence of the frontier, and the conscious creation of an American identity in American arts, guns emerged as a major expression of American masculinity.

Sending a son away from the family to learn manly principles represents a practical reflection of the growing importance of the outside world and individual achievement in achieving manhood. An 1820 advertisement published in Boston for an American Literary, Scientific, and Military Academy promises parents such schooling will instill in their sons the "manly, noble, and independent sentiments which ought to characterize every American, whether citizen or soldier." The rigorous course of study required for such a feat involves not only learning languages, science, mathematics, history, and literature, but also extensive instruction in "artillery duty, the principles of Gunnery, a complete course of Military Tactics," and another course of military strategy. Students also performed military exercises, in addition to regular study, and the school provided each of them with "Arms and accoutrements" of "different sizes, to accommodate those of different ages" (the school accepted boys as early as 11 or 12) (*Boston Commercial Gazette*, March 2, 1820). Although the expense of the Academy would limit the number of men actually exposed to this type of education, this new ideal that an institution other than the family might teach a young man "manly" behavior certainly represented a break from the vision of New England manhood achieved within the confines of the home. Furthermore, the emphasis on military training and handling weapons further demonstrated the burgeoning intersections between masculinity and knowledge of guns.

Historical events such as the rise of the "common man," as embodied by the heroes of the War of 1812, the ascendancy of the public personas of Andrew Jackson, Daniel Boone, Davy Crockett, and their fictional counterpart Nathaniel Bummpo, combined to create a new ideal of manhood, one drawing on guns not just as useful tools, but as symbolically powerful objects. The construction of American masculinity revolving around a mythical portrayal of Old Hickory and the themes of the West emphasized the importance of "earthy wisdom": the ability to "shoot straight, face danger and pain without flinching, and speak from the experience of a rigorous life" (Pugh 1983: 18). This change transformed guns into powerful cultural symbols, imbuing them with the power to create manliness.

One very popular song, "The Hunters of Kentucky," extolled the military prowess of ordinary men in the battle of New Orleans, and served as a campaign song for Andrew Jackson, retaining its influence through his presidency. This song celebrated the fighting prowess of the hunters, particularly their skill with guns, in a way that expressed a connection between gun skill and masculinity. Unlike many war songs, which mention the use of multiple weapons, often including cannon and swords, in this song only rifles are credited with saving New Orleans. The verses emphasize gun use:

For we with rifles ready cock'd,
Thought such occasion lucky,
And soon around the General flock'd
The hunters of Kentucky ...

But Jackson, he was wide awake
And was not scared of trifles;
For well he knew what aim we take
With our Kentucky rifles ...

We did not chose to waste our fire
So snugly kept our places;

But when so near we saw them wink,
We thought it time to stop them;
And 'twould have done you good, I think,
To see Kentucky pop them.
(Woodworth 2005(1831): 222–3)

The lack of fear, and indeed, eagerness to fight exhibited in the verses imply the great skill of the hunters with firearms, while Jackson's confidence in their aim directly states the same. Victory in the battle follows directly from skillful, manly use of their guns.

While these men are working to protect women *and* property—two key components of a patriarchal manhood—they do so as outsiders, almost as independent agents. For example, they are not once identified with the United States, but rather always as Kentuckians, minimizing their personal stake in the battle. Instead, they work to protect others because they are best suited for it; they have the aim of conquering the enemy. The cause that they stand for, the protection of New Orleans, the song equates with guarding women and property: "You've heard, I s'pose, how New Orleans / Is famed for wealth and beauty, / There's girls of ev'ry hue it seems, / From snowy white to sooty; / So Pakenham he made his brags, / If he in fight was lucky, / He'd have their girls and cotton bags, / In spite of old Kentucky" (Woodworth 2005(1831): 222). They protect the white females, the black females, and the cotton bags.

Yet in contrast with colonial visions of manhood where a man protected his own family and property, this song depicts obvious outsiders as fulfilling this role. Described as loners rather than as family men, males create their manly character by hunting rather than via their relationships to any aspect of society. These men, described as half horse, half alligator, and perfectly comfortable in a "mucky" swamp, stand outside society. The work that they do is identified as the work of men, and not only because of the type of work it is. The last line contains a mocking insult to the manliness of all those who, unlike the hunters of Kentucky, either cannot, or did not, protect the women and goods in New Orleans. The song, clearly addressed to a mixed audience, and especially told as a tale to men ("it would have done you good, I think, to see Kentucky pop 'em" would hardly be suitable for a song directed only to women), states "And now, if danger e'er annoys, / Remember what our trade is, / Just send for us Kentucky boys, / And we'll protect you, Ladies" (2005(1831): 223). This not only insinuates that Ladies could not rely on their own men to provide the kind of protection a Kentucky man might offer; in the context of addressing a mixed audience, it is a jibe to the men who might also wish to call for protection, men the Kentuckians look upon as "Ladies."

The same theme of masculinity in relation to gun use also appeared in widely read American fiction. This proves especially important as this developing fiction created the archetype for the American mythological hero and is credited with assisting in the creation of American arts and national identity (Lewis 1955: 77; Wallace 1986:18). The best example of this, James Fenimore Cooper's Nathaniel Bumppo, demonstrates the explicit connections between gun use and the creation of manliness. One of the later installments of the *Leather Stockings* series, *The Deerslayer*, depicts the youthful Bumppo during his first battles and his transition into manhood, both of which heavily and purposefully rely on gun use. Cooper represents Bumppo's transition into manhood by using a "traditional" Indian name-changing ritual, one that he alters to include a gun as the catalyst for growth, and thus the conduit to masculinity (House 1965: 317; Railton 1978: 203).

At the outset of the tale, Cooper reinforces the youthful immaturity of the hero, while leaving room for his great potential. Bumppo goes hunting with a less noble specimen of frontier life, Hurry Harry, who challenges Bumppo to live up to his Delaware name "Deerslayer" and "prove his manhood" by killing a doe. Although Bumppo easily rejects the idea that such actions against a defenseless creature reflect true manliness, he also admits that his name does not reflect an attainment of masculinity, saying: "The Delaware's have given me my name, not so much on account of a bold heart, as on account of a quick eye, and an active foot. There may not be any cowardice, in overcoming a deer, but sartain it is, there's no great valour" (Cooper 1985: 499–500). While he has all the physical abilities of a man, he has yet to test or prove his heart and his skill against another man. Cooper makes it clear that until Bumppo has proved himself he can never fully answer doubts concerning his masculinity that prevent others from taking him seriously. When he and Harry have a disagreement, Harry reminds him: "You're a boy ... mislead and misconsaited" (1985: 499–500). Until Bummpo attains manhood, he remains ineffectual as a moral force, both because he lacks the courage to defend his views, because of his deeply felt uncertainty of his own merit, and because he does not have the proper credentials, in the eyes of those around him, to recommend him as an authority.

In the time that it takes Bumppo to aim his rifle and squeeze the trigger he sheds the uncertainty of youth and claims his new identity as a full-fledged man. After a lone Indian fires upon him, he has an opportunity to shed his first human blood in a fair fight. It is significant that he twice gives up the chance to kill. First, he hesitates to fire on an uncovered man, one at a disadvantage, and then he refuses hand-to-hand combat, which is significant because it demonstrates that Cooper purposely picks the rifle as the means of obtaining manhood, and rejects bloodier tomahawk or knife fighting. While watching his opponent reload, Deerslayer contemplates the possibility of "close assault," but rejects it. Instead "he dropped his rifle to the usual position of a sportsman" and muttered "that may be red-skin warfare, buts it's not a Christian's gift. Let the miscreant charge, and then we'll take it out like men" (Cooper 1985: 594). And take it out like men they do, with Bumppo triumphing over his foe by virtue of his skill. Both fire at the same time, but only the Deerslayer's shot finds its mark. According to Kay Seymour House (1965: 317), "When Natty kills his first Indian, nature testifies to the fairness of his shot; his and his enemy's rifles are discharged so nearly together that 'the mountains, indeed, gave back but a single echo'."

After shooting the Indian, Bumppo approaches his enemy as he draws in his final breaths. After telling the man his name, he predicts that one day he will "bear a more manly title, provided I can 'arn one" (Cooper 1985: 602). The Indian, responding that "Deerslayer" does not befit a warrior, bestows upon Bumppo the name "Hawkeye" with his dying words: "Eye, sartain-finger, light-ning-aim, death. Great warrior, soon—No Deerslayer—Hawkeye—Hawkeye—Hawkeye—Shake hand" (ibid.). And thus, the Deerslayer, through the skill of his rifle, earns a "more manly" title for himself, and enters into adulthood. By choosing the rifle as the proper weapon for a Christian (white) man, fore-grounding Bumppo's superior skill with a rifle, and linking both of these facts to Bumppo's coming of age, Cooper merges gun use with masculinity. In Cooper's model, a boy becomes a man in stages, as Bumppo's journey begins as he becomes the "Deerslayer," and his transition to manhood is completed with his transformation to the warrior "Hawkeye." Significantly, both changes result from his use of a gun.

The idea that a gun could provide a passage into manhood, rather than simply support the duties of men, marks a break from the earliest understanding of guns as they relate to gender. Although loosely associated with masculine tasks, guns in the colonial and Revolutionary periods lacked the cultural power to signify the manliness later ascribed to them. Thus modern understandings of guns as a symbol of manliness do not extend into the early American past. Rather, they grew out of a colonial context in which guns served as useful tools to support a community and family-bound model of manliness. This dominant model, dependent upon relationships with others, did not allow for guns to serve as con-duits to masculinity, since manliness did not depend on skill but on relationships such as marriage and fatherhood, neither of which gun use alone could create. However, as understandings of manliness began to shift, very subtly during the course of the Revolution, and in the early nineteenth century more dramatically, the value of guns as a cultural symbol changed as well. As manliness became less dependent on relationships and more upon individual achievement, suddenly guns provided a skill through which a man might prove himself. The popularization of achievements involving guns through the heroics of riflemen in the War of 1812, the rise of Andrew Jackson to the highest position in the nation, the pervasive influence of frontier characters, both real and fictional, in burgeoning American culture all promoted guns as a cultural symbol of manliness. In this way, the gun became an object that a boy might pick up, and through mastery of it, transform himself into a man.

CHAPTER 12

"I Shot the Sheriff": Gun Talk in Jamaican Popular Music

Carolyn Cooper

Constant references to guns in Jamaican popular music have resulted in an increasing tendency to criminalize the idiom and demonize the culture both locally and in the international marketplace. Simple-minded evaluations of this gun rhetoric often fail to take into account the promiscuous genesis of these discourses, instead representing them as unambiguous signs of the congenital pathology of Jamaican popular culture and its creators. Conversely, I argue that *badmanism* is a theatrical pose that has been refined in the complicated socialization processes of Jamaican youth, who learn to imitate and adapt the sartorial and ideological "style" of the heroes and villains of imported movies. Cinema remains a relatively cheap form of mass entertainment for the urban poor, though cable television networks increasingly facilitate access to the full range of offerings of the North American film and television industry.

There is, as well, an indigenous tradition of heroic "badness" that has its origins in the rebellious energy of enslaved African people who refused to submit to the whip of bondage. Nanny of the Maroons, for example, is memorialized as having possessed supernatural powers; it is said that she used her bottom to deflect the bullets of British soldiers. Nineteenth-century warriors like Paul Bogle and Sam Sharpe kept alive the heroic spirit of resistance to the dehumanizing social and political conditions of colonial Jamaica. Twentieth-century political giants like Marcus Garvey and St William Grant, the latter a champion of the working class and a militant leader in the social and political upheavals of the 1930s in Jamaica, enriched the enduring legacy of resistance against the system, to quote Bob Marley. This heroic anti-slavery, anti-establishment ethos accounts in large measure for much of the ambivalence about "badness" in Jamaican society.

The classic 1972 Jamaican cult film *The Harder They Come* and the much more recent 1999 *Third World Cop* illustrate the indigenization of an imported American culture of "heroism" and gun violence; both films glamorize Hollywood reconstructions of masculinity. These distorted images are greedily imbibed by gullible Jamaican youth searching for role models. In a December

2002 interview with Winford Williams on CVM Television's "On Stage," dance-hall DJ Ninjaman acknowledged the profound impact that *The Harder They Come* had on him as a vulnerable child. That movie created a taste for the feel of the gun. The impressionable boy persuaded his grandmother to buy him a cowboy suit as a Christmas present and, along with it, he acquired his first set of (toy) guns. On stage at the December 2002 "Sting" show, Ninjaman, dressed in a resplendent gold cowboy costume, dramatically handed over to Senior Superintendent Reneto Adams a Glock 17 pistol, symbolizing his rejection of the culture of gun violence and signaling his support for a gun amnesty that would encourage outlaw gunmen to surrender illegal weapons.

The *Gleaner* columnist Melville Cooke gives a sophisticated reading of the theatrical performance of badness in Jamaican culture:

> Ninja Man and Reneto Adams, in their public personae, represent two sides of that much beloved and admired Jamaican personality, the bad man. Ninja Man is the incorrigible, fearless bad man that the supposedly decent citizens of the country would shudder to see at their gate, while SSP Adams is presented as the fearless bad man who stands between the thugs and said supposedly decent citizens.
>
> Make no mistake about it, though, the Ninja and the Saddam are, ultimately, rated for being "real bad man." (Cooke 2003)

Some would argue that SSP Adams is a *real* bad man and Ninjaman merely performs badness in his role as the "Original Gold Teeth, Front Teeth, Gun Pon Teeth Don Gorgon." Having surrendered one gun to SSP Adams, Ninjaman provocatively declared at that Sting 2002 perfomance that he had another gun that he was keeping for rival DJ Beenie Man. This potentially self-incriminating allegation cannot simply be taken at face value. It illustrates the bravura that is such an essential armament of the *braggadocious* dancehall performer; it also exemplifies the ongoing verbal clashes between DJs jousting for dominance of the field.

Furthermore, in "A Wi Run the Gun Them" Pan Head and Sugar Black, in combination DJ/singer style, assert their own mastery of the discourses of the gun, and mockingly claim that Ninjaman is not nearly as bad as the persona he inhabits: "Ninjaman a talk bout him have fourteen gun / Police hold him the other day, dem never hold him with none / A through him talk too much mek dem lock him down."[1] [Ninjaman claims to have fourteen guns. The police caught him the other day, but he had not even one gun on him. It's because he talks so much that they lock him down.]

The opening lines of "A Wi Run the Gun Them" level the playing field on which gunmen of various stripes contend: "Respect! all hortical [bonafide] gunman, whether you a police, soldierman or civilian" (ibid.). Furthermore, Pan Head and Sugar Black engage in a lyrical duel/duet in which the DJ's gun salute to badness—a ritual naming of all the weapons he possesses—is counterpointed with the singer's reworking of Dennis Brown's sweet-sounding lovers' rock melody and pointed political lyrics: "Do you know what it means to have a revolution? / And what it takes to make a solution? / Fighting against the pressure."[2] Here the gun lyrics are deployed in the cause of a revolutionary struggle against oppression.

Writing in support of an egalitarian gun amnesty that does not discriminate between the "good" badman and the "bad" badman, Cooke (2003) underscores the rank double standard in Jamaican society that elevates some privileged people above the law and leaves others groveling far below:

> We cannot demand that Ninja Man be charged for that particular gun and not question why Bruce Golding was not interrogated about the political violence he said he turned his back on. He must know a lot. We would have to exhume Michael Manley, shake his corpse and ask him about his links to "Burry Boy" and how he came to be a part of that infamous funeral.

Cooke here alludes to the fact that supposedly respectable politicians regularly consort with dons, those alternative authority figures and ambiguous outlaw/heroes of Jamaican popular culture who command massive and dreadful respect.

In "Warrior Cause," for example, DJs Elephant Man and Spragga Benz salute a long line of such notorious characters, ascribing to them heroic proportions:

Jamaican:

Well mi come fi big up every warrior
From di present to di past
Hail all who know dem fight for a cause

...

Well some seh dem a bad man
No know di half of it
Don't know a big gill nor a quart of it
Woppy King an Rhygin was di start of it[3]

English:

Well I've come to salute every warrior
From the present to the past
Hail all who know that they fight for a cause.

...

Well some who say they are gangsters
Don't know the half of it
Don't know a big gill or a quart of it
Woppy King and Rhygin were the start of it.

The metaphor of the gill and the quart (for a little and a lot) exemplifies the inventiveness of the DJs' lyrics: a gill, as defined by the *Oxford English: Dictionary* is "[a] measure for liquids, containing one-fourth (or locally, one-half) of a standard pint." A quart is "[a]n English measure of capacity, one-fourth of a gallon, or two pints."

The long list of warriors, with a wonderful assortment of nicknames, includes Feather Mop, Burry Bwoy, Tony Brown, George Flash, Jim Brown, Starky, Dainy, Bucky Marshall, Dudus, Zekes, Ian Mascott, Andrew Phang, Gyasee, Shotta John, Speshie Corn, Claudie Massop, Natty Morgan, Sprat, Sandokhan, Rashi Bull, Cow, Early Bird, Rooster, Chubby Dread, Willy Haggart, George Phang, Tony Welch, Sammy Dread, Randy and Smile Orange.[4] In this roll call of the rougher than rough and the tougher than tough the DJs include even supposed *badman* lawmen: "Laing an Bigga Ford was di police of it/ … / Now Adams come get introduce to it." [Laing and Bigga Ford were the police version of it/ … / Now Adams has come and gotten introduced to it."]

The somewhat ambivalent DJs also salute potential warriors who renounce the calling:

Jamaican:

Big up di youth dem weh steer clear of it
  Weh wuda do nuff tings an dem no hear of it
  Weh know wrong from di right an dem aware of it
  But dem still no have no coward or no fear of it.

English:

Salute the youths who steer clear of it
  Who would do lots of things and wouldn't hear of it
  Who know wrong from right and are aware of it
  But they still aren't cowards and have no fear of it.

It is not only deprived ghetto youth (whether badman or bad cop) who are caught up in the gun culture of Hollywood fantasy and its deadly manifestations in real-life Jamaican society. Jamaican jazz pianist, Monty Alexander, in a rap entitled "Cowboys Talk" on his 1992 CD *Caribbean Circle*, nostalgically recalls the cowboy heroes of his childhood, enigmatically linking their apparent demise with the birth of ska:

When I was a *likl* [little] boy I remember we used to go to pictures. Some people say movies. And some people down in Jamaica say "we going to the flim [sic] show." On a Saturday morning. Matinee. And we used to sit there and watch the greatest cowboy stars on the screen. And I mean Roy Rogers and Gene Autry and all them kind a man dem riding pon the horse. But you know what? Them not riding no more. Is like ghost riders in the ska.[5]

Monty Alexander evokes ska instrumental compositions performed by Don Drummond and the Skatalites, such as "Ringo," "Lawless Street," "Guns of Navarone," and "Ska-ta-shot," the titles of which clearly have their genesis in the assimilated culture of the Hollywood western.

Bob Marley's "I Shot the Sheriff" similarly evokes the seductive gun culture of the Wild West. In a September 1975 interview with the musicologist Dermot Hussey, Marley gives an account of the evolution of the song that emphasizes the power of lyrical weaponry: "People fight me, a di more it better fi me. Becau you see when dem fight me, mi can go sit down an meditate of what they fighting me fa and make a song of it. How you think me write all 'Shot di Sheriff' and all dem tune deh? Just the fight weh me a get inna mi own group. Mi ha fi shoot all sheriff" (Marley 1991) [The more people fight me, the better it is for me. Because when they attack me I can withdraw and meditate about why they are fighting me. And I can compose a song out of that experience. How do you think I got to write songs like "Shot di Sheriff" and all those other tunes? It's because of the fight I got even in my own group. I had to shoot even the sheriff.]

The symbolic power of the ghetto gunman in *The Harder They Come* is amplified because the *shotta* is also a reggae singer, brilliantly played by the redoubtable Jimmy Cliff. Real-life Rhygin was no singer. The Perry Henzell/Trevor Rhone adaptation of the Rhygin legend for film distills the essence of urban revolt: the fusion of reggae music and *badmanism*, shaping the sensibility of duppy-conquering ghetto youth like Bob Marley and his dancehall progeny. Rhygin's control of literal/lyrical and symbolic gunfire in *The Harder They Come* is an excellent example of an oral performance tradition in which masking, spectacle, role-play and sublimation are essential elements. Contemporary Jamaican dancehall music is an organic part of that total theatre of Jamaican popular culture and must be read with the same sophistication that other modes of performance demand.

For Ivan, whose sensibility is decidedly shaped, in part, by the fantasy world of film, reggae music is an urgent expression of contemporary social reality. In Michael Thelwell's novelization of *The Harder They Come* (1980) the protagonist muses on the ideological power of reggae thus:

It seemed to him a sign and a promise, a development he had been waiting for without knowing it. This reggae business—it was the first thing he'd seen that belonged to the youth and to the sufferahs. It was roots music, dread music, their own. It talked about no work, no money, no food, about war an' strife in Babylon, about depression, and lootin' an' shootin', things that were real to him.

"This reggae business" is also a magical enterprise in which a poor ghetto youth, identifying with the heroes of Hollywood fantasy, can rise to international fame and fortune. The *noms-de-guerre* of many DJs, old and new, encode the film origins of their fantasy personae: Dillinger, Trinity, Ninjaman, Red Dragon,

Bandolero. The persistence of this tradition of role-play in contemporary Jamaican dancehall culture makes it difficult sometimes for outsiders to decode local cultural signs accurately. Fusion of the literal and the metaphorical can confuse the issue.

The fact that shooting incidents do occur at some dances, for example, does not invalidate the argument that in many instances gunfire is meant to be purely symbolic. In Jamaican dancehall culture, for example, literal gunfire was often used in the past as a dangerous salute in celebration of the verbal skill of the heroic DJ/singer. Over time, this purely ritual gunfire has been replaced by the flashing of cigarette lighters, and, more recently, the brandishing of illuminated cell phones as the preferred signal of the audience's approval of the DJ/singer's lyrics: a symbol of a symbol; the flash of verbal creativity. With the emergence of the "fire man" Rastafari DJs like Sizzla and Capleton, the lighting of the spray from aerosol cans by enthusiastic fans—a decidedly dangerous activity that ought to be banned—creates a whoosh of all-too-real fire to represent the burning flames of the DJ's rhetoric.

In yet another metaphorical turn, the expression "pram, pram!," a verbal rendering of simulated gunshots, becomes a generic sign of approval of verbal skill beyond the domain of the dancehall. A student at the University of the West Indies, Mona, who knows of my interest in the language of the dancehall, reported that the minister of her church invoked divine gunshots in his 1993 Easter Sunday sermon: "Jesus Christ is risen, pram pram!"—the dancehall equivalent of "Hosannah in the Highest," I suppose. This is the rhetoric of the "lyrical gun," a turn of phrase deployed by Shabba Ranks in the song "Gun Pon Me:"

> *Jamaican:*
>
> When mi talk 'bout gun it is a lyrical gun
> A lyrical gun dat di people have fun
> Fi gyal jump up an just a rail an bomb
> Niceness deh yah an it can't done.[6]

> *English:*
>
> When I talk about a gun it's a lyrical gun
> A lyrical gun for the people to have fun.
> For women to jump up, go wild, and explode:
> Niceness is here and it can't end.

The image of the "lyrical gun" vividly illustrates the function of metaphor and role-play in contemporary Jamaican dancehall culture. "Lyrical" is not a word that one would ordinarily use to describe a gun; "lyrical" is the language of poetic introspection, not willful extermination. "Lyrical gun" is a quintessential dancehall term, the language of subversion and subterfuge: mixing things up, turning them inside out and upside down. A lyrical gun is the metaphorical equivalent of a literal gun. Words fly at the speed of bullets and the lyrics of the DJ hit hard. In this context, the word "lyrical," belonging to the domain of verbal play and fantasy, becomes a synonym of "metaphorical."

"Gun Pon Me" is an extended gun salute to Shabba Ranks's own verbal and sexual potency: the lyrical gun clearly assumes phallic proportions. The moving target at which the DJ fires is spellbound female fans from all over the world who respond energetically to the metaphorical shots he discharges, eagerly picking up the spent shells. By contrast, men are discounted as impotent rivals, easily eliminated by the DJ: "If is a bwoy, yes, him get knock out / An if is a girl she a shock out shock out" (ibid.). [If it's a guy, he'll get knocked out / And if it's a girl she just struts her stuff.]

Shabba militantly declares his mastery of the global field, naming major centers of Jamaican migration: the UK, Canada, and the city/state New York, a world unto itself. The DJ's "route" signifies the diasporic sweep of Jamaican popular culture:

Jamaican:

Born as a soldier Shabba Rankin a no scout
An if is di music, run it without a doubt
Control mi control an rule up mi route
Who don't like me tell dem go to hell
Shabba Rankin lyrics have England under spell
Shabba Rankin lyrics ha Jamaica under spell
If is Canada dem know me as well
Inna New York mi career extend
Wi a bus di gun an dem a pick up shell
Wi a di fire di gun an dem a pick up di shell
If is New York everybody can tell
Pamela, Susan, an di one Rachel
If mi don't DJ di world a go rebel
Tell di whole world seh dem under a spell (ibid.)

English:

Born as a soldier Shabba Rankin is no scout
And if it's the music, I run things without a doubt
I'm in full control, and I decide my route
Whoever doesn't like me, tell them to go to hell
Shabba Rankin's lyrics have England under a spell
Shabba Rankin's lyrics have Jamaica under a spell
In Canada they know me as well
In New York my career is on the rise
We're making the gun explode and they're picking up shells
We're firing the gun and they're picking up shells

In New York everybody can tell
Pamela, Susan, and Rachel.
If I don't deejay the world is going to rebel:
Tell the whole world that they're under a spell.

"Gun Pon Me" is a fascinating example of the way in which the lyrics of the DJs traverse ideological spaces, engendering sound clashes between literal and metaphorical discourse. The unsettling first verse reverberates with what seems to be quite literal gunfire. Shabba, who styles himself as "di bad boy fi di girls dem" [the bad boy for the girls] issues a deadly warning to male informers:

Jamaican:

Mi av mi gun pon mi an mi naa tek it out
Why mi naa tek it out? Too much informer deh bout
An mi no waan shoot someone inna dem mouth.
Tongue a jump up an teeth a jump out
Me a bust di gun an dem a pick up shell
Me a fire di gun an dem a pick up di shell
Can't hide mi gun else a guy woulda tell
Way mi gun big, yes, im head woulda swell
Gone go ring mi name like di tongue inna a bell
Mi ha fi slaughter im an done im mada as well. (ibid.)

English:

I have my gun on me and I won't take it out.
Why won't I take it out?
There are too many informers about
And I don't want to have to shoot anyone in the mouth.
The tongue is jumping up and teeth are jumping out.
I'm making the gun explode and they're picking up the shells.
I'm firing the gun and they're picking up the shells.
I can't hide my gun or else a guy would tell:
My gun is so big, yes, his head would swell
He would go and sound my name abroad
Like a tongue in a bell.
I would have to slaughter him
And then finish off his mother as well.

It is the later use of the modifier "lyrical" that first signifies the song's ambiguous vacillation between the literal and the metaphorical: "If is Pamela pick up lyrical shell / If is Susan she pick up di lyrical shell / An if is Ann-Marie pick up di lyrical shell." [If it's Pamela, she's picking up the lyrical shell / If it's Susan, she's picking up the lyrical shell / And if it's Ann-Marie she's picking up the lyrical shell.] Shabba's firing of his lyrical gun explosively echoes the identical use of the gun metaphor by old-school reggae artists, for example The Ethiopians in their 1970 song, "Gun Man":

> I'm gonna get you down
> I'm gonna gun you down.
> I've got a loaded 45
> It's sweet music
> I've got a loaded 45
> It's soul music.
> Gun, gun, gun, gunman talk.[7]

This conception of music as a "loaded 45"—a lyrical gun—is useful in decoding the rhetoric of gun violence in contemporary Jamaican popular music. Understood in its indigenous context, the meaning of the gun lyrics of the reggae singers and dancehall DJs is much less transparent than might initially appear. Violent, daring talk such as that of the DJ and the rapper can function as a therapeutic substitute for even more dangerous violent action. Cathartic talk does not so much incite to violence, as it controls violence in a socially accepted way. This proposition that violent *talk* is beneficial does, perhaps, have less currency these days in Jamaica, where relatively easy access to guns seems to have made it increasingly unlikely that the cultural traditions that once used talk as a beneficial substitute for physical abuse will be maintained.

Buju Banton's "Mr Nine," from his 2003 CD *Friends for Life*, exemplifies both the complexity of the metaphor of the lyrical gun in Jamaican dancehall culture and the DJ's own ideological development.[8] As in Buju's "Murderer," it is the culture of the gun itself that is under lyrical fire: "I tell unu, all man are created equal / But behind the trigger it's a different sequel."[9] [I tell you, all men are created equal / But behind the trigger it's a different sequel.] Cecil Gutzmore, lecturer in Caribbean Studies at the University of the West Indies, Mona, Jamaica gives a compelling reading of this enigmatic couplet:

> ... "sequel" has a number of meanings appropriate to Buju's context, including "issue, result, upshot". There is even a mediaeval /feudal meaning that has very much to do with the social inequality of lord and villein. And buried within this couplet is the suggestion of a play upon the contradictory notions of equality and inequality. The gun, especially the six-shooter of all those Westerns watched in the land of *The Harder They Come* and which still inhabit the Jamaican popular imagination, is known as the equalizer. This deadly equalizer is the face-to-face eliminator of all those inequalities that developed between that distant, original God-act which created all persons equal and now, when some are so much more equal than others. But the equalizer also imposes a stark inequality between its holder and s/he who is made to stare down its barrel/nozzle.[10]

In "Mr Nine" Buju conjures up a surreal scenario in which personified guns, contesting for the control of territory, critique each other's behavior and, simultaneously, bewail the battles that are being fought by youth in their name. It is as if the big guns themselves have now assumed control of both the society and their own policing, the authority having slipped from human hands:

Jamaican:

Chorus
Mr Nine say to MR 45
M16 and Magnum nah live too right
German Luger too hype
AK mek nuff youths loose [*sic*] dem life

Verse 1
Ar15 control a whole housing scheme
Di one MAC11 run weh gaan a Papine
38 a carry vibes true GLOCK deh pan a rise
380MATIC stick up and a mek a bag a noise
M1 seh im nuh put up wid di foolishness
HK Bomber rule a entire district.[11]

English:

Chorus
Mr Nine said to MR.45
M16 and Magnum are not living too right
German Luger is too hyped up
AK is making a lot of youths loose [*sic*] their life.

Verse 1
Ar15 controls a whole housing scheme.
The MAC11 has run away to Papine.
38 is upset because GLOCK is increasing in power.
380MATIC is on the alert and is making a lot of noise.
M1 says he won't put up with the foolishness.
HK Bomber rules an entire district.

In "Mr Nine" there is a seeming sound clash between what could be heard as a celebratory roll call of these many guns and the DJ's indictment of the culture of gun violence in Jamaica. Buju Banton documents a number of instances in which guns are constantly employed, recalling both legendary moments in the life of particular brands, such as the 303 used to kill Kennedy; as well as the more mundane circumstances in which guns like the pump-rifle, for example, are selected to protect Brinks' employees:

Jamaican:

Walter PPK who bosy like dis
Love have 22 cause anywhere dat fit
303 still a talk bout Kennedy's hit
While chopper cut in a two and split justice
Pump-rifle still a bodyguard di man weh drive di brinks
SLR a definitely soldier man things
MACK 11 di UZI an di M3
All a dem deh belong to di Israelis (ibid.).

English:

Walter PPK who is so boastful
Loves to have a 22 because that fits anywhere.
303 is still talking about Kennedy's hit
While the chopper cuts in two and splits justice.
Pump-rifle is still guarding the man who drives the Brinks truck.
SLR is definitely the soldier's choice.
MACK 11 the UZI and the M3:
All of those belong to the Israelis.

Naming the country of origin of some of these guns, Germany and Israel, Buju thus implicates the manufacturers in the capitalist reproduction of international violence.

Not surprisingly, the DJ gestures towards the culture of the Hollywood western, observing that "Smith and Weston [*sic*] a dat dem give to John Wayne" (ibid.) [Smith and Wesson, that's what they gave John Wayne]. The romanticization of gun violence and the celebration of badness, as in the globalized US film industry, are alluded to in the following lines:

Jamaican:

Tommy was bad boy in is days
When Gatlin talk few witness remain
Him and SMG the two a dem a di same
Pi pi pi 16MM shell
With special and Remington ring bell
Cannon heavy if carry so dem push it pan trolley
Pedal pusher start di riot security keep him quiet
From 1pop deh yah mi know shot a fire
And a ball. (ibid)

English:

Tommy was bad boy in his time.
When Gatling talks few witnesses remain.
He and SMG are both the same.
Pi pi pi 16MM shell
With special and Remington ring bell.
Cannon is heavy to carry, so they push it on a trolley.
As Pedal pusher starts up, the riot squad will keep him quiet.
Once 1pop is here, I know shots are going to be fired
All guns blazing.

In the silences between the firing of the guns, Buju Banton intersperses warnings to the Jamaican people to emancipate ourselves from the tyranny of the gun and the splitting of justice that these weapons engender: "Come now Jamaica now let us live free / And follow Buju Banton hear weh dem seh." (ibid.) [Come now Jamaica, let us live free / And follow Buju Banton. Listen to what he has to say]. In the following lines, as in his classic "Murderer," the DJ much more explicitly denounces the murderous gun culture, with its paradoxical death-in-life ethos: "Every man want gun like is life/ Dem think is the bullet and the shell them make them survive/ Listen Buju di Banton and open up yuh eyes" (ibid.). [Every man wants a gun as if it is life / They think that it's the bullet and the shells that make them survive. / Listen to Buju di Banton and open up your eyes.]

The function of metaphor and roleplay in Caribbean popular culture is not always fully understood within and outside the indigenous context. Thus, the lyrics of Jamaica's dancehall DJs, taken all too literally, have increasingly come under attack at home and abroad. Even more important, perhaps, is the possibility that culture-specific discursive strategies that function to "mask" meaning may, in practice, not be acknowledged as legitimate. There is the presumption of a "universal" (English) language of transparent meaning. The international marketing of reggae/dancehall is raising fundamental questions about cultural identity, cultural autonomy and the right to cultural difference. As Buju Banton's "Mr Nine" so lucidly illustrates, with its ambivalent glorification and renunciation of the gun culture in Jamaica, the battle for the fundamental transformation of Jamaican society must first be fought and won on native soil.

CHAPTER 13

Playing at Hate: War Games, the Aryan World Congress, and the American Psyche

Robert Rinehart

"... You know about the Minnesota Rangers?"

"The militia guys?"

"Yeah. Skinheads. Some old Vietnam veterans, Gulf War veterans, bikers. They go around in long black coats, like in that *Matrix* movie. Even in the summer. Shave their heads... ."

"... I went out to see Dick Worley, he's the leader out there at their war grounds."

"What are the war grounds? " Lucas asked.

"One of those paint-ball places. They play capture the flag, and all that. War games."

John Sandford, Hidden Prey

In the fictionalized world of Lucas Davenport, the veteran Twin Cities' cop of John Sandford's "Prey" novels, the rise of hate groups, undercover militias, and deviant memberships is neatly and slickly aligned with practices like war games, capture-the-flag, and paint-ball. The alignment between leisure activities such as paint-ball and groups professing a variety of anti-government and anti-dominant-society beliefs may or may not exist in real terms; however, the belief system that makes Sandford's "Prey" novels so successful sees such an alignment as plausible, if not credible.

In fact, popular culture texts such as mystery and thriller novels comprise an archipelago of artefacts that, together, are both *based upon* "reality" or fiction and *create* realities and fiction. As Denzin writes of the "mainstream Hollywood cinema," so too might popular novels and popular texts serve to "dramaturgically enact the epiphanal moments of postmodernism" (1991: 63). These texts may be based on reality or not; urban legends blend with fiction, fiction blends with and borrows from factual cases. As Blackshaw and Crabbe (2004: 178) point out, discussing the influence of media practices upon Crabbe's concept of "moral panic" in terms of, particularly, the gang bang/gang rape ("spit-roasting") of one female by various members of a football club in the United Kingdom, "... as the assertion of morality associated with the current crop of sensational sporting headlines suggests, the characterization of 'deviant' practice lives on in the popular imagination as much as it does within the discipline of sociology."

As well as in the popular imagination and the discipline of sociology, the discussions surrounding "deviancy" revolve around political, imbalance-based, racialized, patriarchal power structures like the global media. Blackshaw and Crabbe point out that the consumption of such stories as the alleged rape of a woman by members of a football club has become more important to news outlets as a "presentation of rape and sexual deviance as a titillating performance for widespread public consumption" (2004: 178) as a consumable, seductive tidbit.

In a similar mediated performance, Dao (2005: A10) reports—in the powerful and well-respected *New York Times*—that "an American-born Muslim cleric was convicted ... of inciting followers to wage war against the United States ...". Furthermore, it was pointed out, in post-9/11 rhetoric, that: "... a group of young men, several of them American-born converts, prepared themselves spiritually and physically for waging jihad in defense of Islam, prosecutors said, including *by playing paintball in rural Virginia*" (ibid., emphasis added). Such urban legends, fictionalizations, and factual cases blur, and serve to [re]enact the texts of "larger-than-life persons" who try to "come to grips with the existential dilemmas of postmodernism" (Denzin 1991: 63).

In this chapter, I intend to discuss deviancy, the Aryan Nations (and Christian patriot groups), play, and gun culture as they intersect in the American psyche. The intersections and parallels among such seemingly disparate constructs align with one another within patriarchal, masculinist culture as it is embodied within the socialization of American males. The very strong representation of guns and gun culture within Christian patriot groups—indeed, within many conservative groups calling for their Constitutional "right to bear arms"—fosters a commitment by the culture to reinforce and reproduce such heightened awareness of guns.

Often, groups and individuals who display so-called "deviant" behaviors align somehow with others' imagined expectations—so that, in the case of novels, life can imitate art as well as art imitating life. Or they may merely see their cause, as many of these groups do, as a sort of Christian *jihad*, so that groups like "... the Covenant, Sword and the Arm of the Lord's [book] *Prepare War*" (Aho 1994: 70–1) (which advocates taking up arms against "sodomite homosexuals waiting in their lusts to rape," "negro beasts who eat the flesh of men," and "seed of Satan Jews sacrificing people in darkness") will use hyperbole to attempt to incite their followers to action. But there is a long history involved in the seemingly "deviant" racist tradition of America, so that one comes away from exploration into that tradition wondering which comes first, life which seeks to annihilate other human beings, or art forms celebrating and memorializing philosophies that seek to annihilate other human beings. Enter the concept of "play."

Play is consider by Huizinga (1955: 28) as "voluntary activity or occupation executed within certain fixed limits of time and place, according to rules freely accepted but absolutely binding, having its aim in itself and accompanied by a feeling of tension, joy and the consciousness that it is 'different' from 'ordinary life'." The very juxtaposition of "play" with the concept of "hate" at first seems awkward and jarring; but if the combination is examined, one may see that the two concepts may co-exist, and might in some cases enhance one another. In fact, Huizinga wrote about the "play" element not only in life as grandly viewed, but within certain "civilized" forms of war:

> Fighting, as a cultural function, always presupposes limiting rules, and it requires, to a certain extent anyway, the recognition of its play-quality. We can only speak of war as a cultural function so long as it is waged within a sphere whose members regard each other as equals or antagonists with equal rights; in other words its cultural function depends on its play-quality. This condition changes as soon as war is waged outside the sphere of equals, against groups not recognized as human beings and thus deprived of human rights—barbarians, devils, heathens, heretics and "lesser breeds without the law". (Huizinga 1955: 89–90)

Thus, for Huizinga, the "cultural function" of a "play-quality" within war is dependent upon the warring parties' recognition of some fundamental, agreed-upon, rule structures. Though one warring party may adhere to certain rules based upon an acceptance of "certain limitations for the sake of their own honour" (p. 90), this, in Huizinga's view, lacks the constancy required for a true "ludic" element within war.

As one example of the play element constituted within Christian patriot groups' psyches, "Louis Beam's *Essays of a Klansman* ... details a point system for earning the status of Aryan warrior. Liberal sociologists, for example, are worth but 1/500 a point each; the president of the United States rates a whole point" (Aho 1994: 71). Rules are structured such that "warriors" know their status at any given time.

In the case of what Aho (1990) calls Christian patriots (a generalized—and not terribly accurate—term I also will use throughout to identify the great variety of anti-establishment, anti-government, racist groups, used for brevity), rules do exist, hierarchical power structures abound, and terms of ludic behavior exist as well. If their forms of "play" are seen as "cultural performances," many of the Christian patriots' actions are relatively stable and predictable, like a dance of potential death.

In the case of many of these Christian patriot groups:

> The idea of warfare only enters when a special condition of general hostility solemnly proclaimed is recognized as distinct from individual quarrels and family feuds. This distinction places war at one stroke in the agonistic as well as the ritual sphere. It is elevated to the level of holy causes, becomes a general matching of forces and a revelation of destiny; in other words it now forms part of that complex of ideas comprising justice, fate, and honour. As a sacred institution it is henceforth invested with all the ideal and material imagery common to the tribe. This is

not to say that war will now be waged strictly in accordance with a code of honour and in ritual form, for brutal violence will still assert itself; it only means that war will be seen as a sacred duty and in an honorable light, that it will be played out more or less in conformity with that ideal. (Huizinga 1955: 95)

In much of the Christian patriot rhetoric and ritual behaviors (which, Aho (1990) points out, are not unitary or even always consistent), there is the deep sense of moral justification: the sense of wronged justice, impending fate, and a deeply entrenched, hypermasculinist sense of honor, based in large part on male socialization practices that celebrate rugged individualism, the use and display of survival techniques, and a worldview that is certain and cocksure. In North America, a great deal of masculine socialization, particularly in Survivalist and Christian patriot culture, is also linked with guns and gun culture—but this link is seen as normative male socialization (cf. Jhally 1999).

The threads that commingle popular culture, hate, and masculine identity together remain virtual renderings of linkages until the virtual merges into the real. In the United States, these threads are nowhere more exemplified for popular and populist consumption than by mass-media renderings of school shooting perpetrators. For example, Jeff Weise, the seventeen-year-old Red Lake (MN) High School student who, in the spring of 2005, killed a total of eight people, including himself, "created comic books with ghastly drawings of people shooting each other and wrote stories about zombies. He dressed in black, wore eyeliner and apparently admired Hitler and called himself the 'Angel of Death' in German" (Forlitti 2005). In the popular imaginary, there is a strong connection between what some have come to term "home-grown terrorists" and the popular culture that, it is assumed, socializes them toward their anti-social behaviors and against governmental and societal strictures.

One thing is certain: by most accounts, the "racist underground" movement in America—which is not as underground as most mainstream media would have it—is flourishing, buoyed by mainstream America in the sureness of both its ideals and its aims. In fact, members of various and sundry anti-establishment groups call the dominant government in the United States the Zionist Occupation Government (ZOG), and find that this global statement can neatly encapsulate all their anger and energy towards what they term the Jewish "problem." Of course, in a space that is ideologically framed as a "true" democracy, "good" fights against "evil" constantly (and often they are deeply enmeshed), so that whoever "wins" gets to claim the other as deviant. In the case of popular culture, those who oppose the dominant culture are by definition deviant, since popular culture by its implicit definition depends upon a critical mass, a dominant mainstream support framework. But dominant groups also depend upon "deviance" to establish and retain cultural boundaries of what is viewed as acceptable and what is not acceptable.

Explorations of Deviance Studies

But what is deviance, anyway? Becker (1973) discusses a variety of ways of looking at deviance. There is the laypersons' view of deviance, which Becker terms as "statistical" kinds of deviance: deviance, in this view, is "... anything that differs from what is most common ..." (p. 4). This model follows the dominant/non-dominant cultural norms of society, and sees "out-liers" as deviating from statistical norms set by the majority of members of a society. There is the "medical analogous" model of deviance, which terms the individual who is outside the norm as being in the "presence of a disease" (p. 5). There is the individual who demonstrates a "failure to obey group rules" (p. 8). But Becker, in his early, thorough examination of the concept of "deviance," sees all these definitions as centered around the individual and the individual's actions. He proposes a change in the point of view, one in which there is a different model of deviance from previous models, one that is centered on the actions of societies, in which "*social groups create deviance by making the rules whose infraction constitutes deviance*" (p. 9, italics in original). In this model, society, not the individual, is the primary focus.

This definition, centered on the creation of rules whose existence makes possible the very concept of deviance, puts the onus upon group rather than individual action, upon set-up boundaries that individuals or non-dominant, less powerful groups may or may not resist. In this sense, then, deviance is, of course, socially constructed; but it is also tautologically monitored by those who have set up the original rules. Standpoint epistemology plays a large part in which group(s) are dominant (not merely numerically dominant, but also symbolically and culturally dominant), and which groups stand outside the "normative" behaviors—and what, in fact, constitutes both normative and deviant behaviors. In this sense, then, deviance depends upon normativity in order to remain viable; and also, normativity relies upon deviance to help police the bounds of what is constituted to be normativity.

But deviance is not merely seen as a form of resistance. In discussing punk style, Hebdige (1979) sees deviance as resistance to constructed norms, but also as a form of positive, pro-active emblematics: "the concept of signifying practice ... reflects exactly the group's central concerns with the ideological implications of form, with the idea of a positive construction and deconstruction of meaning, and with what has come to be called the 'productivity' of language" (1979: 118–19).

In Hebdige's earlier worldviews, deviance becomes a statement of form, not merely in terms of resistance to the other, but for its own sake.

Blackshaw and Crabbe not only re-postulate this positive statement of form, but also call for a more nuanced view of deviance, one that goes beyond the simple binaries of "conformist" and "deviant." In this way, and following Rorty, they call for a greater refinement of deviance, to include "ethnocentric communities [that] continually compete for time, space and partnership" (2004: 13).

To approach an understanding of deviance, then, is a multilayered, multifaceted effort that takes into account individual cases and points of view.

In terms of what Flynn and Gerhardt (1989) label "the Silent Brotherhood" in America many groups emerge: among them are such varied-yet-loosely-connected groups as the Aryan Nations Church (the Church of Jesus Christ Christian); the Covenant, the Sword, and the Arm of the Lord (CSA); the National Alliance; the Ku Klux Klan; Posse Comitatus; the "Reformed Church of Christ–Society of Saints (a front of the Socialist Nationalist Aryan Peoples Party)"; the White American Bastion (of the *Bruders Schweigen*, or, the Order); the Ministry of Christ Church; the John Birch Society; and the Christian Patriot Defense League, to name just a few (cf. Flynn and Gerhardt 1989; Aho 1990). The fact of so many slightly different, nuanced groups' existing demonstrates the importance of their individual salience to group members, though some members enter into and exit from a variety of organizations over their lifespans as "Christian patriots" (Aho 1990, 1994).

One interesting fluctuation in group membership is noted by Aho (1990), who describes a striking coincidental timing between white male uncertainty due to economic loss and encroachments by women and minorities, and a growing perception of the ZOG, against which many "Silent Brotherhood" members were encouraged to strive. In this way, Aho implies, Christian patriot groups may act as a barometer for what is considered mainstream and ordered, and what the borders of such order may be within the United States.

These radical-conservative groups, Aho (1990) points out, are self-described as Christian Patriots—thus, they acknowledge their deviance from the normative and/or dominant culture while still professing their "correct" worldview. Embedded within their literature is the acknowledgement and hatred of the ZOG, for example. But their voice and power are symptomatic of dissent itself, rising and falling, respectively, with the cultural, real, and symbolic dominance of more liberal, and then more conservative administrations in the United States. They, just as the radical so-called "eco-terrorists" of the member groups People for the Ethical Treatment of Animals (PETA) and the Earth Liberation Front (ELF), act as cultural balances for the mainstream and more dominant view, as a form of cultural "backlash" against the strictures of the socially-constructed mainstream: in this sense, as well, PETA and ELF are also considered deviant.

But the dominant view waxes and wanes as the media highlight it: thus, at any moment in time, the media may have a story to tell about whatever group they choose—and by the very act of telling the story, the group receives a glimmer of celebrity. The relationship between group, group adherents, and media is one of the key threads of popular and populist culture that inscribes both these Christian Patriots and the groups rejecting their worldviews. And certainly gun culture and the elements of "play" imbricate themselves into the fertile mix, especially when such groups as Richard Butler's Aryan Nations Church attempt to inculcate values into male youth by means of socialization tactics.

Blackshaw and Crabbe note the media effects upon sport practices, now considered "deviant" sport practices because of the construction of such practices in large part by the media itself. In the case of Christian patriots, some of the victims of "consumptive and performative deviance" are obvious: the dead include the Jewish news radio talk-show host Alan Berg, assassinated in his driveway with a fully automatic MAC-10, in Denver, Colorado, in 1984 (Flynn and Gerhardt 1989: 203–10); "in 1979, an alliance of Klansmen and neo-Nazis resulted in the killing of five labor organizers in Greensboro, North Carolina ..." (Langer 2003: 269); Aho lists fifty-one fatalities directly "related to American Right-Wing Activity" between the years 1980 and 1985 (1990: 8–9).

Notwithstanding Blackshaw and Crabbe's difficulty with the very concept of "deviance," Becker's portrayal of deviance seems a good fit for media-saturated determinations of what constitutes deviance from what is considered (by the media) as normative: the idea of deviance is dependent upon "*social groups* [who] *create deviance by making the rules whose infraction constitutes deviance*" (1973: 9)— and key among those social groups are the media.

Butler's Vision of the Aryan Homeland[1]

In the 1960s, Richard G. Butler was a retired aerospace engineer in California, and associated with the founder of Christian Identity, Wesley Swift. Much has been written about Butler; as well, much of it reads like an origination myth, suggesting the self-promotional rhetoric that charismatic leaders learn to reify over time—and that others utilize as encapsulated "truths." The following "facts" of Butler's inception of the Aryan Nations seem to establish a similar kind of origination *mythos* for the group(s):

- In 1973, Butler moves to the Hayden Lake, Idaho, area, intending to create a base for his Church of Jesus Christ Christian. He hosts the "Pacific Kingdom Identity Conference" in 1979, which provides a springboard for his attempts to align such fairly diverse groups as the Ku Klux Klan, neo-Nazis, Posse Comitatus, and others during the 1980s—hoping to establish a "White Homeland" in the Pacific Northwest. In 1982, Butler convenes the first annual "Aryan World Congress." Militant groups from these congresses begin to form, with such known leaders as Robert Mathews splintering away from Butler.[2] Butler attracts more militants, calling for a racial holy war (Northwest Coalition for Human Dignity 2000).
- In 1989, Butler sponsors the Aryan Youth Action Conference, "it's [*sic*] first racist skinhead gathering. The event, held the weekend closest to Hitler's birthday (April 20th), attracts just over 100 attendees. Over the years, conferences have included activities such as Aryan Olympics, survival classes, and swastika lighting" (Northwest Coalition for Human Dignity 2000: 24). Butler continues to reach out to youth annually, and the Aryan Nations sponsor

highly-visible parades in downtown Coeur d'Alene, Idaho (Northwest Coalition for Human Dignity 2000).

- But Butler does receive a lot of attention, some of it worldwide. For example, a Helsinki, Finland, newspaper reports in 1987:

> For 12 years, Butler has commanded a small society in Idaho's backwoods. Into the woods a church, a printing facility, a shooting range, and a watch tower have been built. And the word has spread against the Jews, against the Catholics, against the Blacks, against the Chicanos ... (Hassen, trans., 1987, ms.)

- This kind of attention leads Butler to proclaim his Hayden Lake property as "the world headquarters" for the Aryan Nations.
- Butler drew many like-thinking individuals to his compound, including Floyd Cochran, who was appointed Aryan Nations' chief recruiter, and took the group's racist message to young people with music videos. Calm, articulate, with a knack for the headline-catching phrase, Cochran quickly became the group's national spokesperson. Aryan Nations' chief, the Rev. Richard Butler, proudly called him "the next Goebbels" (Hochschild 1994, http://www.mojones.com/news/update/1994/05/hochschild.html, accessed July 11, 2005).

Aryan Nations Compound Culture

Though there were many "types" of Christian patriots flocking to the Aryan Nations compound in Hayden Lake during the 1980s and 1990s, and though they apparently exchanged ideas and ideological stances in some ways, to classify them all with the same broad strokes would be a gross misrepresentation. Tanner (1995) writes of the inaccurate media phenomenon of glossing different ideological groups together—though, as has already been somewhat established, a variety of similarities between the groups can be understood as well.

Tanner (1995), writing in the mid-1990s, classifies four broad categories of "armed groups and associations" within the United States to be:

- The criminal racists, tax protesters, radical environmentalists, and political groups committed to violent revolution. These are people with narrowly focused agendas who will deliberately break the law in pursuit of their agendas. Examples include the Ku Klux Klan, the Posse Comitatus, the Black Panthers, the Weathermen, the Freemen, and some environmental and animal rights groups.
- Peaceful survivalists, racial separatists, and religious cult groups. These include Mormon polygamists, the Universal Church Triumphant, Bo Gritz, the Branch Davidians, and similar survivalist groups.
- The loners and the Walter Mittys. These are angry individuals who personalize their war with government.
- The armed, but legitimate, political activists. This is a new phenomenon, at

least in this century. These are socially successful people who respect and obey the law, but who are organizing and arming themselves because they fear they may be attacked by agencies of their own government (1995: 43–4).

Chief among the groups gravitating and invited to the Aryan Nations World Congress were groups from the first category, including the National Alliance, Ku Klux Klan, and the Silent Brotherhood/The Order. As well, skinheads flocked to the compound for the summer gatherings. It was a fertile spot for individuals of similar, yet not identical, worldviews.

Among the worldviews the groups shared were attitudes that the former member Floyd Cochran now characterizes as follows:

... nobody in the racist movement gets blamed for anything. My marriage didn't work? It's not my fault, it's because I was a racial activist and my wife couldn't stand it. I didn't graduate from high school? It's because my Jewish English teacher didn't like me. If you couldn't find a job—hey, it's not your fault, it's the Jews'. Or it's because of affirmative action ... even though northern Idaho is 98 percent white! (Hothschild, 1994, http://www.mojones.com/news/update/1994/05/hochschild.html, accessed July 11, 2005)

Another facet of the World Congresses included the physical layout:

... life inside the Idaho compound [included] watchtowers, Nazi and Confederate flags, a wedding in which the young couple marches under arms raised in 'Heil Hitler' salutes. The Aryan Nations' various outposts can contain everything from firing ranges to printing presses to schools for the children. The women do all the cooking. (Hothschild, 1994, http://www.mojones.com/news/update/1994/05/hochschild.html, accessed July 11, 2005, emphasis added)

The gun and weapon culture within the Aryan Nations compound was, by all accounts, pervasive and reflective of a hypermasculinist culture that aligned gun-use with masculinity. According to Flynn and Gerhardt, survivalist groups utilized training camp strategies:

Over the last two decades, America's backwoods became dotted with survivalist training camps. A Klan-run camp in Anahuac, Texas, taught guerrilla warfare techniques. A Christian survival school deep in the Arkansas Ozarks taught urban warfare in a silhouette city constructed Hollywood set-style in the forest. The leader of the Carolina Knights of the KKK, Frazier Glenn Miller, claimed a thousand men would answer his trumpet call at Angier, North Carolina, and that they'd be dressed not in white sheets but in combat fatigues, ready for race war. (1989: 10)

According to the Anti-Defamation League website on Richard Butler, the Aryan Nations compound was "patrolled by a security force of armed guards and dogs" ("Extremism in America," http://www.adl.org/learn/Ext_US/butler. asp?xpicked= 2&item=2, accessed December 15, 2005). One of the primary members of the compound, David Lane, a KKK activist, "... had an AK-47, showing the virtues of it" to everyone around the compound (personal correspondence, Norman Gissel, 5 January 2006). Additionally, "those attending the annual Aryan World Congress also plan[ned] to fire their weapons at a rifle range near Fernan Lake ..." during the World Congress in 2001 (Morlin and Clouse 2001: B1).

Guns and gun culture, for hunting game, are a part of the surrounding Idaho ethos. Thus, one method Butler used to split opposition to his racist tactics was to create some dissonance in the opposition: by dint of his inventing, developing, and supporting a hypermasculinist culture, many of the other groups that were drawn to gun culture, such as survivalists, felt that parts of the message of anti-government freedoms resonated well for them. This tenuous entry into the recruitment of volunteers for his Aryan Homeland in the Pacific Northwest was, to Butler, a valid form of recruitment. Additionally, within the hypermasculinist culture was a concomitant diminished role for women: recall that while there was a school on the compound for children, the women did all the cooking. The advent of women's rights, which were wrought in the larger culture throughout the 1970s, 1980s, and 1990s, created a parallel backlash against feminism, women's rights, and egalitarianism—much like the backlashes against gay rights, and civil rights for people of color, women, and gay and lesbian populations. (The "cult of masculinity," of course, does not always have such an antithetical stance towards persons of color, gay rights, or women's rights; but the popular culture and populist ideologies and stereotypes of these adherents of the "cult of masculinity" reinforce such backlash political stances.)

Also, "Butler had a cult of promoting guns, just because it promoted masculinity" (personal correspondence, Norman Gissel, January 5, 2006). There was a strong sense of a masculine culture within the compound, and particularly during the times of both the Aryan Youth Action Conference held near to Adolf Hitler's birthday, and the Aryan World Congresses held in the summer.

The linkages between gun-use, the Aryan hypermasculinist, hyper-racist philosophy, and masculinity itself tie back to popular culture and populist perceptions (largely media-fed) of "what Christian patriots" should do and ought to do. They carried guns, they target-shot, and some of the armed guards became over-zealous in their use of force—much to the dismay of Butler, who was sued in a claim for damages that arose from one incident. They also "offered paramilitary training in urban terrorism and guerrilla warfare ..." ("Aryan Nations/Church of Jesus Christ Christian, http://www.adl.org/learn/ext_us/ Aryan_ nations.asp?xpicked=3&item=11, accessed August 3, 2005).

Socialization of Children into Aryan Nations: The Academy, the "Adolf Hitler Memorial" Conference

One of the other things the Aryan Nations attempted at the Aryan compound in Hayden Lake was try to indoctrinate children into the racist (what they termed "racialized") doctrine. There was a school on site, the Aryan Nations Academy, and an Aryan Youth Action Conference (sub-headed the "Adolf Hitler Memorial" in 1994), which was begun in 1989 by inviting "neo-Nazi skinheads ... [to] its first racist skinhead gathering, entitled the 'Skinhead Solution Seminar'" (The Northwest Coalition Against Malicious Harassment 1994: 1.21).

Headed by Tom Bentley, the principal of the Aryan Academy encouraged children of residents living in the Aryan Nations compound to attend the school:

In the early 1980s, an "Aryan Nations Academy" was established to inculcate the group's philosophy in the minds of local youngsters. In 1982, an informational mailing claimed that the "academy" had 15 full-time students, preschool through grade eight. In addition, youth conferences attracting numerous skinheads were held in April to coincide with Hitler's birthday. (Aryan Nations/Church of Jesus Christ Christian, http://www.adl.org/learn/ext_us/Aryan_nations.asp?xpicked= 3&item=11, accessed August 3, 2005)

In concert with the attempts to attract youth to the White Supremacist/ Skinhead movement, which was rapidly influencing the Aryan Nations' world-view, an Aryan Youth Action Conference was begun. Skinheads, Aryan leaders, KKK leaders, and so forth met with youth during these conferences. Seeking to find "popular culture" items that would attract youth to the move-ment, activities that supported the masculinist, racist culture were trumpeted, so that:

Johnny Bangeter's Christian Identity Skinheads, affiliated with the Army of Israel from Utah, played as did a Vancouver, British Columbia band, Odin's Law. The Conference also featured Survival Classes, Aryan Olympics, a Swastika burning and a bonfire, drinking and a "slam pit" for dancing to racist rock 'n' roll. [Justin] Dwyer and Elisabeth Bullis were married during the swastika burning. Neo-Nazi Harry Schmidt, the chair of the Washington State Populist Party, also attended the gathering, apparently looking for good "political soldiers" to use as fodder. (The Northwest Coalition Against Malicious Harassment 1994: 1.22)

The blend of skinheads with Aryan youth—and with other so-called "White Supremacist" groups—at the Aryan Youth Action Conferences was a deliberate strategy to create critical mass for the group's goals. Thus, deliberate forms of socialization were performed: youth in attendance could look to the "celebrities" of the Christian patriot and White Supremacist movements, could be entranced by the performance of a "Soldier's Ransom"—a "racist kind of church service where they anoint Aryan soldiers and weapons. There were certain cross-burnings where they would anoint or bless their weapon as part of God's war" (personal correspondence, Bill Morlin, October 25, 2005).

One flyer that was put out for the Aryan Youth Action Conference in 1994 has a caricature of a chiseled male in uniform, legs akimbo, holding a flagpole (which has a Nazi flag, with swastika prominent) in one hand, with a female embracing him, eyes closed. He appears to be boldly looking forward, almost striding towards the future. Next to this cartoon are written: "Youth Speeches, Survival Classes, Skinhead Bands, Aryan Olympics, Swastika Lighting, Book & Flag Burning, Bonfire" (cited from Northwest Coalition Against Malicious Harassment, 1994: 1.21).

The plans to create critical mass by home-growing youth, not unlike Hitler's Youth Groups,[3] however, did not last, at least in this incarnation: Butler died in 2002, and the Aryan Nations' so-called "homeland" was bankrupted, and then transferred to Potter County, Pennsylvania. According to the "Aryan Nations: Kindred Awake!" website (http://www.aryan-nations.org/about.htm, accessed January 16, 2006), the major goals of the organization have changed to "the spread of subversion and the aid of all forms which are a liability and are inimical in nature to the current Judaic-tyrannical state of affairs" in what is described as the "Zionist social control." The website calls, therefore, for an "Aryan jihad," not so much based on armed conflict as on subversion of the so-called "Zionist Occupation Government" structure.

Conclusion: Aryans, Huizinga's "Play," and Gun Culture

Clearly, through much of the often-hysterical rhetoric of the White Supremacist literature (including websites, news reports, and interviews with the participants), and particularly the Aryan Nations' literature, there exist consistent, almost mythic origination stories. Within these stories, gun culture is a given.

The presence of guns, weapons, and destructive force varies from group to group, so that the "Silent Brotherhood" (or The Order) appears to have been a violent arm of the less-overtly violent Aryan Nations group. In the whole of the culture of the Aryan Nations' compound, however, there was a hypermasculinist culture that celebrated weaponry and its use, if only symbolically. As Butler is said to have stated: "The pen may be mightier than the sword, but a .38 always trumps it" (personal correspondence, Tony Stewart, January 5, 2006). There was always the rhetoric of paranoia, and of violence, so that, during and after each World Congress, violent attacks against citizens in the greater Spokane, Washington, area rose (personal correspondence, Bill Morlin, October 25, 2005). There was also the opportunity to learn "urban guerilla warfare techniques," for example from Col. Gordon "Jack" Mohr, who is said to have "conducted a two-day seminar in urban guerilla warfare" (Flynn and Gerhardt 1989:

230). The Congresses appear to have fomented violent action, where speakers called for an "Aryan *jihad*" and such events as gun practice were encouraged. In fact, targets depicting an interracial couple—with just the heads of a white woman and a black man showing—were pasted around the grounds for target practice.

Equally clear is the sense of the Aryan Nations that rules exist. Though the "play" is deadly serious, in this worldview, an "Aryan *jihad*" contains rules: such rules as fairness of weaponry between what they perceive to be the Zionist Occupation Government and the Christian patriot movement exist for these White Supremacist groups. However, since their worldview does not allow for equality between themselves and women, themselves and people of color, and themselves and Jewish (and sometimes Catholic) citizenry, the rules tend toward slippage towards these groups and their members. Thus, the use of guns against unarmed members of these groups appears to be seen as an appropriate usage. One example is the assassination of the unarmed radio host Alan Berg.

Though there is a sense of "play" in the way that Huizinga characterizes it—albeit the deadly, cynical forms of play—many of the Aryan Nations members see themselves as in the fight to establish their own geographical white "homeland." As Richard Butler said, the Aryan Nations' goal is "to form a national racial state. We shall have it at whatever price is necessary. Just as our forefathers purchased their freedom in blood so must we. We will have to kill the bastards" (cited in "MIPT Terrorism Knowledge Base," http://www.tkb.org/Group.jsp?groupID=29, accessed January 31, 2006).

This setting of rules and establishment of rhetorical stances, this call for the understanding of a worldview, smacks of Huizinga's play in the sense that there is a deliberate "notification" of all concerned parties what the goals are, how the Aryans intend to accomplish their goals, and why. Though branches of the Aryan Nations, particularly the Order, called for and accomplished unlawful and violent acts, acts seemingly without rules, it was when the Skinheads—anarchic, non-rule-abiding, and what one person described as "highly dysfunctional" socially (personal correspondence, Tony Stewart, January 5, 2006)—and the White Underground movements came in contact with and influenced the direction of the Aryan Nations, that Huizinga's sense of "play" began to erode.

The use of guns, masculine identity culture, and the socialization of youth in programs geared toward creating the so-called Aryan Homeland were linked together for forty-five years. The effort at establishing a visible, overt Aryan Homeland in the Pacific Northwest was effectively staunched by the counter-establishment of Human Rights groups mostly centered in Idaho. These groups, amazingly enough, did not rely on gun culture or gun-culture mentality to accomplish their ends of social justice; rather, they used education, visibility, and common sense to portray the Aryan Nations as worthy of public ridicule.

CHAPTER 14

The Celebration of Violence: A Live-fire Demonstration Carried Out by Japan's Contemporary Military[1]

Eyal Ben-Ari and Sabine Frühstück

Bombers dropping lethal loads near Tokyo? Tanks shelling targets on the Kanto plain? Infantry soldiers capturing lookout posts and shooting at objectives along the foothills of Mt Fuji? No, these are not part of some imaginary movie depicting a new war in contemporary Japan. All of these activities take place in an annual live-fire exercise carried out by Japan's contemporary military, the Japan Self-Defense Forces (SDF). Held during the first weekend of each September at one of the SDF's major training camps, this event presents the main armaments and capabilities of different units, enacts simplified combat scenarios involving ground and air forces, and entails an exhibition of helicopters, tanks and artillery pieces. Attended by tens of thousands of spectators, reports about the exercise are often broadcast on Japan's major television channels that evening and printed in the major newspapers the following day. Yet what is remarkable in regard to this event is not the use of live fire, since the SDF like all militaries, regularly carries out maneuvers and training. Rather what is significant about the exercise is its context.

The SDF exists in a context marked by powerful constitutional limits, a strong anti-militaristic culture, active pacifist movements and the suspicion constantly voiced by the country's Asian neighbors about Japan's potential for remilitarization (Berger 1998; Hanami 1996: 238). The Japanese public blamed the country's defeat in the Second World War on the "generals," and part of the legacy of that defeat is that the word *military* became synonymous with subjugation, destruction, and disaster. This attitude was magnified by the effects of the atomic bomb which, aside from the sheer misery its use caused hundreds of thousands of people, resulted in a sense of victimhood at the hands both the US and Japan's aggressive wartime military regime. As reflected regularly in opinion polls (Halloran 1994: 13), the experience of the Second World War has led to the emergence of a strong anti-militaristic ethos set against Japan acquiring a large military establishment. One of the most important features of these circumstances has been the institution of strong legal limits—Article 9 of the country's constitution—on Japan's right to maintain armed forces and to sustain any kind of offensive security policy (Arase 1995). Indeed, a central implication of this frame of mind has been that state representatives give precedence to non-violent responses—such as economic diplomacy—to policy issues (Katzenstein 1996).

The existence of Japan's Self-Defense Forces is thus problematic. It exists in a state of limbo: it is a military without explicit recognition of it as such. It now has about 250,000 soldiers (all are volunteers) and, according to official figures, the world's third largest defense budget (about one per cent of the GDP). The SDF is in fact a fully-fledged military establishment complete with three services (ground, maritime and air), the latest military technology (tanks, ships and planes and a variety of state-of-the art weaponry), and all of the usual organizational accompaniments to any military structure (territorial divisions, brigades and training methods). The live-fire exercise that forms the focus of our analysis thus raises a rather peculiar set of issues.

At the most general level, the question this analysis addresses is how are the armed forces portrayed in the context of a society marked by anti-militarism? Yet given that the military (along with the police) is *the* organization most strongly identified with the legitimate use of violence (Boene 1990; Bourdieu 1999: 58-9) such a question is still too general. What needs examination, we argue, are the specific ways in which the military's expertise in handling—managing, controlling, or effecting—violence is represented. More specifically, we ask how violence is both concealed and exposed in the specific historical context of contemporary Japan.

Violence has been the object of rather intense anthropological scrutiny in the past decade or so. This inquiry represents the extension of certain interests that have marked anthropology since its establishment. Two strands, or traditions, of scholarship have been precursors to current concerns. The first comprises works linking violence and ritual. Girard (1977), for example, has argued that ritual controls, channels and represses human violence so as to allow ordered social life. Essential to this point of view is the idea that rites and ceremonies allow the controlled displacement of aggressive impulses (Bouroncle 2000: 55; Schechner 1994; Watson 1996). The second strand of research includes studies focused on the causes of warfare (Haas 1990; Foster and Rubinstein 1989; Rubinstein 1994). This approach has roots either in sociobiology and sees war as providing opportunities for mating and reproduction or competition between individuals (Chagnon 1988), or in ecological theories and regards war as the outcome of inter-group competition for scarce resources such as land, food or trade opportunities (Ferguson 1984).

More recent work has tended to explore other aspects of violence. The stress in much of this newer literature has been on the constructed nature of violence, the symbolism in which it is embedded, and its destructive and traumatic effects (Abbink 2000: xv; Nordstrom and Robben 1995; Sluka 2000a,b). Here the primary links have been made to issues related to cultural representations and images or to the body and personal experience.

At the same time however, and in contrast to sociologists, political scientists, or historians, anthropologists have largely ignored the military (Simons 1999). As a number of scholars have noted, while anthropologists often have studied aspects of conflict among tribal or agricultural societies, they have rarely examined the place of the military in complex industrialized societies (Goldschmidt 1989: 9; Mandelbaum 1989). Moreover, as Krohn-Hansen (1994: 367) stresses, anthropological studies of violence tend to focus on the victim's perspective, often missing out on the perpetrators. This point is surprising because if one wants to understand the contemporary social and cultural significance of violence, then the armed forces would seem to be a key research site. Following Da Matta (1984: 219) because soldiers are materializations of "power in its most instrumental and open—or brutal—form" it is important that we understand the manner by which this form—the potential for violence—is socially and culturally handled. To be sure, anthropologists have long been aware of the power of the state's military arm, but anthropological analyses of the state's use of force or violence have tended (in congruence with the discipline's partiality toward the underdog) to focus almost exclusively on the victims of state actions, or on movements of resistance against the state (Feldman 1991; Sluka 2000a,b; Tambiah 1992). Where military establishments have been studied (or alluded to) they have usually been the armed forces of authoritarian regimes (such as Brazil or Franco's Spain), Third World states, or stateless groups (Kapferer 1988; Nordstrom; 1997 Sluka 2000a,b).

But what of the military establishments of the technologically advanced democracies? The handful of ethnographies published about the armed forces such countries have usually focused on the internal organization of these forces (Ben-Ari 1998; Simons 1997, 1998; Winslow 1997). In these studies, the attention accorded to the use of violence has usually focused on the formal and informal dynamics of field units and on how individuals are conditioned to engage in organized aggression. Yet special historical conditions have made the circumstances of these contemporary militaries problematic. The militaries of today's industrialized democracies are not those of the Cold War and certainly not those of the Second World War. These military establishments are undergoing sweeping shifts in their domestic status, structure, missions and tasks and most importantly, the ways they use force and violence. Their greater participation in peace-keeping and peace-enforcement operations, for example, is indicative of problems centered on justifying the use of state-violence in terms external to any one state (Ben-Ari and El-Ron 2002; El-Ron, Shamir and Ben-Ari 1999; Ignatieff 1998). Similarly, the greater sensitivity of military leaders to the political repercussions of their actions (both domestically and externally) demonstrates the importance of new criteria for assessing military exploits (Boene 2000: 75; MacKinlay 1989). But the most important trend involves changing attitudes toward the use of force and the perpetration of violence (Moskos 2000: 5). Cultural transformations in these societies have led to a very heavy stress on keeping casualties to a minimum, and to a questioning, within the military and especially outside of it, of the morality and justification for using military power (Bellamy 1996: 30; Burk 1998: 12; Moskos, Williams and Segal 2000: 5–6). The recent aggressive incursions into Afghanistan and Iraq ironically attest to this: the violence perpetuated by various "coalition" forces is legitimated by a strong rhetorical stress on precision warfare, a strong control of the dissemination of media reports about the effects of violence (on both sides), and the minimization of casualties.

Let us be clear in this regard. While the use of force is still a major characteristic of contemporary states the terms for using organized violence have become more contested in public arenas in many societies, such as those of Western Europe. That the militaries of the technologically advanced societies are contested institutions raises a host of questions about how they manage their identity as the wielders of the means of violence. Scholars have explored some of the explicit political strategies—gathering support, lobbying for funds, or handling the media, for example—by which these military establishments are handling their problematic situations (Feaver 1999: 235; Burk 1998: 459). Given their heavy stress on the political arrangements that characterize civil-military relations, these studies have done little to explore the cultural imagery and practices by which the militaries of the technologically advanced democracies handle their problematic relation to violence.

Anthropology seems to offer tools for exploring these issues. One can certainly study the "ordinary" (Das and Kleiman 1997: 7), or the hidden or secret side of the state (Feldman 1997) in effecting violence. But anthropology also offers sophisticated tools for the investigation of "public events" (Handelman 1998) or "cultural performances" (MacAloon 1984a: 1): occasions in which a culture or society reflect upon and define themselves, dramatize their collective myths and history, and present themselves with alternatives. Thus for instance, Da Matta (1984), Kertzer (1988), and Fernandez (1986) suggest that political rituals in which the armed forces of various states participate are part of the ways in which the legitimacy, acceptance, and support of the state is presented and acknowledged. But it has been Aijmer (2000: 10) who has underscored the military's peculiar link to violence, observing:

> the violent imagery of the state would incorporate discursive material activities, including the use of uniforms, drills, parades and displays. The uniform communicates danger as well as style and beauty, the drills are choreographed for assumed effectiveness and staged so as to appear threatening for those who are defined as outsiders. Military shows are intended to be visibly pleasing in their display of visual violence.

What Aijmer (2000: 8) seems to be suggesting is that one prime aim of anthropology is to show how violence is domesticated and shaped into a controlled presence in various social institutions through the combined use of discourse, drills and displays. While he does not formulate this point explicitly,

Aijmer seems to posit that the primary means in this regard are the aestheticization and celebration of violence through presentation of its thrilling and seductive aspects (Lofving and Macek 1999). Within US anthropology Lutz and Nonini (1999; see also Nash 1989) have taken up this line of reasoning to show how trans-national economic and political processes have transformed people's livelihood and increased levels of conflict, violence and warfare. Basically, they try to chart the relations between political economy and forms of violence. As they (1999: 73) state, "We view violence less as an epiphenomenon of economic process than a narrative and institutional force requiring its own reckoning and history." In a separate work Lutz (2001) suggests that anthropologists should take up a concept of militarization that avoids a focus on the discrete event of war and draws attention to broader processes of war preparation. Her contention is that we need to understand different aspects of how a society prepares itself for the perpetration of violence (Lutz and Nonini 1999: 73). In a related vein, Chris Hedges (2002) raises the question of what social processes lead to the creation of fantasies about war and to the suspension of self-criticism in regard to the use of violence.

In addition to their general focus on the victims rather than on the perpetrators of state-sanctioned violence, anthropologists have tended to extract information about violence after the fact (Schroder and Schmidt 2001: 13). The great bulk of the documentation has occurred in the wake of violence—most often through collecting and interpreting narratives—and in that manner reconstructing it. Relatively little has been done to document the occurrence or presentation of military violence on the scene.

Against this background, we return to the SDF's live-fire demonstration in order to delineate the questions guiding our analysis. The direct translation of the Japanese word for the demonstration, *enshu*, is "exercise," "maneuver," or "mock battle," but in this context we analyze it as a public event (Handelman 1998). Thus our first set of questions centers on the internal logic of this performance: how is it put together in terms of actions and stages, spatial arrangements and displays, and the timing and tempo of its various movements? What are the messages and experiences that the SDF tries to transmit and create through the event? Our second set centers on the ways in which this internal logic and the messages it carries are related to the negotiations and ties the SDF attempts to create with diverse publics. Through an analysis of the logic of this event, we ask about the messages the SDF attempt to transmit to such groups as politicians, civilian administrators, members of other military organizations, support associations, representatives of the Japanese media, and the "general" public.(2) The third set focuses on how these messages and experiences are related to the problematic status of the SDF in Japanese society: How is the expertise of the SDF in effecting violence *handled*—transformed into an object of entertainment, aesthetic contemplation, or fascination—through the live-fire exercise? Our fourth set of questions relates to the wider implication of our analysis, to the potential contribution of anthropology to the study of those who wield the instruments of violence in contemporary societies: How does our investigation shed light on the problem of how the military in technologically advanced societies controls violence?

The Live-fire Exercise

The live-fire exercise was first organized in 1961, primarily to introduce the latest weaponry and tactics to officer candidates. As the commercial video-tape depicting the 1997 demonstration explains, the life-fire exercise was first held publicly in 1966 as an attempt to "deepen the understanding and knowledge of the SDF in the Japanese population." Today the public event is the culmination of a week of demonstrations with the earlier ones aimed specifically at military personnel (such as students from the National Military Academy or people attending military courses). Only the last two demonstrations (on Saturday and Sunday) are held for a variety of other publics. The publicly held events are our focus.

Tickets for the event are free and are allocated to invited guests—senior politicians and bureaucrats, and local government officials—and to members of the wider interested public (advertisements for the event appear in various magazines) who are chosen according to a lottery. At the same time, the SDF appeals to all of its prefectural support associations to assemble members who would like to be there and keeps tickets for soldiers and officers who want to attend the demonstration. On the tickets are written the names of three television networks that carry cancellation information and that usually broadcast short reports of the event on the evening news. The top line of the one-page brochure that comes with the tickets reads "Fuji General Live-Fire Maneuver: (Japan) Ground Self-Defense Forces" and the dates open to the public.

One large photograph shows helicopters, tanks and a large group of spectators, and another depict soldiers on motorbikes firing machine guns. Smaller photographs show spectators climbing onto a tank, a missile being fired and leaving a great streak of white and gray smoke behind it, a mobile artillery piece, a group of spectators looking at five airplanes that have just gone from flying in formation into different directions, and tanks with many helicopters flying above them. A public relations representative from the Japan Defense Agency (the civilian body overseeing the SDF) told us that between 25,000 and 30,000 people attend the event on a given day, implying that over 50,000 people witness it during a single weekend. The demonstration is held in one of the large firing ranges at the foot of Mt Fuji.

Given the size of the crowds and the mass of soldiers and weapons appearing in the exercise, the whole operation was complex. People arriving in private cars parked in space provided at nearby military bases. Together with those arriving by train, they were bused to the firing range. Many organized groups from the prefectural support associations arrived by tour buses that parked near the viewing stands. At the entrance to the stands were reception areas staffed by noncommissioned officers who took tickets and gave out copies of the program. Five large stands—each seating hundreds of people—were arranged at the front of the firing range. Two stands were allocated to the more important guests: the director of the Japan Defense Agency and other top bureaucratic officials, the chiefs of staff of the three SDF services, high ranking members of the US armed forces, foreign defense attachés, Diet members and representatives of the national government, and the media. The other stands seated local government officials, lower ranking military officers, and some members of the prefectural support association. Adjoining the stands were enormous mats where members of the general public were seated. Many people brought lunch boxes and drinks (some alcoholic) and partook of these during the breaks or after the demonstration.

In front of the stands and mats was an area hundreds of square meters in extent that formed the maneuver area or *stage* for the demonstration. Off in the distant hills a few kilometers away were the targets that the artillery pieces and tanks shot at. A military band playing (Western) martial music stood between the mats and the stage. Behind the stands were a number of commercial booths. Some sold drinks and snacks. Others sold souvenirs: shoes, belts, and lighters with emblems of the SDF and various units; or tie clips, dolls, and telephone cards with pictures of weapons and vehicles. Other booths offered videotapes of weapons or military vehicles, small plastic models of tanks and planes, or jackets with "US Air Force" written on them. Young men stood around the booths and talked about the posters sold or about types of weapons. Also located this area were the public toilets, a small medical center, and a communications station.

Whereas most of the audience was dressed in casual clothing, the invitees wore suits and the senior military officials (Japanese and foreign) wore uniforms. One young man donned a baseball cap with the caption "Peace, People, Japan," a slogan appearing on recruitment posters at the time. Many people bought hats with the word "Rangers" or "Airborne" stitched above "Japan Self-Defense Forces" (all in English). The presence of many families with children in strollers contributed to an atmosphere of an outing. Some people took the opportunity to ask soldiers about their ranks, pointing to their insignia. Finally, numerous people came equipped with video and still cameras, long-range binoculars, and telephoto lenses.

A few minutes past ten, a flow of buses carried female tour guides and dozens of invited guests to the front of the stands. 10:20 a.m., a fleet of jeeps and limousines brought the most important people to their stand. All these guests were met by SDF personnel and shown to their seats. We saw only one Japanese flag flying above the control tent located to the side of the stands. Until the demonstration began at 10:30 a.m., a woman spoke through the public address system, describing the kinds of vehicles we were going to see, the targets to be shot at, and the weapons to be used. At exactly 10:30 a.m. a male announcer took over and said that the demonstration was being presented through the cooperation of the Ground and Air Self-Defense Forces and its aim was "to deepen the understanding of the SDF." He, too, listed the kinds of drills, equipment and armaments we were to witness.

The demonstration began when two yellow and green smoke grenades were set off on hills opposite the stands, defining the boundaries within which the forces were allowed to fire live ammunition. After describing how far different kinds of weapons can fire, the announcer declared that the first performance would be by the air force. Two bombing-runs—one of explosive bombs and the other of fire-bombs—were carried out by Phantom jets, and closely following them a number of helicopters swooshed down across the maneuver area. These runs greatly excited the crowd. From this point onwards, the public address system often patched the audience in to what appeared to be the communications net: We could hear the orders of the commanders to take aim and fire.

Next, two groups of six soldiers parachuted from planes to land where the smoke grenades had been set off. They jumped in staggered formation, and the crowd watched for several minutes as they parachuted down. Immediately following them, another group of paratroopers rappelled down from large helicopters while combat helicopters at the side of the area supplied support fire. Subsequently, two large helicopters landed at the front of the stage: From one emerged a large number of motorcycles, and the other disgorged jeeps. The crowd was thrilled by these performances: We saw many people clap their hands, and we heard shouts of support and a variety of "oos" and "ahs."

The next stage focused on the ground forces: First, to the excitement of the audience, a number of armored personnel carriers rode up to the front of the stage and spewed out soldiers, who ran up to some embankments and shot a variety of small arms at red and white targets. Immediately following them, two anti-mine missiles were fired from jeeps. Three artillery pieces were then presented to us. The announcer explained that, while these pieces could hit targets as far as 30 kilometers distant (he named towns in vicinity that they could reach), because of safety restrictions, here they would only be fired five or six kilometers. After these guns were fired, a single, large, anti aircraft missile was launched, and then four tanks appeared and shot at other targets. All of these displays were accompanied by shouts of "amazing" (*Sugoi!*) and "well done" (*Umai!*).

After a 15-minute break, the second part of the demonstration, consisting of a simulated battle, began. After a few new tanks were introduced and had fired and attacked targets, a number of helicopters rose from the sides of the stands to fire a variety of missiles and machine guns at the same targets. This was the signal to begin an artillery and mortar barrage to provide support fire and smoke screens for the soldiers and vehicles that "fought" within the confines of the stage. The following activities then took place in quick succession: Helicopters fired anti-tank missiles; tanks (going to and from their firing stations) cooperated to shoot at diverse targets; and then two tanks reversed very quickly and stopped about twenty five meters from the first row of spectators. The crowd reacted enthusiastically to the display of power by the tanks (to the combination of size, noise, smell and smoke). Then, two transport planes and two helicopters flew over our heads to drop tens of paratroopers.

The end of the demonstration was marked by a crescendo of activities: A number of smoke bombs erupted to create a backdrop of smoke a few hundred meters behind the stage. Into the corridor that was created between this smoke screen and the front of the maneuver area drove all of the vehicles that had participated in the demonstration, while above them flew the helicopters that had taken part in the event. The sound was deafening, and the sight akin to a movie clip, with vehicles moving from our left to our right. Many people stood up and clapped. The demonstration, which had taken about an hour and forty minutes, was over. In quick succession limousines and jeeps came up to the VIP stand to take the important guests on to lunch at one of the nearby bases.

State Ceremonies: Order and the Instruments of Violence

Handelman (1998: 16) suggests that if public events are constructs designed to carry certain messages and to create certain experiences, then the logic of how they are put together is crucial to how they work. Let us trace out the main elements involved in the logic of the live-fire exercise.

To begin with, the spatial arrangement of people and roles in and around the exercise carries a strong message of order, categorization, and hierarchy. Seating—and the arrangements of ticketing, transporting, and ushering accompanying it—exemplifies this order. Attendees' placement differs according to the following pattern: Members of the general public are asked to sit on large mats set out on the ground whereas others are invited to sit on benches, invited guests are seated in stands specifically allocated to them, and prominent invitees have specially designated seats with their names and titles on them. Ushers and escorts similarly vary, from general escorts who guide the movements of noninvitees to specially designated escorts for the privileged VIPs. Transport also varies and includes private cars, public buses arriving at a bus station in back of the stands, and special tour buses that bring invited guests to the front of the stands. The privileged few—politicians, administrators and generals as well as foreign dignitaries—are not only brought in jeeps and limousines to their stand, but they are also ushered in in full view of the gathering audience.

At first glance then, the demonstration is what Handelman (1998: xxix) calls events of presentation, mirrors held up to social order, reflecting and expressing what their composers desire for society, the form, fantasy, and power of these events deriving directly from social order. Civic events held at the local or regional levels are one example of these kinds of events (Manning 1983). Yet the most well known instances are state mandated occasions such as National Days (Handelman and Katz 1995) or military parades. In this sense, the live-fire maneuver can be likened to a military march-past of the kind that takes place around the world (including recently, in Japan). In such parades, the marching troops as well as the reviewing authorities incarnate the order of the state (Azaryahu 1999; Da Matta 1984: 219; Kertzer 1988: 30). In this case, it is the politicians, senior administrators, and commanders of the three military services who personify the major groups of the Japanese state. These individuals play a double role as both audience and performers: They are there to simultaneously watch the demonstration but also to be themselves "on view" (Ben Ari 1991b).

Other features characterize military parades. First, following Da Matta (1984: 219), parades are marked by a strict separation between performers and audience. Unlike certain religious processions that people can enter or leave at will (Kugelmass 1991), in the military parade there are strictly delimited camps: those who are qualified to be inside the order and the rigid hierarchy of the event and those who are outside of it (Da Matta 1984: 218-19). It is especially the first part of the live-fire demonstration that the separation between the soldiers, the authorities, and general audience is most evident. The general, undifferentiated audience thus sits partitioned off by ropes, to talk, admire, and witness the order presented to it. The separation is thus not only related to practical reasons but it carries messages about the proper loci of power and authority.

Second, as Fernandez (1986: 276) notes, the "military parade is a parade of the 'instruments of violence' of which the nation-state enjoys sole possession and legitimate use". Troops participating in the live-fire exercise embody this very possession of such violent instruments. But, as we have argued, it is precisely this ownership that is contested in the technologically advanced democracies in general, and in Japan in particular. In other words, the SDF's bid for acknowledgement as a professional military establishment is itself especially problematic because it is not just another organization in contemporary Japan. Their professionalism is unlike that of, say, doctors or lawyers. Their professionalism centers on the management and operation of violence.

Didactics, Subordination, and Civil–Military Relations

Given this background, it is not surprising that the most explicit message of the live-fire exercise is the one announced over the loudspeakers at the beginning of the event: That the demonstration's aim is to "to deepen the understanding of the SDF." The organizers of the event attempt to do this in a variety of ways. First, the announcers guide the crowd's understanding and contextualization of the live-fire exercise by providing interpretive frames for what happens in the performance and for the general operation of the SDF. The announcers furnish what seem to be rather uncomplicated data and information, for example, myriad descriptions of specific weapons and vehicles. Yet providing such information is part of what may be termed a celebration of military technology, of having the latest and most advanced techniques. It also resonates with more general emphases found around the world with such "abstract" ideas as the accuracy and precision of "smart bombs" or long-range missiles. The SDF thus tries to associate itself with the latest and most modern forces where, increasingly "technological sophistication replaces brute force as the key to victory" (Moskos 2000: 11–12).

Indeed, our impression is that some people attend the live-fire exercise just as they would go to a gun show. We were told that in 1976, Type 74 tanks were part of the show for the first time, and since then, new weaponry has been presented to the SDF's various publics every year. On the occasion of the Ground Forces' 40th anniversary in 1990, for instance, Type 90 tanks were shown and their firepower displayed for the first time. To this day the live-fire exercise is the only occasion on which new weaponry is not only exhibited to the wider Japanese public but is also fired publicly, an activity that comes closest to the SDF's military role in its most narrow sense.

Second, there is a constant stress on the SDF's acute awareness of issues related to safety. One example is the announcer's explanation that while certain artillery pieces can fire 30 km, the firing range where the demonstration takes place only allows a limit of 6 km. In explaining that it does not shoot shells at distant targets, the SDF actively attempts to transmit the message that it takes into consideration the limits imposed by the placement of its camps and firing ranges near civilian areas. In addition, SDF representatives seem to explain that the forces are law abiding while the overall message is that the use of force is under close supervision and control.

Third, one finds a constant emphasis on cooperation between the different constituent units of the SDF and their interlinkage into one organization. This message is conveyed through the announcements and is embodied in the actual joint maneuvers of the air and ground forces. This stress on the unity, the oneness of the SDF, and its ability to function as a single body reflects the general self-image of contemporary armed forces as based on the flexibility, interoperability, and modularity of a "total force" (Williams 2000: 267). On an implicit level, the emphasis on unity is perhaps related to the SDF's desire to stress its disconnection from the prewar military, especially, from the prewar conflicts that characterized the links between the imperial army and navy.

A fourth point is related to what may be termed the civil-military paradox that exists in any state: "The very institution created to protect the polity is given sufficient power to become a threat to the polity" (Feaver 1999: 214). In the Japanese case, this threat is one that has a historical precedent but is evident in contemporary society in a "widely shared suspicion that antidemocratic forces are afoot in Japan seeking to exploit the security issue to engineer a reactionary takeover" (Berger 1998: 196). Thus, for instance, Japanese historians like Igarashi (2000; also Yoneyama 1999) have contended that the past—specifically, the experience of the Second World War—persists within and festers underneath various phenomena in post-war Japan. Similarly, the central problem addressed in a recent volume on memories of the Asia-Pacific War centers on how memories "are recalcitrant and menacing" and "continue to be unsettling" (Fujitani et al. 2001: 2). Fujitani et al.'s interpretations of the ways these concerns are acted upon by various social critics and movements center either on Japan's continued evasion of national responsibility or on the political maneuvering of its elites. In a related manner, Harootunian (1999: 147-8) worries that recent attempts to revive memorials to Japan's war dead means "returning Japan to a time when people were socialized into performing unhesitant service to the emperor." Against this background, the presence of the politicians and senior bureaucrats at the live-fire demonstration thus also carries concrete messages about the SDF's subordination to civilian leaders. These civilians are there to acknowledge the performance of the soldiers before them and to "play" the role of democratically elected or designated civilian overseers of the SDF in front of the wider public.

Spectacle: Power, Force, and Movement

Much of the above analysis could well apply to any military parade. The live-fire exercise, however, has an added set of features that sets it apart from such processions in terms of how it handles violence. In its enactment of the combat-scenarios, the exercise reveals what is normally hidden in the Japanese context: the real character of the SDF as a military organization, as a body of people charged with the operation of the means of violence. Our contention is that the show of fire power (the central element of the demonstration) takes on the character of spectacle, a dynamic social form that demands movement, action, and change on the part of the human actors who are center stage, and excitement, thrill and pleasure on the part of the spectators (MacAloon 1984b: 244). Indeed, the very term *spectacle* has two connotations: one related to the verb *spectate* and connected to viewing a grand demonstration, and the other related to *spectacular* and implying something that is especially impressive or striking.

To start with, soldiers wearing fatigues, rather than dress uniforms, indicate that some kind of action is going on. But perhaps more importantly, members of the SDF themselves understand the event as a spectacle: One lieutenant colonel used the English term *show* to describe what we were seeing. Yet it is the actual structure and the features of the demonstration that underscore its character as a spectacle. First, consider that almost all of the presentations are accompanied by pyrotechnics that, like fireworks, combine lights and colors, sounds and smells, and even touch. The variety of colors as in the smoke bombs, black gas fumes or the intense hues of the missiles being fired are made all the more impressive against the background of the rather subdued browns and greens of the stage, the soldiers' uniforms, and the camouflage of the vehicles. The variety of sounds heard and reverberations felt during the exercise further amplify the impressiveness of the event. Furthermore, the smell of the sulfur from the weapons or the oil burned by the heavy machinery drifting back to the crowd, adding a tangible olfactory dimension to the demonstration. The armored vehicles that drive near the crowd vibrate almost palpably from the explosive discharges, enhancing the physical appreciation of the exercise.

Next consider movement. Unlike parades, with their lineal, unidirectional movement, the soldiers and vehicles in the exercise move in all directions. For example, each armored vehicle rolls onto the stage and shoots while standing still or while maneuvering. The helicopters move up and down, forwards and backwards, and across the maneuver ground. Finally, the demonstration ends in a climactic, high-speed (and almost deafening) movement of all of the participating vehicles and aircraft. The simultaneous staging of multiple activities—as in three ring circuses—visually presents the disciplined might of the SDF and seeks to overwhelm the audience through a display of mass and magnitude (Handelman 1997: 395). Along the same lines, the visibility of the units and the choreographing of all of the concurrent activities attest to the power of the forces and their unity of purpose. Further, the fact that the targets of the weaponry are not human adds an element of fun to the combat demonstration that further takes the sting out of the violence.

Another indicator of spectators' absorption with the dramatic character of the fire-exercise was their avid photographing of it. Indeed, the use of still cameras and video equipment was greater during the simulated combat-scenario than throughout other stages. Further, for the picture takers, the focal points were very much on the spectacular aspects of the show: the weapons, the movement, and the colors. Finally, several commercially available videotapes about the weaponry used by the ground forces depict scenes primarily taken from the live-fire exercise. Even the SDF's own promotional video repeats the dramatic imagery of the live-fire exercise, for example, showing the motorcycle-riding soldiers emerging from helicopters to fire their weapons. Whereas such a scene is unlikely to unfold in the case of real hostilities, it is the standard fare in the average action movie and provides the opening sequence of the SDF video. Perhaps, like members of other technologically advanced societies, so many Japanese have become what Sontag (1978: 24) calls image junkies. For such people, having an experience often becomes identical with taking a photograph of it, and participating in a public event come more and more to be equated with looking at it in photographic form (Handelman 1997: 397). Taking pictures or videos of the live-fire exercise to view at home not only extends the boundaries of the event beyond its spatiotemporal limits (Ben-Ari 1991a), but is an act of domestication: Violence is transported home to be enjoyed in the comfortable circumstances of one's private space, but in a regulated manner. Conversely, by sending a *trace* of the SDF home, Japan's military is also (in minuscule form) mobilizing the family.

Finally, consider the scripted character of the demonstration. Unlike sports events, the maneuver's outcome is not uncertain, and there is very little space for improvisation or individual creativity left within the general frame of the event. The exercise also differs from the live-fire training that the SDF regularly carries out, which involves hypothetical enemies (sometimes played by friendly forces), is open-ended, and has space for initiative and variation. Rather, because the event is tightly scripted, the emphasis shifts to its more dramatic or imposing aspects. Hence, unlike military parades with their orderly presentation of military and state orders, the live-fire maneuver also involves the *spectacularization* of violence through the combination of fire, colors, noise, smell and movement. It is this spectacularization that turns actions related to soldiering into entertaining displays.

Opening Doors to Tactile Experiences: Between Picnic and Festival

But the day's events are not just about spectacle. In the third part of the demonstration, the SDF handles its problematic monopoly over the means of violence in a manner that compliments the live-fire spectacular. Similar to what happens during open-day festivals held throughout the year in many military bases in Japan (and the world), the SDF invites the public to take a closer view of the helicopters and armored vehicles parked in the maneuver area. Whereas on open-days it is specific bases that host the public, in this case it is the "whole" SDF establishment that entertains its civilian guests. In this respect, the controlled breakdown of boundaries between the audience and the performers can be seen as part of the breaching of limits between society and the SDF. This is done literally by lowering the ropes marking off the hitherto restricted maneuver area and allowing thousands of people into where the vehicles are parked. This breach allows people: people, including children, to touch the vehicles, climb up on them, feel the contrast between their own body size and that of the vehicles, and smell the vehicles' odors.

What is of importance here is that this stage takes place *after* the main part of the event. The audience is allowed to touch and climb on the very vehicles that had previously participated in the fire-exercise. In a sense, then, this part of the day is akin to visiting the back-stage of a theater after a performance to look at the props and meet the actors. The "stylistic choices" governing the photographs taken at this stage underscore these ideas. Almost all of the pictures are composites of family, relatives or friends placed in, on, or near the vehicles, and they often include one of the soldiers in the area. Similarly, this stage of the event provides opportunities for people to speak to soldiers, to those assigned to stand next to the vehicles or to those acting as ushers. Again, as with open-door activities, one of the aims is to bring the SDF closer to the "people" and—among other messages—show that soldiers are "real persons." To follow MacAloon (1984b: 246) this stage partakes of the character of a festival rather than a spectacle because in festival, the roles of actors and spectators are less distinguishable.

The overall mood of festival is heightened by the fact that, except those soldiers or guests on duty, everyone else wears casual clothing. In addition, many people bring food and drinks to consume, chiefly during this stage of the demonstration. Indeed, we saw literally thousands of people spread out private mats over the large ones provided by the SDF, creating little territories within which they held their picnics. Finally, as in Shinto festivals, the booths behind the stands sell soft drinks as well as souvenirs and toys, which were taken home as evidence of participation in this day. In this sense, the commercialization of militaria is another practice by which the violence of the SDF is normalized: Little mementos domesticate the military by bringing its memories home. In a complementary manner, we find that in the controlled breakdown of the boundaries between the military and civilians, the SDF also attempts to encompass, to take in, civilian society

A Rite of Solidarity, a Test of Professionalism

To order tickets, most people contact either the public relations office of the Defense Agency or local public relations offices of bases near their homes. One has to provide one's name, address, phone number, and one's profession in order to receive a ticket. Although anyone who provides these data receives a ticket, provided the application form is filled out early enough, in actuality one does not attend anonymously. Attendance presupposes an act of commitment that enables the military authorities to potentially check one's identity. In addition, depending on where one comes from, the live-fire exercise might involve a considerable financial investment, for public transport, an overnight stay at a hotel, food and drink and probably the purchase of a souvenir.

Although we have used the term *public* up to this point, we do not assume that the audience forms one homogeneous body. Rather, the public is broadly divided into several groups. The most important group comprises members of the prefectural support associations of veterans, family members and friends of SDF personnel. They come from all over Japan to see what their relatives and friends do. Given that these people are convinced of the necessity and legitimacy of the SDF, their participation should be seen as one of partaking in a rite of solidarity. Their understanding and acceptance of the SDF do not need to be deepened. For them the live-fire exercise rather serves as a statement of allegiance and celebration. Such solidarity is also evident in the occasional reacquaintances that take place between friends and colleagues and is further reinforced by people eating and drinking together in small groups. The theme of creating a sense of commonality is closely linked to the much more explicit messages of shared fate, mission, or pride of the SDF which are carried by the demonstration.

Another group includes local government officials from around the country and especially from areas adjacent to military bases. The idea, as one guest told us, is to invite influential local "opinion leaders," partly to ensure their continuing tolerance of the noise and traffic caused by the activities of the SDF in and around training camps and bases during the entire year. But the point is a more general one. The SDF's problematic existence forces it to cultivate ties with hundreds of representatives of local governments on a long-term basis. This live-fire exercise provides the SDF with an opportunity to play host to these people. Many of the invited guests are taken to bases around the area and given lunch at camp dining halls. According to testimonies we received, they ate the same lunch that the soldiers ate, signaling a commonality through eating together.

A third group that attends the live-fire exercise includes SDF personnel: formal guests (like the heads of the three services) or individuals who attend in civilian clothes (but who often wear a cap, shirt or some accessory that identifies them as members of the military). Although some seem to be mainly interested in seeing new weaponry in action, they play two additional roles: They partici-pate in the demonstration as a rite of solidarity and act as experts or professional appraisers of the performers. They thus help to turn the live-fire exercise—at least in the eyes of those who actively participate—into a kind of test of profes-sionalism. As in parades, the smooth running of the demonstration involves ele-ments of flow, efficiency, and control. Indeed, because the synchronization of combined movements is very difficult to achieve, and the challenge for soldiers and officers is to carry out the required movements in the most skilled manner possible. The additional pressure of performing in front of multiple publics, especially higher-ranking peers, intensifies the challenge. Similarly, the presence of foreign commanders and officers should be seen in the content of the recog-nition that the SDF seeks from its own seriousness, expertise and performance from professional others.

Although the exercise has a set script, there is still a risk of failure, of not putting up a good performance. Thus like some rituals, the live-fire exercise is a gamble, a trial (Howe 2000: 76). Such a gamble on the part of those who wage the activity is only significant if they have something to lose. For the military per-sonnel, the risk consists of tarnishing the reputation of the SDF or of their pro-fessionalism. We received hints of this from various officers with whom we talked. A first lieutenant from the signals corps said that although the general structure of the event does not change much from year to year, a military person attending the exercise either looks for new weaponry that is being displayed or at the kinds of details that allow him or her to gauge the SDF's performance. A lieutenant colonel in his early forties noted that the live-fire demonstration is also used as a training exercise, while another noted that it is one of the missions that the Fuji Training School must carry out and that its commanders and sol-diers are evaluated according to their performance in it.

Statements of Existence: The Media, Politicians, and the State

Media representatives attending the live-fire exercise include reporters from Japan's major newspapers and TV stations and persons who are themselves SDF personnel. In contrast to some popular stereotypes, not all of the country's journalists are critical of the SDF. Rather, as several journalists from Japan's mainstream newspapers told us, although there are no formal regulations governing reports on the military, until very recently it was highly controversial to report on the SDF in any other than critical way. In addition, among consumers of mainstream media there is a lack of interest in defense issues, in general, and in the SDF, more particularly. The public relations department of the SDF thus wants to gain exposure and does this, among other ways, by inviting media representatives to such events as the live-fire exercise.

For their part, military photographers and journalists record the event for internal SDF use. Photographs of, and reports on, the live-fire exercise are printed in newsletters and magazines published by the Defense Agency (such as the "Securitarian"), exhibited during open door days, decorate the corridor walls of the SDF's educational institutions (such as the National Defense Academy and the General Staff College) and are disseminated among the SDF in various other contexts. The internal dissemination of the images of the exercise, again, allows the event to transcend its spatial and temporal limits and familiarizes insiders with those self-defining moments that are a part of any organization's history.

The demonstration is a "media event" suggests that one of its primary purposes is to advertise the SDF's existence. The live-fire exercise allows the SDF not only to address certain issues but also to redress, to rectify, some of the problems embedded in its existence in Japanese society. Many officers we interviewed commented about the place of the SDF in Japanese society with sadness and often offered a plea for recognition of the force's importance. Unlike military parades, where politicians directly address the audience, the live-fire demonstration subtly speaks to the politicians and senior administrators present, seeking acknowledgment of the SDF. More concretely, the SDF may use this opportunity to remind politicians that the forces can be used in times of emergency and to plead for support in political arenas normally closed to uniformed representatives of the SDF. This last point is important since the comprehensive rules providing for civilian control over military matters include regulations that prevent uniformed personnel from appearing in parliament or some media forums. Finally, noted earlier, the presence of foreign commanders and officers (especially Americans) can be interpreted as part of the recognition that the SDF seeks from "professional others" for the forces' their seriousness, expertise and performance.

Conclusion

We began with a plea for anthropologists to seriously examine the military establishments of the technologically advanced democracies. Greenhouse (1989: 49) suggests that because of the common premise pervading our discipline that war is pathological and a professional value orientation that opposes armed aggression, key cultural questions about conflict and the armed forces have been ignored. We would add that the essentially distrustful attitude to political authorities that characterizes most professional (Western) anthropologists has been intensified by the legacy of the Vietnam War, still viewed by many researchers as an essentially corrupt undertaking. Consequently, what Greenhouse suggests is that we look at the assumptions underlying discussions about, and the actions of, the armed forces. Central to such an examination is a focus on how the military handles its link to violence. To reiterate a point made earlier, although anthropology has dealt with war and violence, it has not done so in regard to the armed forces of the advanced technological societies, the perpetrators of much violence. Without such a focus, the analysis of sites of suffering and of victims does not inform us about what moves military organizations to participate in making suffering happen and what makes different publics accept the perpetration of violence.

Our argument has been that the Japanese case is an extreme instance of a society marked by skepticism about the military and its use of violence. Further, we have argued that the annual live-fire exercise held by Japan's SDF is a good entry point for examining such skepticism because, as a public event, it constitutes a dense concentration of symbols (and their meanings), because it is considered important by the soldiers and officers who organize and participate in it, and because it epitomizes many kinds of activities that the SDF carries out in relation to various publics. More generally, it is an occasion where the cultural codes that are usually diffused, attenuated, and submerged in the mundane order of things within the SDF lie closest to the behavioral surface. During a performance like the live-fire exercise the codes become more visible not only to the "natives" but also to "external ethnographers."

Although most Japanese citizens know that the SDF exists, for most of them its activities are normally hidden. The demonstration at the foot of Mount Fuji is a complex event that, at once, transmits diverse messages and creates different experiences for the various publics attending it. It brings together, on one occasion, a diverse array of groups who do not, in the normal course of events, interact. Specifically, the live-fire exercise is a complex combination of activities comprising elements of military parades, entertaining spectacles, leisurely picnics or festivals, a rite of solidarity, and a professional test. To put this point differently, the SDF appears to be simultaneously attempting to achieve a number of things in this event: to convince certain publics about its professionalism, to display, entertain and impress with its military power; to explain its various limits; to gain legitimacy and political support, to assure interested publics of its importance. It may well be that the kind of show that we analyze can appear in any advanced technological society. But the fact that it takes place in one that is marked by anti-militarism makes it all the more surprising and interesting.

What are the more general implications of our analysis? Anthropology's most useful contribution has been to document how violence is preeminently collective rather than individual, social rather than a-social or anti-social and culturally interpreted (Abbink 2000: xiii; Aijmer 2000: 1; Riches 1986; Spencer 1996). We would follow Blok (2000) to suggest that in most of the technologically advanced countries the means of violence have been monopolized by the state, and as society has been pacified, people have developed strong feelings about using and witnessing violence. Yet our analysis is not a simple functionalist one. In most of the scholarly literature, violence is seen as something that is problematic and has to be constantly controlled and suppressed. Thus violence has come to be seen as anomalous, irrational, senseless, and disruptive—as the reverse of social order, as the antithesis of 'civilization', as something that has to be brought under control (Blok 2000: 23).

By contrast, we have attempted to show how violence can also be understood as an object of fascination, enjoyment and celebration. Our argument is that the spectacularization, aestheticization and domestication of violence in many technologically advanced societies are carried out precisely because it is so problematic—chaotic and threatening. In this respect we follow recent European theorizing in that by focusing on events as categories of analysis we complement the current postmodernist shift in anthropological research on violence. Many recent (mainly American-based) inquiries into violence have privileged 'experience' as the most authentic form of knowledge and have abandoned an analytical approach in favor of a subjectivist focus on the impact violence has on the everyday life of individuals (Schroder and Schmidt 2001: 7). To be sure, we do not question the fact that experience constitutes an important aspect of violence. But a strongly subjectivist approach will:

> interfere with any effort to view one specific violent confrontation from a historical or comparative perspective. We argue that no violent act can be fully understood without viewing it as one link in the chain of a long process of events each of which refers to a system of cultural and material structures that can be compared to similar structural conditions anywhere else. (Schroder and Schmidt 2001: 7)

Here our analysis follows the investigations of such critical sociologists as Charles Tilly (1985) or Anthony Giddens (1985), who argue that war and the institutions of war-making are integral to the creation of states and to the mobilization of social resources. Such scholars have done much to uncover the main social and (especially) political mechanisms—recruitment, taxation, or propagation of ideologies of citizenship, for example—by which war has become part and parcel of the very dynamics of contemporary countries. Our analysis shows how, given anthropology's long-term preoccupation with the broadly cultural aspects of social life, we can examine the means by which the link between violence and the military is concealed, naturalized or blurred. In 'civilizing' or 'taming' violence, events such as the live-fire exercise seem to suggest that it is controllable and thus more attractive. Such events therefore attempt to render violence as something that is both rational and sensible.

It is worth remembering that these exercises are not the only kind of violence Japanese people are exposed to on daily basis. In a very large array of films, computer games, animations, adult comics and some sports events many Japanese people are "bombarded" with violence (Allison 2000; Gill 1998; Kinsella 2000). Although not all are military in nature, these representations of violence nevertheless are conspicuous in the country's popular culture. One may argue that whatever acceptance the SDF has achieved as the possessor of the means of violence is at least partly due to the population's pre-exposure to violence through these other means. Thus the live-fire exercise should be seen one of many cultural means of taming and normalizing violence in contemporary Japan.

Is the live-fire exercise of the SDF specifically Japanese? The only comparable case that we found in the scholarly literature, reported by Lutz (2001: 246 ff.), involves an event at Fort Bragg in the United States and is remarkably similar to the one we witnessed in Japan. Apart from that, on the basis of our personal impressions, such events also take place in Israel, Britain and Australia. It would thus seem, and here we are speculating, that the live-fire exercise is an example of a kind of transnational military culture. Theoretically, our argument is that the emulation and mimicking of one military establishment by another is one of the processes that take place within what may be called a world system of the military profession. Within this system, professional knowledge and practices are produced and disseminated from world centers through various institutions and arrangements such as the curricula and seminars of military universities and colleges, military attaches, joint maneuvers, experience in multi-national forces, journals and books, or personal networks. In the Japanese case, of course, it is the American military establishment that has been the center for the production of such knowledge and practices emulated by the SDF. First, the SDF's formal structures of combat and training are modeled on the US system. The SDF has three services with an internal division of labor similar to the US forces, and its techniques for training military personnel are basically the same as those practiced in the United States. Second, combined exercises and drills are a major mechanism for linking the SDF to American armed forces deployed in Japan and East Asia. These maneuvers include all three services and have been held since 1986 both in Japan and in the United States. The repertoire of practices arising from the US military occupation and residual influence on Japan for fifty years is part of this world system of military knowledge and practices.

Finally, we must be wary of automatically attachming a negative value to violence. Despite the moral difficulty involved making this point, it is important to understand how people may enjoy violence. It turns out that violence not only belongs to the realm of the pathological but is also woven into the very fabric normal everyday life. Along these lines, Schroder and Schmidt (2001: 5–6) suggest that the performative aspect of violence is crucial to an understanding of what it can achieve. It appears that in many societies whose members do not directly experience violent acts, this "performative quality makes violence an everyday experience ... without anybody actually experiencing physical hurt every day" (2001: 5–6). When members of an audience come to see an entertaining spectacle, they are not constantly thinking about the fact that they are looking at means of violence. The same effect can be had, say, through attending a fireworks show. The audience seems to be contemplating technological power, or the aesthetics of the sublime. It is in and around this point that we can most clearly see the seduction involved on the part of the military and the readiness of the public to be seduced. Indeed, what we showed here is the ease with which violence is aestheticized, prettified, packaged, marketed and celebrated.

Notes

CHAPTER 1: THE SOCIAL LIFE OF GUNS: AN INTRODUCTION

1. Estimating the number of firearms in the world is extremely difficult, owing to: unavailable data regarding guns owned by certain governments, hidden caches of weapons, unregistered and unreported civilian-owned arms, and uneven definitions of firearms used by different studies. The Small Arms Survey project, sponsored by the United Nations, is the most thorough and detailed estimate (Small Arms Survey 2001, 2002), and the 2002 survey estimates that 638,900,000 firearms exist globally (see also Peck 2002), including privately-owned guns as well as those used by armed forces, police, and non-state military groups. This number does include such weapons as rocket launchers. Michael Klare (1999: 21) writes that the number of guns in use ranges "from 500 million to a billion, of which some 200–250 million are owned by private individuals and public agencies in the United States."
2. This photograph, reprinted with the permission of Tom Rosseel, appears on the website he produces for his club Airsoft Brugge. Located in Bruges, Belgium, members travel both domestically and abroad to use their recreational weapons.

CHAPTER 2: GUNSCAPES: TOWARD A GLOBAL GEOGRAPHY OF THE FIREARM

1. Guns are not actually manufactured (to any considerable degree) in the Netherlands. Burrows is indicating, what is confirmed in the *UN Small Arms Report* of 2002, that numerous firearms move through customs in the Netherlands, which is one of the major transit centers for the legal transfer of weapons.

CHAPTER 3: GUN POLITICS: REFLECTIONS ON BRAZIL'S FAILED GUN BAN REFERENDUM IN THE RIO DE JANEIRO CONTEXT

1. Viva Rio (VR), a large Brazilian NGO, was created in 1993 in response to two massacres of unarmed civilians by military policemen: the Candelária massacre and the Vigário Geral shantytown massacre. VR works with the poorest communities in Rio to find practical solutions to the problems of gun crime. They work with the local police to set up a system for storing and recording guns that are seized, with the aim of tracing the source of guns and ensuring that they are not reintroduced into the community, and they pilot projects of community policing (Amnesty International 2003). They also created a partnership with the Instituto de Estudos da Religião

(ISER) to collect and publish materials on firearms in Brazil, much of which had been scattered in different bureacracies around the country.

2. Sales figures, likewise, follow the production figures closely, because the value of production is actually measured in terms of sales figures. According to Dreyfus, Lessing and Purcena (2005: 66), the most comprehensive and current data on total SALW production in Brazil comes from the Annual Study of Industry by Product (Pesquisa de Indústria Anual – Produto, PIA-Product) available only since 1998. Because the PIA-Product Survey defines the value of production in terms of sales figures, the numbers regarding production and sales of guns in Brazil are consistently parallel.

3. See: http://www.brazilianartists.net.

4. See: http://www.nraila.org/Issues/Articles/Read.aspx?ID=67.

5. Halbrook (1994, 2000) has written more scholarly versions of this chapter.

CHAPTER 4: OF GUNS, CHILDREN AND THE MAELSTROM: DETERMINING PURPOSIVE ACTION IN ISRAELI-PERPETRATED FIREARM DEATHS OF PALESTINIAN CHILDREN AND MINORS

1. The author is deeply and gratefully indebted to Arizona State University and its College of Public Programs, the Applied Research Institute-Jerusalem, the Palestinian American Research Center, B'Tselem, the Palestine Red Crescent Society, faculty and staff of the Institute of Forensic Medicine at Al Quds University, and the directorate and staff of Ramallah Hospital. In addition, heartfelt individual thanks must be extended to Dr. Mohammad Ghanayem, Dr. Jad Isaac, the Ishaq family, Ing. Valdemar Ramos Hernández, and a number of other individuals who, through commission or omission, made this preliminary research possible. The most profound thanks, by far, are extended to the Thaljiya family of Bethlehem, Palestine, for allowing me into their home and for sharing their unrelenting sorrow with me.

2. "My rage … empire, assassin of children."

3. Other methods of death-inducement are tank shelling, roadblocks impeding mothers giving birth from reaching hospitals, airplane/helicopter bombing and missile-firing during assassinations of activists, "tear" gas intoxication, and being run over by soldiers or illegal settlers.

4. Courtesy of ICRC-affiliated Palestinian medical relief organizations, I handled these so-called rubber bullets once removed from the corpses of children. They are steel balls the size of marbles, and are simply coated with a thin layer of Teflon.

5. All data were garnered from the website of the Palestinian Centre for Human Rights (www.pchrgaza.org), an affiliate of the International Commission of Jurists, among other international organizations. These data are often more conservative in their quantitative and documentary estimates and reporting than other Israeli and Palestinian websites.

6. Eliminated from these tallies were the following: back shots, abdominal shots, limb shots, pelvic and hip shots, deaths by shelling, deaths by explosive missiles in assassination attempts, deaths where data as to corporal location of the fatal wound were not available from the sources used, being run over by either IDF soldiers or illegal settlers, and deaths through gassings or inability to reach proper medical services in time.

CHAPTER 8: DRAWING A VIRTUAL GUN

1. In memory of my maternal grandfather, Peter Efthim, an avid hunter, veteran of the First World War and survivor of the deadly effects of mustard gas.
2. The student spent 5 hours as a participant observer in a pro-gun chatroom.
3. A label the student and I used for what happened to her when she challenged their beliefs.

CHAPTER 9: "GUN RIGHTS ARE CIVIL RIGHTS": RACISM AND THE RIGHT TO KEEP AND BEAR ARMS IN THE UNITED STATES

1. Concealed carry legislation (CCW) varies state to state; as of the date of writing, 38 states have some version of CCW. This man was referring to "Restrictive May Issue" discretionary policies, wherein the issuance of permits is left to the discretion of county sheriffs, no matter what requirements the applicant meets.
2. The District of Columbia's Firearms Control Regulation Act prohibits the possession of handguns not registered with city police prior to September 24, 1976 and re-registered by February 5, 1977.
3. Some of the activists profiled here also appear in the book *People For and Against Gun Control* (Bijlefeld 1999).
4. According to the CDC, homicide is the leading cause of death for black males aged 15–17, and handguns were involved in 78 per cent of homicides. Despite overall nationwide decreases in handgun-related crimes after 1993, the only demographic that did not indicate a decrease in handgun-homicides was that of black males between the ages of fifteen and twenty-four, for whom the leading cause of death is gun violence (Bureau of Justice Statistics 2002).

CHAPTER 10: MAN TO MAN: POWER AND MALE RELATIONSHIPS IN THE GUNPLAY FILM

1. This distinction is made consistently throughout the text, with the exception of direct quotations from others and words such as "gunshot" and "handgun," for which no graceful substitute could be found. Such a distinction has been made by others (Diaz 1999; Gibson 1994; Wilkinson and Fagan 1996).
2. In fact, the man with a gun is the *sine qua non* of entire genres of cinema: Westerns, Police/Detective Films, War Films, Action Films, etc.
3. While this is not as true today as it was during the heyday of the gunplay film, gun violence is still a man's world—both statistically and ideologically.
4. For an account of how radically US ideas about violence were changing in at this time see Gibson 1994; Hofstadter 1971; Jeffords 1989.
5. See Gibson (1994) for an extensive investigation of the "New Warrior" figure.
6. While Stone may have been more openly critical of cinema violence, and Tarantino more celebratory, the fact remains that both directors saw that film violence had come to refer primarily to itself, and were able to articulate the ways in which this rendered Peckinpah's strategy untenable.
7. This is not to suggest that Hong Kong action films don't have their own deep and

intricate codes of male relationships *vis-à-vis* violence (see Stringer 1997).

8. The connections between these working-class heroes and the middle-class portions of the white male viewership are complicated. It is entirely possible that these figures—police officers, seamen, Vietnam veterans—more purely embodied a fantasized "deep masculinity" than middle-class heroes could have. There are striking parallels between the modern "crisis" of middle-class masculinity and similar movements in the early twentieth century (Bederman 1995).

9. The use of "heterosexual" as an opposition to "homosocial" should not be taken to imply that heterosexual relationships are privileged over homosexual—just that mature, loving heterosexual relationships would be preferable to the violence-mediated homosociality that structures these films. Mature, loving homosexual relationships would be equally preferable, but they are clearly impossible within the logic of gunplay films.

10. Serial killers, the closest real thing to horror-film monsters, have almost never been found to use firearms (Roth 1994: 4).

11. The connection between knives and sexual aggression is not confined to gunplay films: a study of prison inmates found that criminals who had used knives, but had never used firearms, were "much more likely" to be in prison on a charge of rape (see Wright 1986).

12. The "good" terminator of *T2*, that is—the bad terminator of the original film not only uses knives, but fashions them out of his own body, thus penetrating other men's bodies with his own.

13. That being said, the question remains of the role of the knife in the "final fight," that ultimate confrontation between the hero and the anti-hero. The requirements of the final fight deserve fuller investigation; but, for the sake of brevity, it can be said simply that because the final fight is in fact a resolution of the homosocial intimacy that has been denied and postponed throughout the film, it is the most likely place for a knife to appear in any given film.

14. The outlaw Johnny Ringo is allowed to wield a gun in the defense of the eponymous stagecoach. Perhaps John Carpenter had this in mind while filming a similar plot in 1976's *Assault on Precinct 13*.

CHAPTER 12: "I SHOT THE SHERIFF": GUN TALK IN JAMAICAN POPULAR MUSIC

1. Pan Head and Sugar Black, "A Wi Run the Gun Them," Track 20, *Buju Banton Meets Garnett Silk and Tony Rebel at the Super Stars Conference*, Rhino Records Ltd., n.d., RNCD 2033.

2. The word in the original Dennis Brown song is "oppression," not "pressure."

3. Spragga Benz and Elephant Man, "Warrior Cause," Track 6, *Strictly The Best*, Volume 27, VP Records, VPCD1639, 2001.

4. I am indebted to Sean Mock Yen of the Radio Education Unit, University of the West Indies, Mona, for the transcription of the song text.

5. Monty Alexander, Track 5, *Caribbean Circle*, Chesky Records, JD80, 1992.

6. Shabba Ranks, "Gun Pon Me," Track 4, *As Raw As Ever*, Epic Records, EK 47310, 1991.

7. The Ethiopians, "Gun Man," Track 12 *The Ethiopians*, Trojan Records, CDTRL 228,1988; 1986.

8. "Mr Nine" is co-authored with Gregory Isaacs.

9. Buju Banton, "Murderer," Track 3, *'Til Shiloh*, Loose Cannon, 314-524 119-2, 1995.

10. Extracted from a longer version of Chapter 1, "Border Clash: Sites of Contestation," in which Gutzmore gives a detailed critique of Andrew Ross's dismissive reading of "Murderer" as, first, "censorious" and later, "quite conventional;" the former appears in Ross's paper, "The Structural Adjustment Blues," 1; and the latter in "Mr. Reggae DJ, Meet the International Monetary Fund," in *Real Love: In Pursuit of Cultural Justice*, New York: New York University Press, 1998: 41.

11. Buju Banton, "Mr Nine," Track 19, *Friends for Life*, VP Records/Atlantic, 0 7567 83634 2, 2003.

CHAPTER 13: PLAYING AT HATE: WAR GAMES, THE ARYAN WORLD CONGRESS, AND THE AMERICAN PSYCHE

1. Many of the primary documents, taken from the Aryan Nations and from Richard Butler's compound near Hayden Lake, Idaho, were retained after the bankruptcy of the Aryan Nations by Tony Stewart, a North Idaho College political science professor. I am particularly indebted to him for his patience and assistance in giving me access to much of the documentation discussed in this section.

2. Mathews, frustrated with the pace of the *jihad* against the ZOG, established the Order, or Silent Brotherhood, and died in 1984 on Whidbey Island, WA when FBI agents and a task force held a siege and tear-gassed him inside a cabin. Mathews refused to leave the cabin as it burned (Flynn and Gerhardt 1989).

3. The Hitler Youth was a logical extension of Hitler's belief that the future of Nazi Germany was its children. The Hitler Youth was seen as being as important to a child as school was. Movements for youngsters were already part of German culture in the 1920s, when the Hitler Youth had been created. By 1933 its membership stood at 100,000.

CHAPTER 14: THE CELEBRATION OF VIOLENCE: A LIVE-FIRE DEMONSTRATION CARRIED OUT BY JAPAN'S CONTEMPORARY MILITARY

1. This chapter is a slightly abridged version of an essay originally published in 2003 in *American Ethnologist* 30(4), pp. 540–55. Between July 1998 and August 1999 we carried out over 14 months of fieldwork, conducting over seventy interviews with soldiers, officers, and "external experts" such as foreign military attaches. This chapter is based on attendance at two live-fire exercises on the first Saturday and Sunday of September 1998. We wish to thank Efrat Ben-Ze'ev, Don Handelman, Eva Illuz, Anna Simons, Nurit Stadler, as well as the participants at the Ph.D. Kenkyukai of International House, Tokyo, and at the seminar of the Department of East Asian Studies of the Hebrew University.

References

Abbink, Jon (2000). Preface: Violation and Violence as Cultural Phenomena. In *Meanings of Violence: A Cross Cultural Perspective*, ed. Goran Aijmer and Jon Abbink, pp. xi–xvii. Oxford: Berg.

Abdel-Nabi, S. (2001). The Death of a Palestinian Child, *The Washington Report on Middle East Affairs*, Washington, DC, September 30, 2001, XX(6): 95–6.

Afflitto, F. M. (2000). The Homogenizing Effects of State-Sponsored Terrorism: The Case of Guatemala. In *Death Squad: The Anthropology of State Terror*, ed. J. A. Sluka, pp. 114–26. Philadelphia: University of Pennsylvania Press.

Afflitto, F. M. (2001). Internal grant proposal, College of Public Programs, Arizona State University, Tempe, AZ, Fall.

Afflitto, F. M. and ARIJ (Applied Research Institute–Jerusalem) (2001–2). Spatial models/spatial and interview data collected, December, 2001–January, 2002.

Aho, J. (1990). *The Politics of Righteousness: Idaho Christian Patriotism*. Seattle, WA: University of Washington Press.

Aho, J. (1994). *This Thing of Darkness: A Sociology of the Enemy*, Seattle, WA: University of Washington Press.

Aijmer, Goran (2000). Introduction: The Idiom of Violence in Imagery and Discourse. In *Meanings of Violence: A Cross Cultural Perspective*, ed. Goran Aijmer and Jon Abbink, pp. 1–22. Oxford: Berg.

Aijmer, Goran and Jon Abbink (eds) (2000). *Meanings of Violence: A Cross Cultural Perspective*. Oxford: Berg.

Albina, M. (2002). Palestinian Children Show Signs of Trauma, *World Vision*, October 8, at www.wvi.org.

Alexander, Monty (1992). Track 5, *Caribbean Circle*, Chesky Records, JD80.

Aljazeera, from Agence France Presse (2004). Israeli MP: Arabs are "worms", Aljazeera.net, http://english.aljazeera.net/NR/exeres/AEA5A403-CA53-4DA7-B34F-82B372367375.htm.

Allen, Paul (1801). "Original Poems, Serious and Entertaining". *Early American Imprints, Series II: Shaw–Shoemaker, 1801–1819*. Northwestern University Library, accessed November 15, 2005. http://infoweb.newsbanl.com.turing.library.northwestern.edu/.

Allison, Anne (2000). *Permitted and Prohibited Desires: Mothers, Comics and Censorship in Japan*. Berkeley, CA: University of California Press.

Almagor, Uri (1978). *Pastoral Partners: Affinity and Bond Partnership among the Dassanetch of South-west Ethiopia*. Manchester: Manchester University Press.

Al Mezan Center for Human Rights (2004). The Slaughter of Children in the Occupied Palestinian Territories (OPT) must Stop Now, *Press Room-Press Release, Reference*: 69/2004, October 12.

Amar, Paul E. (2003). Reform in Rio: Reconsidering the Myths of Crime and Violence, *NACLA* 37(2): 37–42, 44.

Amayreh, K. (2004). Palestinian Children Killed by Israel, Aljazeera.net, Saturday, April 10, http://english.aljazeera.net/NR/exeres/C3994F6B-9576-4702-94E3-73EA1470182E.htm, accessed April 10, 2004.

Amayreh, K. (2005a). Israel Rights Group Slams Army Reports, Aljazeera.net, Wednesday, September 7, http://english.aljazeera.net/NR/exeres/554FAF3A-B267-

427A-B9EC-54881BDE0A2E.htm, accessed September 7, 2005.

Amayreh, K. (2005b). Israel Accused of Covering Up Murders, Aljazeera.net, Monday, June 27, http://english.aljazeera.net/NR/exeres/554FAF3A-B267-427A-B9EC-54881BDE0A2E.htm, accessed September 7, 2005.

Amnesty International (1996–2005). Report. London: Amnesty International.

Amnesty International (2001). "People End Up Dying Here": Torture and Ill-treatment in Brazil, October 18, 2001, pp. 1–29.

Amnesty International (2003). Women in Brazil Take a Stand Against Guns, *The Wire*, February 2003, http://web.amnesty.org/web/wire.nsf/print/February2003Brazil, accessed October 24, 2005.

Anderson, Myrdene (1987). Tools and Toys: Human Implementation in Evolutionary and Cross-cultural Perspective (Tools and Toys II). In *153rd Annual Meeting of the American Association for the Advancement of Science*, Chicago, February.

Anderson, Myrdene (ed.) (2004). *Cultural Shaping of Violence: Victimization, Escalation, Response*. Ashland, OH: Purdue University Press.

Anonymous (1992). Unintentional Firearm-Related Fatalities Among Children, Teenagers – United States, 1982–1988, *Journal of the American Medical Association*, 268 (4): 451–2.

Anonymous (1999). Two Million Children Killed in Wars since 1987, *Society* 36(2): 2.

Anonymous (2002). The War's Effect on Palestinian Children, *The Washington Report on Middle East Affairs*, 21(9): 91–2.

Appadurai, Arjun (1996). *Modernity at Large*. Minneapolis: University of Minnesota Press.

Arafat, C., with Boothby, N. (2003). A Psychosocial Assessment of Palestinian Children, *U. S. Agency for International Development*, July 2003.

Araizaga, Jorge Carrasco (2005). Matar Con Permiso [Kill With Impunity]. *Proceso* 1491: 26–9 (May 29).

Arase, David (1995). A Militarized Japan? *The Journal of Strategic Studies*, 18(3): 84–103.

Ardener, Shirley (1987). A Note on Gender Iconography: The Vagina. In *The Cultural Construction of Sexuality*, ed. Pat Caplan. New York: Routledge.

Arnold, M. W., G. H. F. Neto and J. N. Figueiroa (2002). Years of Potential Life Lost by Children and Adolescent Victims of Homicide, Recife, 1997, *Journal of Tropical Pediatrics* 48(2): 67–71.

Assal, Adel and Edwin Farrell (1992). Attempts to Make Meaning of Terror: Family, Play, and School in the Time of Civil War, *Anthropology and Education Quarterly* 23(4): 275–90.

Azaryahu, Maoz (1999). The Independence Day Parade: A Political History of a Patriotic Ritual. In *The Military and Militarism in Israeli Society*, ed. Edna Lomsky-Feder and Eyal Ben-Ari, pp. 89–116. Albany, NY: State University of New York Press.

Baker, J. (1984). 'Seventeenth-Century English Yeoman Foodways at Plimouth Plantation'. In *The Dublin Seminar for New England Folklife: Annual Proceedings 1982: Foodways in the Northeast*, ed. P. Benes. Boston: Boston University Press.

BBC News (2005a). London attacks. 21 July attacks. What happened. http://news.bbc.co.uk/1/shared/spl/hi/uk/05/london_blasts/what_happened/html/21_07_05.stm, accessed July 26, 2006.

BBC News (2005b). London Attacks. 21 July Attacks. Investigation. Suspects, http://news.bbc.co.uk/1/shared/spl/hi/uk/05/london_blasts/investigation/html/suspects.stm, accessed July 26, 2006.

BBC News (2005c). London Attacks. 21 July Attacks. The Menezes Killing. Introduction. 1. The Stakeout, http://news.bbc.co.uk/1/shared/spl/hi/uk/05/london_blasts/tube_shooting/html/stakeout.stm accessed July 26, 2006.

BBC News (2005d). London Attacks. 21 July Attacks. The Menezes Killing.

Introduction. 2. The Pursuit, http://news.bbc.co.uk/1/shared/spl/hi/uk/05/london_blasts/tube_shooting/html/pursuit.stm, accessed July 26, 2006.

BBC News (2005e). London Attacks. 21 July Attacks. The Menezes Killing. Introduction. 3. The Station, http://news.bbc.co.uk/1/shared/spl/hi/uk/05/london_blasts/tube_shooting/html/station.stm, accessed July 26, 2006.

Beaton, A. C. (1950). Record of the Toposa Tribe, *Sudan Notes and Records*, XXXI: 129–32.

Beauchemin, E. (2004). Troubled Children in a Troubled Land, *Radio Netherlands*, August 25.

Becker, H. S. (1973[1963]). *Outsiders: Studies in the Sociology of Deviance*. New York: The Free Press.

Bederman, G. (1995). *Manliness and Civilization: A Cultural History Of Gender and Race in The United States, 1880–1917*. Chicago: University of Chicago Press.

Bellamy, C. (1996). *Knights in White Armour: The New Art of War and Peace*. London: Random House.

Bellesiles, M. (2000). *Arming America: The Origins of a National Gun Culture*. New York: Alfred A. Knopf.

Bellesiles, M. (2002). Exploring America's Gun Culture, *William and Mary Quarterly*, LIX: 241–68.

Ben-Ari, Eyal (1991a). Posing, Posturing and Photographic Presences: A Rite of Passage in a Japanese Commuter Village, *Man* 26: 87–104.

Ben-Ari, Eyal (1991b). Transformation in Ritual; Transformation of Ritual: Audiences and Rite in a Japanese Commuter Village, *Ethnology* 30(2): 135–47.

Ben-Ari, Eyal (1998). *Mastering Soldiers: Conflict, Emotions and the Enemy in an Israeli Military Unit*. Oxford: Berghahn Books.

Ben-Ari, Eyal and Efrat El-Ron (2002). Blue Helmets and White Armor: Multi-Nationalism and Multiculturalism Among UN Peacekeeping Forces, *City and Society* 13(2): 271–302.

Benson, A. (ed.) (1937). *The America of 1750. Peter Kalm's Travels in North America, The English version of 1770*, 2 Vols. New York: Wilson-Erickson.

Berger, Thomas U. (1998). *Cultures of Antimilitarism: National Security in Germany and Japan*. Baltimore, MD: Johns Hopkins University Press.

Bijlefeld, M. (1999). *People for and against Gun Control: A Biographical Reference*. Westport, CT and London: Greenwood Press.

Black Panther Party for Self-Defense. *Platform* (2004). Retrieved December 14, 2004, from www.africawithin.com/studies/black_panther_party1.htm.

Blackshaw, T. and T. Crabbe (2004). *New Perspectives on Sport and 'Deviance': Consumption, Performativity and Social Control*. London: Routledge.

Blake, Gerald (1997). *Imperial Boundary Making: The Diary of Captain Kelly and the Sudan–Uganda Boundary Commission of 1913*. Oxford: British Academy.

Blanchard, K. V. F. (2000). *Black Man With a Gun: A Responsible Gun Ownership Manual for African Americans*. Baltimore, MD: American Literary Press, Inc.

Blok, Anton (2000). The Enigma of Senseless Violence. In *Meanings of Violence: A Cross Cultural Perspective*, ed. Goran Aijmer and Jon Abbink, pp. 23–38. Oxford: Berg.

Bloodsworth-Lugo, Mary and Carmen R. Lugo-Lugo (2005). The War on Terror and Same-Sex Marriage: Narratives of Containment and the Shaping of U.S. Public Opinion, *Peace and Change: A Journal of Peace Research*, 30(4): 469–88.

Boene, Bernard (1990). How Unique Should the Military Be? A Review of Representative Literature and Outline of Synthetic Formulation. *European Journal of Sociology* 31(1): 3–59.

Boene, Bernard (2000). Trends in the Political Control of Post-Cold War Armed Forces. In *Democratic Societies and their Armed Forces: Israel in a Comparative Perspective*, ed.

Stuart A. Cohen, pp. 73–88. London: Frank Cass.

Boston News Letter, Early American Newspapers, Series I, 1690–1876 (microcard). Young Research Library, University of California, Los Angeles.

Boston News Letter, Boston Evening Post, The Boston Chronicle, and *The BostonGazette*, Early American Newspapers, Series I, 1690–1876,Northwestern University Library, November 15, 2005, http://infoweb.newsbanl.com.turing.library.northwestern.edu/.

Bourdieu, Pierre (1977). *Outline of a Theory of Practice*, trans. Richard Nice. Cambridge: Cambridge University Press.

Bourdieu, Pierre (1999). Rethinking the State: Genesis and Structure of the Bureaucratic Field. In *State/Culture: State-Formation After the Cultural Turn*, ed. George Steinmetz, pp. 53–75. Ithaca, NY: Cornell University Press.

Bourgois, Philippe (1995). *In Search of Respect: Selling Crack in El Barrio*. Cambridge: Cambridge University Press.

Bouroncle, Alberto (2000). Ritual, Violence and Social Order: An Approach to Spanish Bullfighting. In *Meanings of Violence: A Cross Cultural Perspective*, ed. Goran Aijmer and Jon Abbink, pp. 55–76. Oxford: Berg.

Breen, C. (2003). The Role of NGO's in the Formulation of Compliance with the Optional Protocol to the Convention on the Rights of the Child on Involvement of Children in Armed Conflict, *Human Rights Quarterly* 25(2): 453–82.

Brownlow, C. and L. O'Dell (2002). Ethical Issues for Qualitative Research in On-line Communities, *Disability and Society*, 17(6): 685–94.

Bruce-Briggs, B. (1976). The Great American Gun War, *Public Interest*, 1976: 37–62.

B'Tselem (2005a). "Casualties," http://www.btselem.org/english/statistics/Casualties.asp.

B'Tselem (2005b). "Use of Firearms," http://www.btselem.org/English/Firearms/.

Bureau of Justice Statistics (2002). *Firearms and Crime Statistics*. Washington, DC: US Department of Justice.

Burk, James (1998). Introduction, 1998: Ten Years of New Times. In *The Adaptive Military: Armed Forces in a Turbulent World*, ed. James Burk, pp. 1–24. New Brunswick, NJ: Transaction Books.

Burrows, Gideon (2002). *The No-nonsense Guide to the Arms Trade*. Oxford: New Internationalist Publications.

Bush's Possession of Saddam's Gun Both Freudian and Traditional (2004). [Editorial, Roundup: Media's Take] *New York Times*, June 21, http://www.nytimes.com/2004/06/21/politics/21letter.html.

Butler, Judith. (1990). *Gender Trouble*. London: Routledge.

Cadigan, D. (2004). An Open Letter "Killing Children is No Longer a Big Deal", *The Modern Tribune*, October 23.

Caldeira, Teresa (2000). *City of Walls: Crime, Segregation, and Citizenship in São Paulo*. Berkeley and Los Angeles: University of California Press.

Caldeira, Teresa (2002). The Paradox of Police Violence in Democratic Brazil, *Ethnography* 3(3): 235–63.

"Cattle rustling sparks famine." (1999). *Daily Nation* (Nairobi, August 11).

Chagnon, Napoleon (1988). Life Histories, Blood Revenge and Warfare in a Tribal Population, *Science* 239: 985–92.

Chase, Kenneth (2003). *Firearms: A Global History to 1700*. Cambridge: Cambridge University Press.

Chew, Huibin Amee (2005). Why the War is Sexist. *Monthly Review* November 22, http://mrzine.monthlyreview.org/chew221105.html, accessed November 29.

Christian/Base21 Media Activists (2003). Zionist Occupation Kill 565 Palestinian Children during Intifada, Base 21 Newsdesk/www.base21.org, July 4.

Clayton, Liz (2000). "Drought in Kenya" *Horn of Africa Crisis* 4(8).

CNN (2000). Palestinian Children Moved by Boy's Killing, October 9, www.CNN.com.

Coe, M. and S. Coe (1984). Mid-Eighteenth-century Food and Drink on the Massachusetts Frontier. In *The Dublin Seminar for New England Folklife: Annual Proceedings 1982: Foodways in the Northeast,* ed. P. Benes. Boston: Boston University Press.

Colonial Office, Public Records Office, Kew Gardens, London (henceforth CO).

CO 533/380/13 'Memorandum on the History of the Boundary between Kenya and Uganda'.

CO 533/419/8 'Slave Raids on the Kenya-Abyssinian Frontier'.

CO 533/421/4, 'Disarmament of Frontier Tribes & Abyssinian Raids'.

CO 822/1559 'From Governor of Uganda to Ian N. Macleod, Secretary of State for the colonies dated December 18, 1959 titled "Revision of the Kenya-Uganda Inter-territorial Boundary".

CO 822/3050, 'Visit to Karamoja by E.G. Le Tocq to K.A. East Esq. Commonwealth Relations Office of April 8, 1963'.

CO 927/161/5 'Anthropological and Sociological Research Study of the Turkana and Jie Peoples of Kenya and Uganda by P.H. Gulliver 1952'.

Conant, Jeff (2006). Propagating Popular Resistance: The Poetics, Public Relations, and Fetish of Zapatismo. *LiP: Informed Revolt,* 2006 Winter edition: 40–8.

Connell, Robert. (2000). Arms and the Man: Using the New Research on Masculinity to Understand Violence and Promote Peace in the Contemporary World. In *Male Roles, Masculinities and Violence: A Culture of Peace Perspective,* ed. Ingeborg Breines, Robert Connell, and Ingrid Eide, pp. 21–33. Paris: Unesco Publishing.

Coogan, Tim Pat (1995). *The Troubles: Ireland's Ordeal 1966–1996 and the Search for Peace.* Boulder, CO: Roberts Rinehart.

Cook, C. (n.d.). The Impact of the Conflict on Children, from the organizational website, If Americans Knew, what every American needs to know about Israel/Palestine.

Cooke, Melville (2003). Ninja Man, Reneto Adams – Both above the Law, *The Gleaner,* Friday, January 3, A4.

Cooper, James Fenimore (1985[1841]). *The Deerslayer: or, The First War Path.* New York: The Library of America.

Cooper, J. (1991). Cooper's Corner, *Guns & Ammo,* 1991: 104.

Cotterell, Arthur (1981). *The First Emperor of China.* London: Macmillan.

Cottrol, R. J. (1999). A Liberal Democrat's Lament, *The American Enterprise Magazine Online,* September/October.

Cottrol, R. J. and R. T. Diamond (1991). The Second Amendment: Toward an Afro-Americanist Reconsideration, *Georgetown Law Journal,* 80: 309–61.

Cowell, Alan and Don Van Natta Jr. (2005). Britain Says Man Killed by Police Had No Bomb Tie, *The New York Times,* July 24, 2005, p. 1.

Cramer, C. E. (1995). The Racist Roots of Gun Control, *Kansas Journal of Law and Public Policy,* 4: 17.

Cukier, Wendy (2005). Commentary: The United State is Set Again to Block International Efforts to Fight the Illegal Trade in Guns, Catering to the Powerful National Rifle Association, Shooting Times Research Center, Canada NewsWire.

Da Matta, Roberto (1984). Carnival in Multiple Planes. In *Rite, Drama, Festival, Spectacle: Rehearsals Toward a Theory of Cultural Performance,* ed. John J. MacAloon, pp. 208–40. Philadelphia: Institute for the Study of Human Issues.

Dao, J. (2005). Muslim Cleric Found Guilty in the "Virginia Jihad" Case, *The New York Times,* April 27, p. A10.

Das, Veena and Arthur Kleiman (1997). Introduction. In *Violence and Subjectivity,* ed. Veena Das, Arthur Kleiman, Mmphela Ramphele and Pamela Reynolds, pp. 1–18. Berkeley, CA: University of California Press.

Defence for Children International – Palestine Section (2004). "Status of Palestinian

Children's Rights: Israel's violations of the right to life and security and the rights of children deprived of their liberty during the second Intifada (29 September 2000–30 June 2004)", Jerusalem.

Deming, David (2001). Guns and Vaginas: A Personal Perspective on Free Speech and Sexual Harassment in Oklahoma, *Sexuality and Culture* 5 (4): 43–65.

Denzin, N. K. (1991). *Images of Postmodern Society: Social Theory and Contemporary Cinema*. London: Sage Publications.

Denzin, N. K. (1999). Cybertalk and the Method of Instances. In *Doing Internet Research: Critical Issues and Methods for Examining the Net*, ed. S. Jones, pp. 107–25.Thousand Oaks, CA: Sage.

Derven, D. (1984). Wholesome, Toothsome, and Diverse: Eighteenth-Century Foodways in Deerfield, Massachusetts. In *The Dublin Seminar for New EnglandFolklife: Annual Proceedings 1982: Foodways in the Northeast*, ed. P. Benes. Boston: Boston University Press.

Dias, Carolina Lootty (2005).Small Arms Control Legislation in Brazil: From Vargas to Lula. In *Brazil: The Arms and the Victims*, pp. 26–49. Rio de Janeiro: Viva Rio/ISER.

Diaz, T. (1999). *Making a Killing: The Business of Guns in America*, New York: New Press.

Dicken-Garcia, H. (1998). The Internet and continuing historical discourse, *Journalism and Mass Communication Quarterly*, 75(1): 19–27.

Dickson-Gomez, J. (2002). Growing up in Guerrilla Camps: The Long-term Impact of being a Child Soldier in El Salvador's Civil War, *Ethos* 30(4): 327–52.

"Disarmament Gets Under Way." (2005). *The Standard* (Nairobi 31 May).

Dorf, M. (2002). What does the Second Amendment Mean Today? In *The Second Amendment in Law and History*, ed. C. Bogus. The New Press: New York.

Dreyfus, Pablo, Benjamin Lessing, and Julio César Purcena (2005). The Brazilian Small Arms Industry: Legal Production and Trade. In *Brazil: The Arms and the Victims*, pp. 50–93. Rio de Janeiro: Viva Rio/ISER.

Dreyfus, Pablo and Marcelo de Sousa Nascimento (2005). Small Arms Holdings In Brazil: Toward a Comprehensive Mapping of Guns and Their Owners. In *Brazil: The Arms and the Victims*, pp. 94–145. Rio de Janeiro: Viva Rio/ISER.

Early, Frances and Kathleen Kennedy (eds) (2003). *Athena's Daughters: Television's New Women Warriors*. Syracuse, NY: Syracuse University Press.

Eber, G. B., J. L. Annest, J. A. Mercy, and G. W. Ryan (2004). Nonfatal and Fatal Firearm-related Injuries among Children Aged 14 Years and Younger: United States, 1993–2000. *Pediatrics* 113(6): Part 1, 1686–91.

Edberg, Mark C. (2004). *El Narcotraficante: Narcocorridos and the Construction of a Cultural Persona on the U.S. Mexico Border*. Austin, TX: University of Texas Press.

Ehrenreich, Ben (2005). The Guerilla War Against Cheap Lettuce, *The Believer*, www.alternet.org/story/29655, accessed December 27, 2005.

El-Haddad, L. (2005). "Israeli army commander released", Aljazeera.net, Monday, February 7, http://english.aljazeera.net/NR/exeres/554FAF3A-B267-427A-B9EC54881BDE0A2E.htm.

Ellis, John (1975). *The Social History of the Machine Gun*. New York: Pantheon.

El-Ron, Efrat, Boas Shamir and Eyal Ben-Ari. (1999). Why Don't They Fight Each Other? Cultural Diversity and Operational Unity in Multinational Forces, *Armed Forces and Society* 26(1): 73–98.

El-Sarraj, E. (1996). Palestinian Children and Violence, Conference paper at "The Impact of Armed Conflict on Children", Belfast, Northern Ireland, February 2–5, 1996, organized by Save the Children–Belfast.

Enloe, Cynthia (2004). *The Curious Feminist: Searching for Women in a New Age of Empire*. Berkeley, CA: University of California Press.

Fay, S. (1801). *An oration delivered at Concord on the anniversary of American Independence,*

July 4ᵗʰ, 1801, Early American Imprints, Series II: Shaw Shoemaker, 1801–1819. Northwestern University Library, November 15, 2005, http://infoweb.newsbanl. com.turing.library.northwestern.edu/.

Feaver, Peter D. (1999). Civil–Military Relations, *Annual Review of Political Science* 2: 211–41.

Feldman, Allen (1991). *Formations of Violence: The Narrative of the Body and Political Terror in Northern Ireland.* Chicago: University of Chicago Press.

Feldman, Allen (1997). Violence and Vision: The Prosthetics and Aesthetics of Terror. In *Violence and Subjectivity,* ed. Veena Das, Arthur Kleiman, Mmphela Ramphele and Pamela Reynolds, pp. 46–78. Berkeley, CA: University of California Press.

Ferguson, R. B. (ed.) (1984). *Warfare, Culture and Environment.* Orlando, FL: Academic Press.

Ferme, Mariane (2001). *The Underneath of Things: Violence, History, and the Everyday in Sierra Leone.* Berkeley, CA: University of California Press.

Fernandez, James (1986). *Persuasions and Performances: The Play of Tropes in Culture.* Bloomington, IN: Indiana University Press.

Fingerhut, L. A. and K. K. Christoffel (2002). Firearm-related Death and Injury among Children and Adolescents, *The Future of Children,* 12(2): 24–37.

Fingerhut, L. A., D. D. Ingram, and J. J. Feldman (1992a). Firearm and Nonfirearm Homicide Among Persons 15 through 19 Years of Age: Differences by Level of Urbanization, United States, 1979 through 1989, *Journal of the American Medical Association* 267(22): 3048–53.

Fingerhut, L. A., D. D. Ingram, and J. J. Feldman (1992b). Firearm Homicide among Black Teenage Males in Metropolitan Counties, *Journal of the American Medical Association* 267(22): 3054–8.

Finkleman, P. (2002). "A Well Regulated Militia": The Second Amendment in Historical Perspective. In *The Second Amendment in Law and History,* ed. C. Bogus. The New Press: New York.

Flynn, K. and G. Gerhardt (1989). *The Silent Brotherhood: Inside America's Racist Underground.* New York: The Free Press.

Forlitti, A. (2005). Shooter Seemed Fascinated with Death: Students Say There May Have Been Warning Signs, http://aolsvc.news.aol.com/news/article.adp?id= 20050322101809990009, accessed March 23, 2005.

Foster, Mary LeCron and Robert A. Rubinstein (eds) (1989). *Peace and War: Cross-Cultural Perspectives.* New Brunswick, NJ: Transaction Books.

Foucault, Michel (1963). *The Birth of the Clinic.* New York: Random House.

Foucault, Michel. (1975). *Discipline and Punish: The Birth of the Prison.* New York: Random House.

Fujitani, T., Geoffrey M. White and Lisa Yoneyama (2001). Introduction. In *Perilous Memories: The Asia-Pacific War(s),* ed. T. Fujitani, Geoffrey M. White and Lisa Yoneyama, pp. 1–29. Durham, NC: Duke University Press.

Funk, T. Markus (1999). Gun Control in America: A History of Discrimination against the Poor and Minorities. In *Guns in America,* ed. Jan E. Dizard, Robert Merrill Muth, and Stephen P. Andrews, Jr., pp. 390–402. New York: New York University Press.

Garbarino, J. and K. Kostelny (1996). The effects of political violence on Palestinian children's behavior problems: a risk accumulation model, *Child Development* 67(1): 33–45.

Garbarino, J., C. P. Bradshaw and J. A. Vorassi (2002). Mitigating the Effects of Gun Violence on Children and Youth, *The Future of Children* 12(2): 72–85.

Geffray, Christian (2001). Brazil: Drug Trafficking in the Federal State of Rondônia, *International Social Science Journal* 169: 443–50.

Geltman, P. (1997). Genocide and the Plight of Children in Rwanda, *Journal of the*

American Medical Association, 277(4): 289–94.

Giacaman, R., A. Abdullah, R. Abu Safieh, and L. Shamieh (2002). Schooling at Gunpoint: Palestinian Children's Learning Environment in War Like Conditions: The Ramallah/al-Bireh/Beitunia Urban Center, Palestinian American Research Center, December 1.

Gibbs, Nancy (2003). Saddam's Capture, *Time,* December 22.

Gibson, J. (1994). *Warrior Dreams: Paramilitary Culture in Post-Vietnam America.* New York: Hill and Wang.

Gibson, K. (1989). Children in Political Violence, *Social Science and Medicine,* 28(7): 659–67.

Giddens, Anthony (1985). *The Nation-State and Violence.* Cambridge: Polity.

Gill, Tom (1998). Transformations of Magic: Some Japanese Super-Heroes and Monsters. In *Japanese Popular Culture: Gender, Shifting Boundaries and Global Cultures,* ed. D. P. Martinez, pp. 33–55. Cambridge: Cambridge University Press.

Girard, Rene (1977). *Violence and the Sacred.* Baltimore, MD: Johns Hopkins Press.

Gluckman, Max (1956). *Custom and Conflict in Africa.* Oxford: Oxford University Press.

Gluckman, Max (1965). *Politics, Law and Ritual in Tribal Societies.* Oxford: Oxford University Press.

Gold, G. (2003). Rediscovering Place: Experiences of a Quadriplegic Anthropologist, *The Canadian Geographer,* 47(4): 467–79.

Goldschmidt, Walter (1989). Personal Motivation and Institutionalized Conflict. In *Peace and War: Cross-Cultural Perspectives,* ed. Mary Lecron Foster and Robert A. Rubinstein, pp. 3–14. New Brunswick, NJ: Transaction.

Goldstein, Donna M. (2003). *Laughter Out of Place: Race, Class, Violence, and Sexuality in a Rio Shantytown.* Berkeley and Los Angeles: University of California Press.

Goodrich, L. Carrington and Feng Chia-sheng (1946). The Early Development of Firearms in China, *Isis* 36: 114–23.

Grassroots International (2000). Palestinian Children: A Childhood Denied, Grassroots International, *Palestine Now,* July 26.

Grech, Jacob (1991). An Arms Sale Here and an Arms Sale There, *Social Alternatives* 10(4): 7–8.

Green, Richard (1992). *Sexual Science and the Law.* Cambridge, MA: Harvard University Press.

Greenhouse, Carol J. (1989). Fighting For Peace. In *Peace and War: Cross-Cultural Perspectives,* ed. Mary Lecron Foster and Robert A. Rubinstein, pp. 49–60. New Brunswick, NJ: Transaction.

Grossberg, L. (1992). *We Gotta Get Out of This Place: Popular Conservatism and Postmodern Culture.* New York: Routledge.

Grossman, D. (1995). *On Killing: The Psychological Cost of Learning to Kill in War and Society.* Boston: Little, Brown.

Gruber, I. (2002). Of Arms and Men: *Arming America* and Military History, *William and Mary Quarterly,* LIX: 217–22.

Haas, Amira (2000). "Don't Shoot Till You Can See They're Over the Age of 12", *Ha'aretz,* November 20, 2000, Tel Aviv, Israel.

Haas, Jonathan (1990). *The Anthropology of War.* Cambridge: Cambridge University Press.

Halbrook, Stephen (1994). *That Every Man Be Armed: The Evolution of a Constitutional Right.* Oakland, CA: The Independent Institute.

Halbrook, Stephen (2000). Nazi Firearms Law and the Disarming of the German Jews, *Arizona Journal of International and Comparative Law* 17(3): 483–535.

Halloran, Richard (1994). Is Japan a Military Threat to Asia? *Arms Control Today,* 24: 12–17.

Hanami, Andrew K. (1996). Japan. In *The Political Role of the Military*, ed. Constantine P. Panopoulos and Cynthia Watson, pp. 235–55. Westport, CT: Greenwood Press.

Handelman, Don (1997). Rituals/Spectacles, *International Social Science Journal*, 153: 387–99.

Handelman, Don (1998). *Models and Mirrors: Towards an Anthropology of Public Events*. Oxford: Berghahn Books.

Handelman, Don and Elihu Katz (1995). State Ceremonies of Israel: Remembrance Day and Independence Day. In *Israeli Judaism: The Sociology of Religion in Israel*, ed. Shlomo Deshen, Charles Liebman and Moshe Shokeid, pp. 75–85. New Brunswick, NJ: Transaction.

Hanley, D. C. (2001). Israel's Spin-Doctors Wage War of Images and Words Against Palestinian Rock Children, *The Washington Report on Middle East Affairs* XX(1): 21–4.

Haraway, Donna (1985). A Manifesto for Cyborgs: Science, Technology, and Socialist Feminism in the 1980s, *Socialist Review* 80: 65–107.

Harcourt, Bernard E. (2004). On Gun Registration, the NRA, Adolf Hitler, and Nazi Gun Laws: Exploding the Gun Culture Wars, University of Chicago, http://ssrn.com/abstract=557183.

Harcourt, Bernard (2006). *Language of the Gun*. Chicago: University of Chicago Press.

Harootunian, Harry (1999). Memory, Mourning, and National Morality: Yasukuni Shrine and the Reunion of State and Religion in Postwar Japan. In *Nation and Religion: Perspectives on Europe and Asia*, ed. Peter van der Veer and Hartmut Lehmann, pp. 144–60. Princeton, NJ: Princeton University Press.

Hassen, L. (trans.) (1987). Nazi Country in Idaho's Wilderness, Helsingin Sanomat— Kuu Kausiliite (February 3), manuscript.

Hearn, Kelly (2005a). As Brazil Votes to Ban Guns, NRA Joins The Fight, in *The Nation* (web), November 7, 2005, http://www.thenation.com/doc/20051107/hearn.

Hearn, Kelly (2005b). The NRA Takes On Gun Control, in *Alternet*, October 25, 2005, http://alternet.org/story/27279/.

Hebdige, D. (1979). *Subculture: The Meaning of Style*. London: Routledge.

Hedges, Chris (2002). *War Is a Force That Gives Us Meaning*. New York: Public Affairs.

Heinecken, Dawn (2003). *The Warrior Women of Television*. New York: Peter Lang.

Hertslet, Sir Edward (1909). *Map of Africa by Treaty*, 3rd edition, Vol. II, Nos. 95 to 259. London: His Majesty's Stationery Office.

Heston, Charlton (1999). The Second Amendment: America's First Freedom. In *Guns in America: A Reader*, ed. Jan E. Dizard *et al.*, pp. 199–204. New York: New York University Press.

Hill, J. and T. Wilson (2003). Identity Politics and the Politics of Identities, *Identities: Global Studies in Culture and Power*, 10: 1–8.

Hill, L. (2004). *The Deacons for Defense: Armed Resistance and the Civil Rights Movement*. Chapel Hill, NC: University of North Carolina Press.

Hinton, Alexander Laban (ed.) (2002). *Genocide: An Anthropological Reader*. Malden, MA: Blackwell Publishers Inc.

History Learning Site, "The Hitler Youth," http://www.historylearningsite. co.uk/hitler_ youth.htm, accessed February 2, 2006.

Hochschild, A. (1994). Changing Colors: Once a Rising Star in the White Supremacist Movement, Floyd Cochran Now Attacks Racism with Equal Fervor. Is He for Real?, *Mother Jones*, 19(3): 55–9.

Hoffman, Danny (2005). Violent Events as Narrative Blocs: The Disarmament at Bo, Sierra Leone, *Anthropological Quarterly* 78(2): 329–53.

Hofstadter, R. (1970). America as a Gun Culture. In *American Violence: A Documentary History*, ed. R. Hofstadter and M. Wallace. New York: Knopf.

Hofstadter, R. (1971). Reflections on Violence in the United States. In *American Violence:*

A Documentary History, ed. R. Hofstadter and M. Wallace, pp. 3–43. New York: Vintage Books.

Holston, James and Teresa P. R. Caldeira (1998). Democracy, Law, and Violence: Disjunctions of Brazilian Citizenship. In *Fault Lines of Democracy in Post-Transition Latin America*, ed. F. Agüero and J. Stark, pp. 263–96. Coral Gables, FL: North–South Center Press at the University of Miami.

Hooker, Richard J. (1981). *Food and Drink In America, A History*. Indianapolis, IN/New York: The Bobbs-Merrill Company.

Hosley, William (1999). Guns, Gun Culture, and the Peddling of Dreams. In *Guns in America*, ed. Jan E. Dizard, Robert Merrill Muth, and Stephen P. Andrews, Jr., pp. 47–85. New York: New York University Press.

House, K. S. (1965). *Cooper's Americans*. Columbus, OH: Ohio State University Press.

Howe, Leo (2000). Risk, Ritual and Performance, *Journal of the Royal Anthropological Institute* 6: 63–79.

Huggins, Martha (ed.) (1991). *Vigilantism and the State in Modern Latin America: Essays in Extra Legal Violence*. New York: Praeger.

Huggins, Martha (2000). Legacies of Authoritarianism: Brazilian Torturers' and Murderers' Reformulation of Memory, *Latin American Perspectives* 27(2): 57–78.

Huizinga, J. (1955). *Homo Ludens: A Study of the Play Element in Culture*. Boston: Beacon Press.

IANSA (International Action Network on Small Arms) (2005). Brazilian Gun Referendum Approaches: A Historic Opportunity to Make People Safer From Gun Violence, October 19, 2005, Press Release, http://www.iansa.org/regions/samerica/dirty-tricks.htm, accessed on November 18, 2005.

Igarashi, Yoshikuni (2000). *Bodies of Memory: Narratives of War in Postwar Japanese Culture, 1945–1970*. Princeton, NJ: Princeton University Press.

Ignatieff, Michael (1998). *The Warrior's Honor: Ethnic War and the Modern Conscience*. London: Chatto and Windus.

"Illicit firearms proliferation and the implications for security and peace in the Sudan, Kenya, and Uganda border region: report of the research carried on the Sudan side of the common border" (2001). *AFRICANEWS* Vol. 68 (November).

Innes, Sherrie A. (1999). *Tough Girls: Women Warriors and Wonder Women in Popular Culture*. Philadelphia: University of Pennsylvania Press.

Innes, Sherrie A. (ed.) (2004). *Action Chicks: New Images of Tough Women in Popular Culture*. New York: Palgrave Macmillan.

Jabr, S. (2004). The Children of Palestine: A Generation of Hope and Despair, *The Washington Report on Middle East Affairs* 23(10): 18–19.

Jameson, Fredric (1991). *Postmodernism, or, The Cultural Logic of Late Capitalism*, Durham, NC: Duke University Press.

Jeffords, S. (1989). *The Remasculinization of America: Gender and the Vietnam War*. Bloomington, IN: Indiana University Press.

Jensen, Robert (2002). Blow Bangs and Cluster Bombs: The Cruelty of Men and Americans, retrieved November 28, 2005 from http://uts.cc.utexas.edu/~rjensen/freelance/blowbangs.htm.

Jhally, S. (1999). *Tough Guise: Violence, Media, and the Crisis in Masculinity*. Northampton, MA: Media Education Foundation.

Kalm, P. (1770). *The America of 1750, Peter Kalm's Travels in North America, The English version of 1770*, 2 Vols. New York: Wilson-Erickson.

Kalof, Linda, Amy Fitzgerald, and Lori Baralt (2004). Animals, Women, and Weapons: Blurred Sexual Boundaries in the Discourse of Sport Hunting, *Society and Animals*, 12 (3): 237–51.

Kamau, Peter (1999). More Starve to Death in Turkana, *Africa News Service*, November.

Kann, M. (1998). *A Republic of Men: The American Founders, Gendered Language, and Patriarchal Politics*, New York: New York University Press.

Kapferer, Bruce (1988). *Legends of People, Myths of State: Violence, Intolerance, and Political Culture in Sri Lanka and Australia*. Washington, DC: Smithsonian Institution Press.

Kapp, C. (2001). Violence against Children Widespread, says Human Rights Report, *The Lancet* 358(9288): 1166–7.

Katzenstein, Peter J. (1996). *Cultural Norms and National Security: Police and Military in Postwar Japan*. Ithaca, NY: Cornell University Press.

Keller, A. and B. Zilversmidt (2001). The Other Israel, *Al Awda News*, December 15.

Kennet, L. and J. L. Anderson (1975). *The Gun in America: The Origins of a National Dilemma*. Westport, CT: Greenwood Press.

Kenya National Archives, Nairobi: DC/ISO/2/5/5, "The Kenya / Sudan Boundary and the Elemi Triangle", a report from the Provincial Commissioner. Northern Frontier Province Isiolo District Reports.

Kenya National Archives, Nairobi: PC/NFD1/1/2, The Kenya Colony and Protectorate (Boundaries) Order in Council 1921, ref. SR & O.1921/1134 (REV. XI).

Kertzer, David I. (1988). *Ritual, Politics and Power*. New Haven, CT: Yale University Press.

Kheel, Marti (1995). License to Kill: An Ecofeminist Critique of Hunters' Discourse. In *Animals and Women: Theoretical Explorations*, ed. Carol J. Adams and Josephine Donovan. Durham, NC: Duke University Press.

Kinsella, Sharon (2000). *Adult Manga: Culture and Power in Contemporary Japanese Society*. London: Curzon.

Klare, Michael (1999). The Kalashnikov Age, *The Bulletin of the Atomic Scientists*, January/February: 18–21.

Kleck, Gary (1991). *Point Black: Guns and Violence in America*. New York: Aldine De Gruyter.

Kleiman, Arthur and Joan (1997). The Appeal of Experience; The Dismay of Images: Cultural Appropriations of Suffering in Our Times. In *Violence and Subjectivity*, ed. Veena Das, Arthur Kleiman, Mmphela Ramphele and Pamela Reynolds, pp. 1–23. Berkeley, CA: University of California Press.

Kohn, Abigail A. (2001). Their Aim Is True, ReasonOnline, reason.com/0105/fe.ak.their/shtml.

Kohn, Abigail A. (2004). *Shooters: Myths and Realities of America's Gun Cultures*. Oxford: Oxford University Press.

Kopel, David B. (1992). *The Samurai, The Mountie, and The Cowboy: Should America Adopt the Gun Controls of Other Democracies?* Buffalo, NY: Prometheus Books.

Kopel, David B. (ed.) (1995). *Guns: Who Should Have Them?* Amherst, NY: Prometheus Books.

Kramnick, I. (ed.) (1976). *Common Sense*, by Tom Paine (1776). New York: Penguin Books.

Krohn-Hansen, Christine (1994). The Anthropology of Violent Interaction, *Journal of Anthropological Research* 50: 367–81.

Kugelmass, Jack (1991). Wishes Come True: Designing the Greenwich Village Halloween Parade, *Journal of Asian Folklore* 104: 445–65.

Lamphear, John (1994). The Evolution of Ateker 'New Model' Armies: Jie and Turkana. In *Ethnicity and Conflict in the Horn of Africa*, ed. Katsuyoshi Fukui and John Markakis. London: James Currey.

Lan, David (1985). *Guns and Rain: Guerrillas and Spirit Mediums in Zimbabwe*. Berkeley, CA: University of California Press.

Langer, E. (2003). *A Hundred Little Hitlers: The Death of a Black Man, the Trial of a White Racist, and the Rise of the Neo-Nazi Movement in America*. New York: Picador.

Latour, Bruno (1999). *Pandora's Hope: Essays on the Reality of Science Studies.* Cambridge, MA: Harvard University Press.

Lawrence, Denise (1982). Parades, Politics and Competing Urban Images: Doo Dah and Roses, *Urban Anthropology* 11(2): 155–76.

Leddy, E. (1987). *Magnum Force Lobby.* Lanham, MD: University Press of America.

Leeds, Elizabeth (1996). Cocaine and Parallel Polities in the Brazilian Urban Periphery: Constraints on Local-Level Democratization, *Latin American Research Review,* 31(3): 47–83.

Leisy, E. E. (1923). "The American Historical Novel (On American Themes) Before 1860: The Early Novels of James Fenimore Cooper (1821–1831)". Urbana, IL: an abstract of a thesis.

Lemert, Charles and Garth Gillan (1982). *Michel Foucault: Social Theory as Transgression.* New York: Columbia University Press.

Lessing, Benjamin (2005). The Demand for Firearms in Rio de Janeiro. In *Brazil: The Arms and the Victims,* pp. 202–21. Rio de Janeiro: Viva Rio/ISER.

Lester, W. (1999). Men, Women Differ Widely on Gun Control in AP Poll, *San Diego Union-Tribune,* p. 8 (September 8).

Levy, G. (2004). Israel's War on Children, *Ha'aretz,* December 7, Tel Aviv, Israel.

Lewis, R.W. B. (1955). *American Adam: Innocence, Tragedy and Tradition in the Nineteenth Century.* Chicago: The University of Chicago Press.

Lindgren, J. (2002). Fall from Grace: Arming America and the Bellesilles Scandal, *Yale Law Journal,* 111: 2195–233.

Lindgren, J. and J. Heather (2002). Counting Guns in Early America, *William and Mary Law Review* 43: 5.

Ling, Wang (1947). The Invention and Use of Gunpowder and Firearms in China, *Isis* 37 (1947): 160.

Lobo, Irene (2005). Proposal To Ban Guns in Brazil Fails to Win a Single State, *Brazil Magazine,* October 24, 2005, http://www.brazzilmag.com/content/view/4295/2/, accessed January 24, 2006.

Lofving, Staffan and Ivana Macek (1999). Introduction: On War – Revisited. *Antropologiska Studier* 66–67: 2–14.

Lombard, Anne (2003). *Making Manhood: Growing up Male in Colonial New England.* Cambridge, MA: Harvard University Press.

Lott, Jr., J. R. (2003). Guns, crime and health, *The World and I,* 18(10): 32–5.

Luke, Brian (1998). Violent Love: Hunting, Heterosexuality, and the Erotics of Men's Predation, *Feminist Studies* 2 (3): 627–53.

Lutz, Catherine (2001). *Homefront: A Military City and the American Twentieth Century.* Boston: Beacon Press.

Lutz, Catherine and Donald Nonini (1999). The Economies of Violence and the Violence of Economies. In *Anthropological Theory Today,* ed. Henrietta L. Moore, pp. 73–113. London: Polity Press.

Lyons, Tanya (2004). *Guns and Guerilla Girls: Women in the Zimbabwean Liberation Struggle.* Trenton, NJ: Africa World Press, Inc..

MacAloon, John J. (1984a). Introduction: Cultural Performances, Cultural Theory. In *Rite, Drama, Festival, Spectacle: Rehearsals Toward a Theory of Cultural Performance,* ed. John J. MacAloon, pp. 1–15. Philadelphia: Institute for the Study of Human Issues.

MacAloon, John J. (1984b). Olympic Games and the Theory of Spectacle in Modern Societies. In *Rite, Drama, Festival, Spectacle: Rehearsals Toward a Theory of Cultural Performance,* ed. John J. MacAloon, pp. 241–80. Philadelphia: Institute for the Study of Human Issues.

MacKinlay, J. (1989). *The Peacekeepers: An Assessment of Peacekeeping Operations at the Arab–Israeli Interface.* London: Unwin Hyman.

Maero, Titus and Diana Etsabo (2002). Twenty Pokot Girls Hospitalized After Circumcision, *The East African Standard* (Nairobi, June 24).

Main, G. (2002). Many Things Forgotten: The Use of Probate Records in *Arming America*, *William and Mary Quarterly*, LIX: 211–16.

Malcolm, J. (1994). *To Keep and Bear Arms: The Origins of an Anglo-American Right*. Cambridge, MA: Harvard University Press.

Malkki, Liisa H. (1995). *Purity and Exile: Violence, Memory, and National Cosmology Among Hutu Refugees in Tanzania*. Chicago: The University of Chicago Press.

Mandelbaum, David G. (1989). Anthropology for the Second Stage of the Nuclear Age. In *Peace and War: Cross-Cultural Perspectives*, ed. Mary Lecron Foster and Robert A. Rubinstein, pp. 309–19. New Brunswick, NJ: Transaction.

Mann, C. and F. Stewart (2000). *Internet Communication and Qualitative Research: A Handbook for Researching Online*. Thousand Oaks, CA: Sage.

Mann, Nyta (1993). Lethal Shop of Horrors, *New Statesman Society*, 6(269): 12.

Manning, Frank E. (1983). Cosmos and Chaos: Celebration in the Modern World. In *The Celebration of Society*, ed. Frank E. Manning, pp. 3–32. Bowling Green, OH: Bowling Green University Popular Press.

Marley, Bob (1991). [Interview with Dermott Hussey]. Track 20, *Talkin' Blues*, Tuff Gong Records, 422-848 243-2.

Marshall, R. (1993). Special Report: Sowing Dragonseed: Israel's Torment of Children Under Occupation, *The Washington Report on Middle East Affairs*, 11(9): 29–31.

Marshall, R. (2002). Children are a Chief Target as the Israelis 'De-develop' Palestinian Society, *The Washington Report on Middle East Affairs*, 21(9): 6–8.

Máusse, M. A. (1999). The Social Integration of the Child Involved in Armed Conflict in Mozambique, *Monograph 37: Child Soldiers in Southern Africa*, April 1999, http://www.iss.co.za/Pubs/Monographs/No37/TheSocialReintegration.html.

Mburu, Nene (2001). Firearms and Political Power: The Military Decline of the Turkana of Kenya 1900–2000, *Nordic Journal of African Studies*, 10(2): 148–62.

Mburu, Nene (2002). The Proliferation of Guns and Rustling in Karamoja and Turkana Districts: the Case for Appropriate Disarmament Strategies, *The Journal of Peace, Security and Development* 2(2).

Mburu, Nene (2003). Delimitation of the elastic Elemi Triangle: pastoral conflicts and official indifference in the Horn of Africa, *African Studies Quarterly* 6(4).

Mburu, Nene (2005). *Bandits on the Border: The Last Frontier in the Search for Somali Unity*. Trenton, NJ: Africa World & The Red Sea Press.

McCaughey, Martha and Neal King (eds) (2001). *Reel Knockouts: Violent Women in the Movies*. Austin, TX: University of Texas Press.

McClurg, A. J., D. B. Kopel, and B. P. Denning (eds) (2002). *Gun Control and Gun Rights*. New York: New York University Press.

McGreal, C. (2004). Palestinian children never safe from Israeli bullets, *Guardian*, September 17, accessed on web.

McMahon, S. (1985). A Comfortable Subsistence: The Changing Composition of Diet in Rural New England, 1620–1840, *The William and Mary Quarterly*, 3rd ser., Vol. 42, No. 1: 26–65.

McNamara, P. (2001). Palestinian Children Bear the Brunt of Violence and Occupation, Counterpunch.org, October 15.

McNeill, William H. (1982). *The Pursuit of Power: Technology, Armed Force, and Society since A.D. 1000*. Chicago: University of Chicago Press.

Mermet, J. (1998). International Law Concerning Child Civilians in Armed Conflict, *The American Journal of International Law*, 92(4): 802–4.

MIPT Terrorism Knowledge Base, http://www.tkb.org/Group.jsp?groupID=29, accessed January 31, 2006.

Morlin, B. and T. Clouse (2001). Aryans to March, Burn Cross: Gathering to be at State Park Since Compound Confiscated, Spokane *Spokesman-Review* (4 July): B1.

Morton, David (2006). Gunning for the World, *Foreign Policy* 152: 58–67.

Moskos, Charles (2000). Towards a Postmodern Military? In *Democratic Societies and Their Armed Forces: Israel in a Comparative Perspective*, ed. Stuart A. Cohen, pp. 3–26. London: Frank Cass.

Moskos, Charles C., John Allen Williams and David R. Segal (2000). Armed Forces After the Cold War. In *The Postmodern Military: Armed Forces After the Cold War*, ed. Charles Moskos, John Allen Williams and David R. Segal, pp. 1–13. New York: Oxford University Press.

'Move in and get Guns but Commit no Crimes' (2005). *The Standard* (Nairobi, May 30).

Muggah, Robert and Eric Berman (2001). Humanitarianism under Threat: The Humanitarian Impact of Small Arms and Light Weapons, *Small Arms Survey*, 66.

Murnan, J., J. A. Dake, and J. H. Price (2004). Association of Selected Risk Factors with Variation in Child and Adolescent Firearm Mortality by State, *The Journal of School Health*, 74(8): 335–40.

NAACP (National Association for the Advancement of Colored People) v. A.A. Arms, Inc. *et al.* (United States District Court Eastern District of New York 1999).

Nash, June (1989). *From Tank Town to High Tech: The Clash of Community and Industrial Cycles.* Albany, NY: State University of New York Press.

Navarro, Fernanda (2005). A New Way of Thinking in Action; The Zapatistas in Mexico – A Postmodern Guerilla Movement? In *Cultural Studies: From Theory to Action*, ed. P. Leistyna, pp. 106–15. Malden, MA: Blackwell Publishing.

Newsbrief, source unknown (2004). Israelis Kill More Palestinian Children, Wednesday, October 13, 2004, updated October 29, 2004.

Nisbet, Lee (ed.) (2001). *The Gun Control Debate: You Decide*, 2nd edn. Amherst, NY: Prometheus Books.

Nordstrom, Carolyn (1997). *A Different Kind of War Story.* Philadelphia: University of Pennsylvania Press.

Nordstrom, Carolyn (2004). *Shadows of War: Violence, Power, and International Profiteering in the Twenty-first Century.* Berkeley, CA: University of California Press.

Nordstrom, Carolyn and Antonius C. G. M. Robben (eds) (1995). *Fieldwork Under Fire: Contemporary Studies of Violence and Survival.* Berkeley, CA: University of California Press.

Northwest Coalition Against Malicious Harassment (1994). *The Northwest Imperative: Church of Jesus Christ Christian—Aryan Nations.* Seattle, WA: Northwest Coalition Against Malicious Harassment.

Northwest Coalition for Human Dignity (2000). *A Lasting Legacy: Aryan Nations' Impact on the Inland Northwest.* Seattle, WA: Northwest Coalition for Human Dignity.

O'Connell, Robert L. (1989). *Of Arms and Men: A History of War, Weapons, and Aggression.* New York: Oxford University Press.

O'Duffy, Brendan (1995). Violence in Northern Ireland, 1969–94: Sectarian or Ethno-National? *Ethnic and Racial Studies* 18(4): 740–72.

Ogola, O. (2000). Kenyans Move into Uganda with their Cattle to Escape Drought, *CNN Report* (August 27).

Ohito, David (2005). Influx of Firearms Worrying, *The Sunday Standard* (Nairobi, May 29), p. 13.

Oketch, Oscar and Anthony Lokwang (1999). 20 cows per gun, *New Vision* (Kampala, October 25).

Olson, L. (1991). *Emblems of American Community in the Revolutionary Era: A Study in Rhetorical Iconology.* Washington, DC: Smithsonian Institution Press.

Ombati, Cyrus (2005). Seven Killed in Bandit Attacks, *The Standard* (Nairobi, June 1), p. 7.

Onyang, Sylvester (1996). Karimojong Rustlers Raid Kenya, Rock Border Peace, *The Monitor*, (Kampala, 18 November).

"Operation to disarm North Rift residents starts today" (2005). *The Standard*, Nairobi, 30 May.

Palestine Red Crescent Society (2005). Conflict Deaths by Age and Gender, http://www.palestine.org/Conflict%20Deaths%20by%20Age%20&%20Gender.htm.

Palestinian Center for Human Rights, Gaza (2005). Data Sets, www.pchrgaza.org.

Past Peak Archives (2005). http://www.pastpeak.com/archives/2005/07/no_bulky_jacket.htm, accessed July 26, 2006.

Peck, Don (2002). The Gun Trade, *Atlantic Monthly* 290 (5): 46–7.

Penhallow, S. (1726). *The history of the wars of New-England, with the Eastern Indians. Or, A Narrative of Their Continued Perfidy and Cruelty, from the 10th of August,1703 to the peace renewed 13th of July, 1713. And from the 25th of July 1722. To their submission 15th December, 1725. Which was ratified August 5th 1726*, Early American Imprints, Series I: Evans, 1639–1800. Northwestern University Library, Evanston, IL, November 15, 2005, http://infoweb.newsbank.com.turing.library.northwestern.edu/.

PETA (People for the Ethical Treatment of Animals) (2005). Research Center Concludes That Hunters 'Compensate' for Diminutive Genitalia by Acting Out Domination Fantasies, retrieved May 25, 2005 from http://www.peta.org/mc/NewsItem. asp?id=6168.

Phillips, Tom (2005). Brazil Votes on Deadly Obsession With Guns, *Guardian Unlimited*, October 22, 2005.

Phythian, Mark (2001). The Price of Success, *The World Today* (January): 8–10.

Pitcavage, Mark (1996). Welcome to a New World (Disorder): A Visit to a Gun Show, retrieved November 29, 2005 from http://www.militia-watchdog.org/gunshow. asp.

Poniatowska, E. (1971/1991). La Noche de Tlatelolco, Testimonios de Historia Oral, Ediciones Era, S.A. de C.V., 49th Edition, Mexico, D.F., Mexico.

Poniatowska, Elena (1999). *Las Soldaderas*. Mexico City: INAH (National Institute of Anthropology and History).

Poulton, Robin E. (). The Kalashnikov in Afghanistan, Tajikistan and the other 'Stans', *Asian Affairs*, 2001 (October): 295–9.

Pugh, D. (1983). *Sons of Liberty: The Masculine Mind in Nineteenth Century America*, Westport, CT: Greenwood Press.

Quam, Michael D. (1997). Creating peace in an armed society: Karamoja, Uganda, 1996, *Africa Studies Quarterly*, 1 (1).

Radabaugh, J. (1954). The Militia of Colonial Massachusetts, *Military Affairs*, 18: 1–18.

Railton, S. (1978). *Fenimore Cooper: A Study of His Life and Imagination*. Princeton, NJ: Princeton University Press.

Rakove, J. (2002a). The Second Amendment: The Highest State of Originalism. In *The Second Amendment in Law and History*, ed. C. Bogus. The New Press: New York.

Rakove, J. (2002b). Words, Deeds, and Guns: *Arming America* and the Second Amendment, *William and Mary Quarterly*, LIX: 205–10.

Rawson, E. (ed.) (1672). *The General Laws and Liberties of the Massachusetts Colony: Revised & Reprinted, by Order of the General Court holden at Boston*, Early American Imprints, Series I: Evans. Northwestern University, Evanston, IL, May 18, 2005, http://infoweb.newsbank.com.turing.library.northwestern.edu/.

Reel, Monte (2005). Brazilians Reject Measure to Ban Sale of Firearms: Issue Defeated Decisively in National Vote, *The Washington Post*, October 24, p. A13.

Reich, K., P. L. Culross, and R. E. Behrman (2002). Children, youth, and gun violence: Analysis and recommendations, *The Future of Children*, Los Altos, Summer, 2002, 12(2): 4–23.

Relatives for Justice (1995). *Collusion, 1990–1994: Loyalist Paramilitary Murders in the North of Ireland*. Derry: Relatives for Justice.

Renner, Michael (1998). Curbing the Proliferation of Small Arms, *State of the World*, pp. 131–48.

Renner, Michael (1999). Arms Control Orphans, *The Bulletin of the Atomic Scientists* 55(1): 22–6.

Resende, Juliana (2005). Gunshot wounds "endemic" in Rio de Janeiro: Undeclared War Between Authorities and Drug Dealers, *San Francisco Chronicle*, November 18, p. A19.

Riches, David (ed.) (1986). *The Anthropology of Violence*. Oxford: Blackwell.

Rinehart, R. E. (1998). *Players All: Performances in Contemporary Sport*, Bloomington, IN: University of Indiana Press.

Rivero, Patricia S. (2005). The Value of the Illegal Firearms Market in the City of Rio de Janeiro. In *Brazil: The Arms and the Victims*, pp. 146–201. Rio de Janeiro: Viva Rio/ISER.

Roberts, L., R. Lafta, R. Garfield, J. Khudairi and G. Burnham (2004). Mortality Before and After the 2003 Invasion of Iraq: Cluster Sample Survey, *The Lancet*, 364(9448): 1857–68.

Robey, R. (1972). *Diary of Samuel Sewall, 1674–1729*, 2 Vols. New York: Arno Press.

Rohter, Larry (1999). Brazil, High in Shootings, Is Proposing To Ban Guns, *The New York Times*, June 13, p. 19.

Rohter, Larry (2002). Ipanema Under Siege: Rio's Gangs Flex Harder, *The New York Times*, October 20, Week in Review, p. 4.

Rohter, Larry (2005). Gun-Happy Brazil is Hotly Debating a Nationwide Ban, *The New York Times*, October 20, p. A3.

Rolston, Bill (2003). *Drawing Support 3: Murals and Transition in the North of Ireland*. Belfast: Beyond the Pale.

Ron, J. (2000). "Savage Restraint: Israel, Palestine and the Dialectics of Legal Repression." *Social Problems*. 47/4: 445–72.

Ross, John (2003). Guns, Trade, and "Control", *NACLA Report on the Americas* 37(2): 18–19.

Roth, J. (1994). *Firearms and Violence*, Washington, DC: US Dept. of Justice, Office of Justice Programs, National Institute of Justice.

Roth, R. (2002). Counting Guns: What Social Science Historians Know and Could Learn about Gun Ownership, Gun Culture, and Gun Violence in the United States, *Social Science History*, 26(4): 700–8.

Rotundo, E. A. (1987). Learning about Manhood: Gender Ideals and the Middle Class Family in Nineteenth Century America. In *Manliness and Morality: Middle Class Masculinity In Britain and America, 1800 – 1940*, ed. J. A. Manfan and J. Walvin. New York: Palgrave Macmillan.

Rubinstein, Robert A. (1994). Collective Violence and Common Security. In *Companion Encyclopedia of Anthropology*, ed. Tim Ingold, pp. 983–1009. London: Routledge.

Russell, Philip (2005). *The Chiapas Rebellion*. Austin, TX: Mexico Resource Center.

"Rustlers Elude Security Officers, Steal Livestock" (2005). *The Standard* (Nairobi, June 1).

Ryan, D. (1979). *A Salute to Courage: The American Revolution as Seen Through Wartime Writings of Officers of the Continental Army and Navy*. New York: Columbia University Press.

Sade-Beck, Liav (2004). Internet Ethnography: Online and Offline, *International Journal of Qualitative Methods*, 3(2): 1–14.

Sait, M. S. (2004). Have Palestinian Children Forfeited Their Rights?, *Journal of Comparative Family Studies*, 35(2): 211–28.

Sandford, J. (2004). *Hidden Prey*. New York: Berkley Books.

Save the Children (2004). Rights of Palestinian Children "Compromised", *Save the Children Report*, March 9.

Savitz, D. A., N. M. Thang, I. E. Swenson, and E. M. Stone (1993). Vietnamese Infant and Childhood Mortality in Relation to the Vietnam War, *American Journal of Public Health*, 83(8): 1134–8.

Savran, D. (1998). *Taking it Like a Man: White Masculinity, Masochism, and Contemporary American Culture*. Princeton, NJ: Princeton University Press.

Schechner, Richard (1994). Ritual and Performance. In *Companion Encyclopedia of Anthropology*, ed. Tim Ingold, pp. 613–45. London: Routledge.

Schleunes, K. A. (1996). "Did the Children Cry?" Hitler's War against Jewish and Polish Children, 1939–1945, *The American Historical Review*, 101(2): 520.

Schrag, C. O. (1997). *The Self after Post-modernity*, New Haven, CT: Yale University Press.

Schroder, Ingo W. and Bettina E. Schmidt (2001). Introduction: Violent Imaginaries and Violent Practices. In *Anthropology of Violence and Conflict*, ed. Bettina E. Schmidt and Ingo W. Schroder, pp. 1–24. London: Routledge.

Schwoerer, L. (2000). To Hold and Bear Arms: The English Perspective. In *The Second Amendment in Law and History*, ed. C. Bogus. The New Press: New York.

Seierstad, Asne (2004). *The Bookseller of Kabul*. Boston: Back Bay Books.

Seligman, N. (2000). NRA Leader LaPierre's "Homogenization" Quote Most Recent Addition to NRA History of Racist Commentary, *Violence Policy Center Press*, May 16.

Sharf, B. (1999). Beyond Netiquette: The Ethics of Doing Naturalistic Discourse Research on the Internet. In *Doing Internet Research: Critical Issues and Methods for Examining the Net*, ed. S. Jones, pp. 243–57. Thousand Oaks, CA: Sage.

Sharret, C. (1999). Foreword. In *Mythologies of Violence in Postmodern Media*, ed. C. Sharret, p. 10. Detroit, MI: Wayne State University Press.

Sherril, R. (1973). *The Saturday Night Special and Other Guns with which Americans Won the West, Protected Bootleg Franchises, Slew Wildlife, Robbed Countless Banks, Shot Husbands Purposely and by Mistake, and Killed Presidents—Together with the Debate Over Continuing Same*. New York: Charterhouse.

Simons, Anna (1997). *The Company They Keep: Life Inside the U.S. Army Special Forces*. New York: The Free Press.

Simons, Anna (1998). How Ambiguity Results in Excellence: The Role of Hierarchy and Reputation in U.S. Army Special Forces, *Human Organization* 57(1): 117–23.

Simons, Anna (1999). War: Back to the Future?, *Annual Review of Anthropology* 28: 73–108.

Singer, P. W. (2001–2). Caution: Children at War, *Parameters*, Carlisle Barracks, Winter 2001/2002, 31(4): 40–56.

"Slaughter in Turkana" (1997). *The Weekly Review* (Nairobi, September 26).

Slocum, John David (1995). "Screening Violence: Film Narratives and Postwar America", Ph.D. dissertation, New York University.

Slotkin, R. (1992). *Gunfighter Nation: The Myth of the Frontier in Twentieth-Century America*. New York: Maxwell Macmillan International.

Slovak, K. (2002). Gun violence and children: Factors related to exposure and trauma, *Health and Social Work*, (27)2: 104–12.

Sluka, Jeffrey A. (1989). *Hearts and Minds, Water and Fish: Support for the IRA and INLA in a Northern Irish Ghetto* (Contemporary Ethnographic Studies, Vol. 4). Greenwich, CT and London: JAI Press.

Sluka, Jeffrey A. (ed.) (2000a). *Death Squad: The Anthropology of State Terror*. Philadelphia: University of Pennsylvania Press.

Sluka, Jeffrey A. (2000b). "For God and Ulster": The Culture of Terror and Loyalist Death Squads in Northern Ireland. In *Death Squad: The Anthropology of State Terror*, ed. Jeffrey A. Sluka, pp. 127–57. Philadelphia: University of Pennsylvania Press.

Sluka, Jeffrey A. (2000c). Introduction: State Terror and Anthropology. In *Death Squad: The Anthropology of State Terror*, ed. Jeffrey A. Sluka, pp. 1–45. Philadelphia: University of Pennsylvania Press.

Small Arms Survey (2001). *Profiling the Problem*. Oxford: Oxford University Press [A Project of the Graduate Institute of International Studies, Geneva].

Small Arms Survey (2002). *Counting the Human Cost*. Oxford: Oxford University Press [A Project of the Graduate Institute of International Studies, Geneva].

Smith, Robert A. (1994). Lost Children: Family Day at an Arms Fair, *Friends Journal* (2): 26–7.

Soares, Luiz E. (2000). "Violence and Politics in Rio de Janeiro", talk given at Columbia University, New York, October 5.

Sobchack, V. (1976). The Violent Dance: A Personal Memoir of Death in the Movies. In *Graphic Violence on the Screen*, ed. T.Atkins, pp. 79–94. New York: Monarch Press.

Sontag, Susan (1978). *On Photography*. New York: Farrar, Straus and Giroux.

Spencer, Jonathan (1996). Violence. In *Encyclopedia of Social and Cultural Anthropology*, ed. Alan Barnard and Jonathan Spencer, pp. 559–60. London: Routledge.

Spencer, Paul (1998). Age Systems and Modes of Predatory Expansion. In *Conflict, Age and Power in Northeast Africa*, ed. Esei Kurimoto and Simon Simonse. London: James Currey.

Spitzer, R. J. (1995). *The Politics of Gun Control*. Chatham: Chatham House Publishers.

Spitzer, R. (2002). Lost and Found: Researching the Second Amendment. In *The Second Amendment in Law and History*, ed. C. Bogus. New York: The New Press.

Storey, John (1998). *An Introduction to Cultural Theory and Popular Culture*, 2nd edn. Athens, GA: University of Georgia Press.

Stringer, J. (1997). Your Tender Smiles Give Me Strength, *Screen*, 38: 1.

Sweet, D. (2005). More than Goth: The rhetorical reclamation of the subcultural self, *Popular Communication*, 3(4): 239–64.

Symmes, T. (1725). *Historical Memoirs of the Late Fight at Piggwacket, with a Sermon Occasion'd by the Fall of the Brave Capt. John Lovewell and Several of his Valiant Company, in the Late Heroic Action There*, Early American Imprints, Series I: Evans. Northwestern University, Evanston, Illinois, November 15, 2005, http://infoweb.newsbank.com.turing.library.northwestern.edu/.

Tahmassebi, S. (1991). Gun Control and Racism, *George Mason University Civil Rights Law Journal*, 2: 67.

Tambiah, Stanley J. (1992). *Buddhism Betrayed? Religion, Politics and Violence in Sri Lanka*. Chicago: Chicago University Press.

Tanner, M. (1995). Extreme prejudice: How the media misrepresent the militia movement, *Reason*.

Taylor, L. (2004). Children and War: A Historical Anthology, *Canadian Journal of History*, April, 39(1): 208–9.

Thabet, A. A. M., Y. Abed, and P. Vostanis (2002). Emotional Problems in Palestinian Children Living in a War Zone: A Cross-sectional Study, *The Lancet* 359(9320): 1801–4.

Thelwell, Michael (1980). *The Harder They Come*. London: Pluto (p. 221).

Thomas, Mark (2005). Selling Torture in London's Docklands, *New Statesman*, September 26.

Thompson, Chris (2005). War Pornography, *East Bay Express*, September 21.

Tilly, Charles (ed.) (1985). *The Formation of National States in Western Europe*. Princeton, NJ: Princeton University Press.

Tonso, W. (1982). *Gun and Society: The Social and Existential Roots of the American Attachment to Firearms*. Lanham, MD: University Press of America.

Tonso, W. (1985). Gun Control: White Man's Law, *Reason* magazine (December).

Tonso, W. (ed.) (1989). *The Gun Culture and Its Enemies.* Bellevue, WA: Second Amendment Foundation Press.

Turner, Bryan S. (1984). *The Body and Society.* Oxford: Basil Blackwell.

Tyson, T. B. (1999). *Radio Free Dixie: Robert F. Williams and the Roots of Black Power.* Chapel Hill, NC and London: The University of North Carolina Press.

United Nations (n.d.). Impact of Armed Conflict on Children: Special Concerns, http://www.un.org/rights/concerns.htm, accessed 3/11/2005.

US Department of Justice, Bureau of Justice Statistics (2006). Homicide trends in the United States, http://www.ojp.usdoj.gov/bjs/pub/pdf/htius.pdf. Also available online at: http://www.ojp.usdoj.gov/bjs/homicide/gender.htm#osex.

US House of Representatives (1989). *Hearing Before the Select Committee on Children, Youth, and Families.* Washington, DC: US Government Printing Office.

Wakabi, Wairagala (2004). The Arms Smugglers, *New Internationalist*, 362: 20–1.

Wald, Elijah. (2001). *Narcocorrido: A Journey into the Music of Drugs, Guns, and Guerillas.* New York: Rayo.

Wallace, J. (1986). *Early Cooper and His Audience.* New York: Columbia University Press.

Wanyonyi, Tim (1998). The Changing Nature and Scope of Cattle Rustling, *Daily Nation* (Nairobi, December 26).

Warigi, George (2000). Who's Fuelling Cattle Rustling by the Pokot?, *The East African* (Nairobi, February 14).

Watson, James L. (1996). Fighting with Operas: Processionals, Politics and the Spectre of Violence in Rural Hong Kong. In *The Politics of Cultural Performance*, ed. David Parkin, Lionel Caplan and Humphrey Fisher, pp. 145–60. Oxford: Berghahn.

Weiner, Tim and Ginger Thompson (2001). U.S. Guns Smuggled Into Mexico Aid Drug War, *New York Times*, May 19, 2001.

Weitzer, Ron (1990). *Transforming Settler Societies: Communal Conflict and Internal Security in Northern Ireland and Zimbabwe.* Berkeley, CA: University of California Press.

Wilkinson, D. L. and J. Fagan (1996). Role of Firearms in Violence "Scripts": The Dynamics of Gun Events Among Adolescent Males, *Law and Contemporary Problems*, 59: 55–89.

Willard, M. W. (1968). *Letters on the American Revolution, 1774–1776.* Port Washington, NY: Kennikat Press, Inc.

Williams, D. C. (2003). *The Mythic Meanings of the Second Amendment: Taming Political Violence in a Constitutional Republic.* New Haven, CT and London: Yale University Press.

Williams, John A. (2000). The Postmodern Military Reconsidered. In *The Postmodern Military: Armed Forces After the Cold War*, ed. Charles C. Moskos, John A. Williams and David Segal, pp. 265–78. New York: Oxford University Press.

Williams, R. F. (1998 (orig. 1962)). *Negroes with Guns.* Detroit: Wayne State University Press.

Wilson, Lisa (1999). *Ye Heart of A Man: The Domestic Life of Men in Colonial New England.* New Haven, CT: Yale University Press.

Wilson, S. M. and L. C. Peterson (2002). The Anthropology of Online Communities, *Annual Review of Anthropology*, 31: 449– 67.

Winslow, Donna (1997). *The Canadian Airborne Regiment in Somalia: A Socio-cultural Inquiry.* Canada: Minister of Public Works and Government Services.

Woodworth, S. (2005). *Melodies, Duets, Trios, Songs, and Ballads, Pastoral, Amatory, Sentimental, Patriotic, Religious, and Miscellaneous. Together with Metrical Epistles, Tales, and Recitations.* Ann Arbor, MI: University of Michigan Library, http://name.umdl.umich.edu/ABK3633.0001.001.

Worsnop, Richard L. (1994). Gun Control, *CQ Researcher*, 4(22): 1–28.

Wright, F. (n.d.). "Studies Confirm Occupation's Harm to Palestinian Children", *Bethlehem Media Net*, the voice of the voiceless.

Wright, J. (1986). *The Armed Criminal in America*, Washington, DC: US Department of Justice, National Institute of Justice.

WRP (Workers' Revolutionary Party) (2005). Investigators Met boss Blair – IPCC urges Home Secretary. http://www.wrp.org.uk/news/580n, accessed July 26, 2006.

Yoneyama, Lisa (1999). *Hiroshima Traces: Time, Space and the Dialectics of Memory*. Berkeley, CA: University of California Press.

Younes, R. (2003). Israel's Psychological Terrorism: Flashback; 500,000 Palestinian Children Suffer from Post-Traumatic Stress Disorder, *The Washington Report on Middle East Affairs*, 22(2): 26–7.

Zimring, F. E. (1985). Violence and Firearms Policy. In *American Violence and Public Policy: An Update of the National Commission on the Causes and Prevention of Violence*, ed. L. A. Curtis, pp. 133–52. New Haven, CT and London: Yale University Press.

Zimring, F. and G. Hawkins (1997). *Crime is Not the Problem: Lethal Violence in America*, p. 106. New York: Oxford University Press.

Zornick, George (2005). The Porn of War, *The Nation*, October 10, retrieved November 28, 2005 from http://www.thenation.com/doc/20051010/the_porn_of_war.

Zoroya, G. (2002). Fear, Rage Fester Inside West Bank Children, *USA Today*, August 6, http://www.usatoday.com/news/world/2002-08-06-curfew- cover_x.htm.

Index

Adams, Gerry 61, 64
Afghanistan 3, 7, 95, 96, 127, 181
Ahern, Bertie 56, 61
Aijmer, Goran 2, 181, 182, 196
Alcohol, Tobacco, and Firearms (ATF) 26, 103
Almagor, Uri 72
Al Qaeda 18
Amin, Idi 75
Amnesty International 29
Appadurai, Arjun 24
Aryan Nations 166, 170–7, 203
Arabic 99

Becker, Harold 169, 171
Berg, Alan 171, 177
Boone, Daniel 147, 148
Bourdieu, Pierre 23
Brazil 9, 19, 28–33, 35–41, 180, 200
Bummpo, Nathaniel 148, 150
Bush, George W. 1, 108
Butler, Richard 171–4, 176, 177

Canada 24, 37, 104, 121, 159
Chase, Kenneth 5
China 4, 17
Chiapas 25, 26
Cooper, James Fenimore 150–1
Cottrol, Robert 113, 114, 120
Crockett, Davy 148

Deming, David 97
Democratic Unionist Party (DUP) 56, 57, 61, 62, 64, 68, 69
Denzin, Norman 102
Diamond, Raymond 113, 114
disarmament 10, 27, 31, 34, 36, 37, 56–70, 72, 73, 75, 78, 81, 83

El Salvador 58
Enloe, Cynthia 7

Farsi 99

firearms, see guns
Foucault, Michel 22
Fox, Vicente 19

Garvey, Marcus 153
gender 16, 17, 39, 112
  feminism 90, 92
  masculinity 20–2, 85, 89, 92, 93, 94, 125–37, 141–52 passim
  women
    as gun users 20, 92, 93
    as gun victims 17, 131
    as sex objects 85–97 passim
Giddens, Anthony 196
Grant, St William 153
gun control organizations
  The International Action Network on Small Arms (IANSA) 36
  Viva Rio 30, 32, 33, 37, 39
gun films
  Bonnie and Clyde 127
  Boyz N the Hood 128, 130
  Commando 27, 128
  Death Wish 128
  Die Hard 125, 127, 130–2, 134, 135
  Dirty Harry 127, 128, 130
  Lethal Weapon 127, 128, 131, 132, 135–7
  Jackie Brown 87, 96
  Magnum Force 128, 131
  Menace II Society 128, 130, 131
  Natural Born Killers 129
  Pulp Fiction 129
  Rambo: First Blood Part II 128, 130, 132, 135
  Reservoir Dogs 129
  To Live and Die in L.A. 128, 131
  The Wild Bunch 127, 129, 130, 132
gunpowder 4
guns
  amount of 3–4, 17–18, 30
  and children 15–16, 17, 30, 42–55 passim, 65, 131, 174, 175

exchanges and buybacks 15, 17, 21, 27
and hunting 89, 90, 91, 93, 94, 95,
 115, 116, 117, 123, 143, 145,
 147–50
laws (Second amendment) 2, 101, 112,
 141
and pornography 88, 89, 92, 93, 95, 96
as sex objects 94
toy guns 3, 6, 7, 15, 16, 21, 22
 (Airsoft) 5, 8–9
 (paintball) 19, 165, 166
types
 .303 rifle 3, 24
 .357 Magnum 6, 19
 .43 rifle 106
 .44 104
 Barretta 19, 106
 Glock 6, 19, 154, 162
 Kalashnikov (AK-47) 1, 2, 5, 17, 19,
  20, 24, 27, 76, 80, 174
 M-16 5
 MAC-10 171
 machine guns 5, 125

habitus 22–4
Handelman, Don 186, 204n1
Harcourt, Bernard 23, 37, 38
Hebdige, Dick 169
Hedges, Chris 182
Heston, Charlton 111
Hitler, Adolf 37–8, 41, 168, 171–6, 203n
Hoffman, Danny 27
Hong Kong 129
Huizinga, Johan 166–8, 176–7

Indonesia 58
Intifada (Al Aqsa) 42, 46, 47, 50, 52–4
internet 98–110 passim, 176
Iraq 1, 18, 96, 181
Irish Republican Army (IRA) 56–70
 passim
Israel 17, 18, 19, 42–55, 197
Israeli Defense Forces (IDF) 42–52
 passim

Jackson, Andrew 148
Jamaica 153–64 passim
Japan 5, 16
 Japan Defense Agency 183, 184, 192,
  194
 Japan Self-Defense Forces (SDF) 11,
  190–7

Kabila, Joseph 8
Kalashnikov, Mikhail 5
Karamojong 76
Kenya 71–84
 Ngoroko 78
Kubrick, Stanley 91
Ku Klux Klan 113, 118, 170–3

Latour, Bruno 23
Lynch, Jessica 95

Maasai 72
MacAloon, John 191
Mai Mai militia 7
Marley, Bob 153
Maxim, Hiram 5
McNeill, William 5
Merleau-Ponty 22
Mexico 15, 18, 19, 21, 22, 24, 25, 58
Miller, David 24
Minutemen 21
Mozambique 2, 58

narcocorridos 25
National Association of Colored Peoples
 (NAACP) 118, 119, 121, 124
New Orleans 18, 149
New York City 21
Nordstrom, Carolyn 58
Northern Ireland
Nugent, Ted 110

O'Connell, Robert 5
Oslo Accords 44

Palestine 42–55 passim
Paine, Thomas 146
paintball, see toy guns
 Paisley, Ian 56
play 3, 6, 7, 9, 11, 15, 16, 20–2, 23, 87,
  88, 89, 91, 92, 93, 95, 97, 125–38
 passim, 158, 159, 164, 165–77
 passim
Polsby, Daniel 26
Pokot 73–5
pro-gun organizations
 Citizens Committee for the Right to
  Keep and Bear Arms (CCRKBA)
  117
 National Rifle Association (NRA) 6,
  9, 23, 36, 41, 107, 108, 111–24
 passim

Second Amendment Foundation (SAF) 117

Western Missouri Shooters Alliance (WMSA) 118

race/racism 16, 111–24 passim
gun laws as racist 112–17
white supremacy 112
whiteness 99, 101, 165–77 passim
religion 68–9
Christian *jihad* 166, 176–7
Christianity 73, 74, 82, 95, 96, 151, 166–8, 170–5, 177
Islam 95, 96, 166
Revolutionary Armed Forces of Columbia (FARC) 40
Rio de Janeiro 28–41 passim
Ross, John 19

Second Amendment, *see* gun laws
São Paulo 36, 40
Seierstad, Asne
Sinn Fein 57, 60–4, 68, 69
Schwarzenegger, Arnold 104
Selden, Samuel 145
Soares, Luiz Eduardo 39
Somalia 19
Spencer, Paul 72
Sudan 78

Tarantino, Quentin 87, 129
Tillim, Guy 7–8
Tilly, Charles 196
Toposa 79–82
Turkana 75–9

Uganda 73
United Nations 17, 27, 36, 104, 199
United States 1, 2, 3, 5, 6, 11, 15, 17, 18, 19, 21, 24, 33, 37, 43, 85–97 passim, 98, 99, 101, 103, 104, 107, 109, 111–24 passim, 149, 166, 167, 168, 170, 172

Vargas, Paulino 25
Ventura, Zuenir 29
Villa, Pancho 26
violence 11, 28, 29, 42–55, 77, 87, 88, 90, 94, 95, 168, 176, 178–98
terrorism 32, 35, 40, 41, 54, 95, 96, 168, 170, 174
9/11 89, 95
war 58
and sociobiology 179
wars
American Revolution 139–52 passim
Iraq war 40, 41, 96
Mexican Revolution 25–6
Rwanda 8, 11
Sierra Leone 20, 27, 44
Vietnam 195
War in Northern Ireland 56–70
War of 1812 142, 148, 152
World War II 188
Zapatista Rebellion 25–6
weapons (non-firearms) 20, 95
bows and arrows 77
crossbows 4
fighter planes 18, 178, 179
grenade launchers 19
knives 134
spears 77
tanks 178, 179
wrist knife 77
Weaver, Randy 103
women, *see* gender

Zapata, Emiliano 26
Zapatistas (Zapatista Liberation Army) 26
Zinser, Adolfo Aguilar 19
Zimbabwe 20
Zimring, Franklin 123